Elasticsearch Guidebook

From Basics to Expert Proficiency

Contents

Introduction

Elasticsearch is a powerful open-source search and analytics engine built on top of Apache Lucene. Designed for horizontal scalability, reliability, and real-time search capabilities, Elasticsearch is capable of handling large volumes of structured, semi-structured, and unstructured data. Its distributed nature means it can scale out to hundreds of nodes and petabytes of data. This makes it an invaluable tool in today's data-intensive environments.

The purpose of this book is to provide a comprehensive guide to Elasticsearch, ranging from basic concepts to advanced techniques. It is intended for those new to Elasticsearch, as well as professionals looking to deepen their understanding and proficiency. Every chapter is crafted to be self-contained while contributing to an overall understanding of the system.

We begin with an exploration of what Elasticsearch is and the history of its development. This background sets the stage for understanding why Elasticsearch has become a crucial tool in modern data management and analytics. You will learn about the core features, architecture, and an overview of the ecosystem, which includes various tools and plugins that extend its capabilities.

Once the groundwork is laid, the focus shifts to the practical aspects of setting up your Elasticsearch environment. This encompasses installation procedures for various operating systems, configuration settings, and how to get Elasticsearch running smoothly on your system. By the end of this section, you will be well-equipped to commence your journey in Elasticsearch.

Core concepts are fundamental to mastering any technology. Accordingly, the next part of the book delves into the fundamentals of Elasticsearch, including its document model, indexing techniques, cluster architecture, and essential terminology. These concepts form the foundation of your Elasticsearch knowledge, enabling you to understand, utilize, and troubleshoot the system effectively.

Elasticsearch's prowess lies in its ability to index and manage data efficiently. In the subsequent sections, you will learn to index documents, manage data, and employ various techniques to ensure data integrity and performance. These practices are essential for maintaining a robust Elasticsearch environment.

Equally important are Elasticsearch's search and query functionalities. This book provides a detailed examination of the query DSL, full-text search techniques, sorting, pagination, and more. By mastering these topics, you will be able to craft sophisticated queries that are both efficient and effective.

Aggregations and analytics form another critical area of focus. Elasticsearch excels at providing near real-time analytics capabilities, making it ideal for applications requiring fast, ad-hoc queries. This part of the book introduces various types of aggregations and demonstrates how to leverage them for complex analytical tasks.

Scaling and performance tuning are next on the agenda. Here, you will learn to scale your Elasticsearch clusters effectively, optimize performance, and ensure high availability. These insights are vital for administrators who need to maintain large-scale deployments.

Security and access control cannot be overlooked in any modern application. Elasticsearch offers robust security features, from basic authentication to granular role-based access control. This book covers these features in depth, ensuring you can secure your Elasticsearch instances against unauthorized access and data breaches.

Monitoring and maintenance are ongoing tasks for any Elasticsearch deployment. This section provides guidance on critical metrics to monitor, tools for diagnostics, and regular maintenance tasks to keep your clusters running smoothly. Practical exercises reinforce these concepts, helping you to implement effective monitoring solutions.

Finally, the book explores extending Elasticsearch functionality with plugins. This includes installing popular plugins, developing custom plugins, and enhancing various capabilities of your Elasticsearch deployment. These extensions can significantly enhance the utility of Elasticsearch in specialized use cases.

Throughout the book, practical exercises and real-world examples are provided to reinforce the concepts discussed. By the end of your reading, you will possess a thorough understanding of Elasticsearch and the skills to apply this knowledge in real-world applications.

This guide aims to be your definitive resource on Elasticsearch, empowering you to leverage its full potential in your projects.

Chapter 1

Introduction to Elasticsearch

Elasticsearch is an open-source search and analytics engine that excels in handling large volumes of diverse data types efficiently in real-time. Built on Apache Lucene, it offers scalability and reliability through its distributed architecture. This chapter provides a foundational understanding of Elasticsearch, covering its origins, key features, basic architecture, and various use cases. Additionally, it introduces the essential terminology and ecosystem components, setting the stage for a hands-on exploration of Elasticsearch's capabilities.

1.1 What is Elasticsearch?

Elasticsearch is a powerful, open-source search and analytics engine that has garnered widespread adoption for its flexibility and performance. Built on top of Apache Lucene, a high-performance, full-featured information retrieval library, Elasticsearch extends the capabilities of Lucene and provides a distributed, multitenant-capable architecture to achieve scalability and reliability.

At its core, Elasticsearch offers robust functionality for full-text search, structured search, and analytics. One of its defining attributes is its ability to handle large volumes of diverse data types. Whether dealing with textual documents, numerical data, geospatial information, or complex JSON objects, Elasticsearch provides a seamless and efficient mechanism to ingest, index, store, and search data in near real-time.

Key features that make Elasticsearch stand out include its distributed nature, horizontal scalability, document-oriented storage, and RESTful API, which eases integration with a myriad of application platforms.

Elasticsearch leverages a distributed model, meaning it is designed to work across a cluster of nodes, each node participating in storing a portion of the data and providing search capabilities. This architecture enables horizontal scaling, where additional nodes can be added to the cluster to accommodate data growth seamlessly. This model not only enhances fault tolerance by replicating data across multiple nodes but also improves performance by distributing search and indexing tasks.

Being document-oriented signifies that Elasticsearch manages data in the form of JSON documents, each containing a self-contained and indexed set of fields. This schema-less architecture allows for dynamic data structures and reduces the overhead associated with strict schemas. Indexing documents in JSON format is efficient and aligns well with the modern web's preference for flexible, portable data interchange formats.

The RESTful API further strengthens Elasticsearch's integration capabilities. Through straightforward HTTP requests, clients can interact with the Elasticsearch cluster to perform a plethora of operations, including creating indices, managing documents, querying data, and even monitoring cluster health. The RESTful approach makes Elasticsearch accessible from virtually any programming language or platform that can issue HTTP requests.

To solidify understanding, an exemplary HTTP request to index a document in Elasticsearch is shown below:

```
PUT /my-index-000001/_doc/1
{
  "user": "kimchy",
  "post_date": "2009-11-15T14:12:12",
  "message": "Trying out Elasticsearch, so far so good?"
}
```

In response to this request, Elasticsearch will return a JSON output indicating the result of the indexing operation:

```
{
  "_index": "my-index-000001",
  "_type": "_doc",
  "_id": "1",
  "_version": 1,
  "result": "created",
  "_shards": {
    "total": 2,
    "successful": 1,
    "failed": 0
  },
  "_seq_no": 0,
  "_primary_term": 1
}
```

The search capability in Elasticsearch is equally expressive, enabling complex queries through a rich domain-specific language (DSL). For example, a basic search for documents with a message containing the word "Elasticsearch" can be accomplished as follows:

```
GET /my-index-000001/_search
{
  "query": {
    "match": {
      "message": "Elasticsearch"
    }
  }
}
```

Executing this query will yield a response listing all documents that match the search criteria, along with metadata about the search itself.

Another critical aspect of Elasticsearch is its indexing strategy. An index in Elasticsearch is akin to a database in relational database management systems. Each index can contain multiple types, and each type can have multiple documents. The indexing process involves breaking down documents into searchable tokens, creating an optimized data structure that allows for fast retrieval.

Elasticsearch achieves this through an inverted index, where terms extracted from documents point to the document IDs containing them. This index structure ensures searches are performed efficiently, even across large datasets.

With Elasticsearch's ability to combine batching (bulk processing) and near real-time searching, it manages the trade-off between performance and immediacy effectively.

To sum up Elasticsearch's role in modern data ecosystems, it aids organizations in quickly deriving insights from their data, making it an indispensable tool in scenarios ranging from log and event data analysis to enterprise search solutions and beyond.

1.2 History and Evolution of Elasticsearch

Elasticsearch, originally developed by Shay Banon, emerged as a robust and highly performant search engine, evolving significantly over the years. The origins trace back to the early 2000s when Banon sought a solution to handle complex search requirements for a recipe application he aimed to build. This journey began with the introduction of Compass, a first attempt at an open-source search engine.

Compass, built as an abstraction atop the Apache Lucene library, provided significant search capabilities but also revealed the need for more extensive scalability and flexibility. Apache Lucene, a high-performance, full-featured text search engine library, laid the groundwork with its intricate indexing and searching capabilities, crucial for full-text searches.

By 2010, recognizing the limitations of Compass in adapting to real-world scaling needs, Banon initiated a new project—Elasticsearch. This project was intended to harness the core strengths of Lucene while addressing the scalability and operational challenges encountered with Compass. Thus, Elasticsearch was born as a distributed, RESTful search and analytics engine built directly atop Lucene.

Elasticsearch rapidly gained traction due to its simple yet powerful REST API, providing ease of integration with various applications. Furthermore, its distributed nature allowed for seamless scaling, enabling users to manage and query extensive data sets efficiently. Elasticsearch's ability to handle near real-time search results fulfilled the growing demands of modern applications.

Over the years, Elasticsearch has seen numerous releases with significant enhancements. Key milestones include:

- **Version 0.4.0** (2010) - The initial release showcased the fundamentals of distributed search and indexing. It introduced basic features such as auto-sharding and support for JSON over REST.
- **Version 1.0.0** (2014) - Marked a pivotal step with a more stable and feature-rich framework. This version introduced index aliases, the ability to rename indexes and provided enhanced stability with a better query DSL (Domain Specific Language).
- **Version 2.0.0** (2015) - Focused on robustness and ease of use. Key introductions included federation capabilities for cross-cluster search and enhancements in resiliency and security.

- **Version 5.0.0** (2016) - Renumbered to align with other Elastic Stack products (Elastic Beats, Logstash, Kibana). This release brought significant performance improvements, enhanced numerical capabilities for better aggregation performance, and simplified versioning.
- **Version 6.0.0** (2017) - Continued enhancement in aggregations APIs and better handling of terms. It incorporated stronger security measures and better infrastructural support for large-scale deployments.
- **Version 7.0.0** (2019) - Introduced a range of performance optimizations, including faster ingestion, reduced noise in search results using improved rank algorithms, and support for frozen indices to manage low-access data.

Elasticsearch's evolution extended beyond mere version upgrades. Its integration with the Elastic Stack—composed of Beats for data shippers, Logstash for data transformation and ingestion, and Kibana for visualization—formed a comprehensive suite for end-to-end data search and analytics, significantly broadening its adoption.

This period also witnessed the emergence of cloud-based Elasticsearch solutions, such as Amazon Elasticsearch Service and Elastic Cloud—offered directly by Elastic NV, the company behind Elasticsearch. These services provided fully managed and scalable instances of Elasticsearch, simplifying operations for users and ensuring high availability and security.

The development community surrounding Elasticsearch grew vibrantly with active contributions, making it one of the most popular and widely used search engines in various sectors, from e-commerce to enterprise search, logging, and security intelligence. As Elasticsearch progressed, crucial concepts like index lifecycle management, machine learning integrations, and security enhancements, including role-based access control and audit logging, were introduced.

Significant efforts were also made in optimizing the underlying infrastructure. Innovations like the introduction of vectors for approximate nearest neighbor (ANN) search for advanced search capabilities and enhancements in the ingest pipelines, enriched the Elasticsearch ecosystem.

The continued commitment to open-source principles, coupled with strong community support and innovative enhancements, ensured that

Elasticsearch remained at the forefront of search and analytics technology. These advancements have extended its applications, making it an indispensable tool in the big data landscape, capable of handling the ever-growing data challenges in the modern techno-industrial era.

```
# Downloading and Installing Elasticsearch
wget https://artifacts.elastic.co/downloads/elasticsearch/elasticsearch-7.10.0-x86_64.
    rpm
sudo rpm -ivh elasticsearch-7.10.0-x86_64.rpm

# Starting Elasticsearch
sudo systemctl start elasticsearch.service

# Enabling Elasticsearch auto-start on boot
sudo systemctl enable elasticsearch.service
```

Executing the above commands will set up a basic instance of Elasticsearch ready for data ingestion and querying. The systemctl commands ensure that the Elasticsearch service starts automatically, reducing manual intervention and ensuring continuous availability.

Elasticsearch's historical evolution illustrates a trajectory of continuous improvement and adaptation to meet the demands of high-performance, scalable search solutions. This ongoing development is a testament to its foundational role in modern data architectures.

1.3 Key Features and Benefits of Elasticsearch

Elasticsearch offers a plethora of functionalities tailored to handle vast data arrays, providing seamless integration, advanced search capabilities, and remarkable performance. This section delves into its core features and their consequent benefits to practitioners and enterprises alike.

- **1. Real-Time Data Ingestion and Search:** Elasticsearch is designed to perform searches and analytics in near real-time. This feature is crucial for applications that require immediate feedback. The indexing occurs within seconds of data ingestion, ensuring that users have access to the most current data without latency.
- **2. Distributed Architecture:** Elasticsearch follows a distributed architecture, ensuring high availability and resilience. The data is split into shards, each of which can have multiple replicas distributed across multiple nodes. This distribution promotes fault

tolerance and allows for horizontal scaling, enabling the addition of more nodes to handle increased data load seamlessly.

- **3. Scalability:** Scalability is inherent to Elasticsearch, facilitated through its shard-based architecture. Adding or removing nodes is simplified, allowing Elasticsearch clusters to scale out by distributing the workload. This flexibility supports the handling of large datasets and high query rates efficiently.
- **4. Advanced Search Capabilities:** Elasticsearch's search capabilities are robust, supporting a variety of query types, including full-text search, structured search, and geo-location search. The use of the Lucene library as the foundation allows Elasticsearch to provide powerful search functionalities such as term level, full-text, and spatial search, among others.
- **5. Aggregation Framework:** The powerful aggregation framework in Elasticsearch enables the execution of complex analytics over large sets of data. Aggregations help in summarizing and dissecting data across many dimensions, supporting statistical and faceted search capabilities. This is particularly beneficial for deriving insights and performing detailed analysis.
- **6. RESTful API:** Elasticsearch provides a comprehensive and intuitive RESTful API for interacting with the system. This API allows for easy integration with various clients and supports a wide range of operations, such as indexing documents, conducting searches, and managing clusters. The simplicity of the API makes Elasticsearch accessible to developers and easy to integrate into applications.
- **7. Document-Oriented:** Elasticsearch stores complex entities as structured JSON documents, making it highly versatile for different types of data. The document-oriented nature simplifies data representation and allows for schema-less storage, which can adapt to the varying structure of the data ingested.
- **8. Schema-Free and Dynamic Mapping:** Elasticsearch supports dynamic mapping, which automatically detects and indexes the schema of JSON documents, easing the indexing process. However, it also provides the flexibility to define mappings explicitly, catering to specific needs for search and analysis.
- **9. Full-Text Search and Analyzers:** Elasticsearch excels in full-text search capabilities. It incorporates analyzers to index tex-

tual data in a way conducive to efficient and accurate searches. These analyzers can tokenize text, filter stop words, stem words to their root forms, and more, enhancing search relevance and performance.

- **10. High Availability:** High availability is ensured through replication of shards. Elasticsearch allows one or more replicas of each shard, which facilitates quick recovery and query distribution, ensuring continuous availability even if some nodes fail.

- **11. Security Features:** With the introduction of various security tools and plugins, Elasticsearch provides robust security features such as encryption, user authentication, role-based access control (RBAC), and audit logging. These features are essential for protecting data integrity and confidentiality in production environments.

- **12. Snapshot and Restore:** The snapshot and restore functionality in Elasticsearch allows for creating backups of the indexed data at any point in time and restoring it when necessary. This feature is vital for data recovery and maintaining data integrity over long-term operations.

```
GET /my_index/_search
{
  "query": {
    "match": {
      "message": "search term"
    }
  }
}
```

```
{
  "took": 10,
  "timed_out": false,
  "_shards": {
    "total": 5,
    "successful": 5,
    "skipped": 0,
    "failed": 0
  },
  "hits": {
    "total": {
      "value": 100,
      "relation": "eq"
    },
    "max_score": 1.0,
    "hits": [
      {
        "_index": "my_index",
        "_type": "_doc",
        "_id": "1",
        "_score": 1.0,
        "_source": {
          "message": "search term"
        }
      }
    ]
  }
}
```

The benefits of these features translate into significant operational advantages. Elasticsearch enables high-speed search and analytics capabilities across large datasets, which can be critical for businesses that deal with real-time data processing and require instant insights. Its robust architecture ensures data redundancy, operational resilience, and scalability, providing an optimal solution for enterprise-grade search and analytic applications.

1.4 How Elasticsearch Works: Basic Architecture

Elasticsearch's architecture is designed to provide high availability, scalability, and robust search capabilities. At its core, it relies on a distributed, RESTful search and analytics engine built on top of Apache Lucene. Each component in the architecture works cohesively to ensure effective data indexing, storage, and retrieval. Understanding the key elements of the Elasticsearch architecture is essential for leveraging its full potential.

A cluster comprises one or more nodes, and each node can host multiple indices. Clusters enable high availability and failover, ensuring data is replicated and distributed across different nodes, which guarantees data redundancy and system robustness. Nodes within a cluster communicate and collaborate to process and serve search queries, manage indexes, and handle indexing requests.

Node Types and Roles:

In Elasticsearch, nodes have specific roles depending on their purpose within the cluster. The primary node types are:

- **Master Node:** Responsible for managing the cluster's overall state and configuration. It handles operations related to adding or removing nodes, creating or deleting indices, and splitting or merging index shards. The master node also coordinates changes across the cluster, ensuring consistency and synchronization.
- **Data Node:** Stores data and executes data-related operations such as indexing, search, and aggregation. Data nodes are responsible for managing the actual storage and retrieval of documents and are pivotal for the cluster's data handling performance.
- **Ingest Node:** Preprocesses documents before they are indexed. Ingest nodes can apply various transformations, enrichments, or filters on the incoming document data, such as removing unwanted fields or adding additional metadata.
- **Coordination Node:** Handles user requests by routing search and index requests and aggregates results from different data nodes. Any node can act as a coordination node, ensuring that the workload is balanced and managed efficiently.
- **Machine Learning Node:** Executes machine learning jobs within the cluster, which could include anomaly detection, forecasting, and data categorization. These nodes require more substantial computational resources due to the nature of machine learning operations.

Shard and Replica Management:

Elasticsearch indexes can be divided into smaller units called shards. This sharding mechanism enables efficient storage, search, and retrieval of large datasets by distributing data across multiple nodes. Each index in Elasticsearch is split into a specified number of primary shards, and each shard is a self-contained instance of Apache Lucene.

Shards can have replicas, which are essentially copies of primary shards. Replicas ensure data redundancy and high availability. By default, each primary shard has one replica, but this can be configured based on the required redundancy levels and available resources. Shard replication ensures that the system can tolerate node failures without data loss.

Data Distribution and Rebalancing:

When a new index is created, the primary shards are assigned across data nodes based on available resources and the current distribution of data. Elasticsearch employs a balanced sharding strategy to ensure that no single node is overwhelmed with excessive data. If the cluster's configuration changes, such as adding or removing nodes, Elasticsearch automatically redistributes shards to maintain balance across the cluster.

For example, consider creating an index with five primary shards and one replica. If the cluster consists of three data nodes, the primary shards and their replicas will be distributed among these nodes to ensure optimal balance and redundancy. Elasticsearch continuously monitors data node utilization and performs rebalancing as required.

Indexing and Search Flow:

The process of indexing involves taking incoming documents and transforming them into a format that allows for efficient search and retrieval operations. Indexing leverages various text analysis techniques, tokenizers, and filters to break down the document content into structured terms that Elasticsearch can manage.

A typical indexing request involves the following steps:

1. The document is sent to the coordination node, which acts as an entry point.
2. The coordination node analyzes and processes the document, applying any necessary transformations via ingest nodes.
3. The document is then forwarded to the primary shard where it should be stored.
4. The primary shard indexes the document and simultaneously updates its replica shards to ensure redundancy.

The search operation is similarly distributed. A search request follows these steps:

1. The search query is sent to the coordination node.
2. The coordination node distributes the search request across relevant shards (both primary and replica).
3. Each shard executes the search query independently and returns its results to the coordination node.
4. The coordination node aggregates the results and returns a consolidated response to the requester.

Cluster State and Metadata:

Maintaining a consistent and up-to-date cluster state is crucial for Elasticsearch's distributed nature. The cluster state includes metadata regarding the indices, mappings, and shard allocation. The master node is responsible for ensuring the consistency of this state across the cluster. It utilizes the Zen Discovery module to handle node discovery and master election processes, guaranteeing coordination and communication across nodes.

Snapshot and Restore:

Elasticsearch supports snapshot and restore capabilities to facilitate backup and recovery operations. Snapshots capture the state and data of an index or a cluster at a specific point in time. These snapshots can be stored in remote repositories like AWS S3 or on a shared filesystem, providing resilience against data loss.

Creating a snapshot involves the following steps:

1. Register a snapshot repository using an accessible storage location.
2. Trigger a snapshot request either manually or via a scheduled job.
3. Elasticsearch captures the incremental state of the indices and stores them in the registered repository.

Restoring from a snapshot recovers the indices to their previous state, providing a robust mechanism for disaster recovery or data migration. The snapshot and restore process ensures minimal disruption to cluster operations.

```
PUT /_snapshot/my_backup/snapshot_1
{
```

```
  "indices": "index_1,index_2",
  "ignore_unavailable": true,
  "include_global_state": false
}
```

This baseline knowledge of Elasticsearch's basic architecture sets the stage for more advanced configurations and operations, equipping users with the understanding necessary for efficient and effective data management.

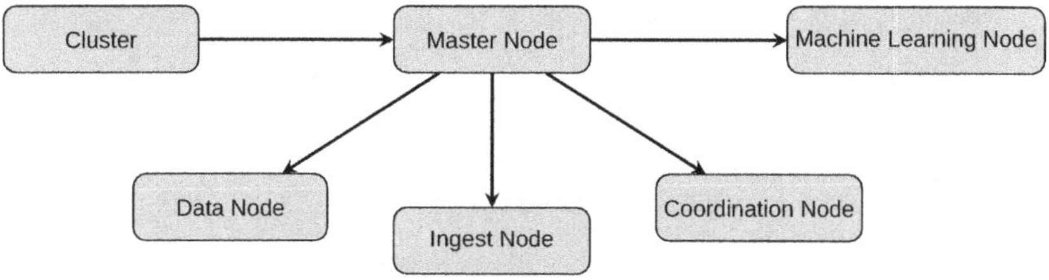

1.5 Use Cases for Elasticsearch

Elasticsearch's versatility and robustness make it suitable for a multitude of use cases across various industries. Its core capabilities include full-text search, structured search, analytics, and data visualization. This section delineates some of the most prevalent applications of Elasticsearch, demonstrating its adaptability and efficacy in real-world scenarios.

Log and Event Data Analytics

One of the most significant applications of Elasticsearch is in logging and event data analytics. Organizations utilize Elasticsearch to aggregate, analyze, and visualize logs from various sources, including application logs, system logs, and security logs. By indexing log data in near-real time, Elasticsearch enables quick searches and correlations, aiding in troubleshooting, performance monitoring, and security incident analysis.

```
PUT /logs/_doc/1
{
  "@timestamp": "2023-10-01T14:12:12",
  "log_level": "ERROR",
  "message": "NullPointerException at line 45",
  "service": "PaymentService"
}
```

Search Engine for E-Commerce

In e-commerce platforms, Elasticsearch serves as the backbone of the product search functionality. It allows users to search for products using various criteria such as keywords, categories, price ranges, and attributes. Elasticsearch's powerful full-text search capabilities, combined with features like autocomplete and spell correction, enhance user experience by providing relevant and accurate search results quickly.

```
GET /products/_search
{
  "query": {
    "bool": {
      "must": [
        { "match": { "name": "smartphone" } },
        { "range": { "price": { "gte": 300, "lte": 800 } } }
      ],
      "filter": [
        { "term": { "availability": "in_stock" } }
      ]
    }
  }
}
```

Real-Time Application Monitoring

Elasticsearch is instrumental in monitoring the health and performance of applications in real-time. By collecting and analyzing metrics such as CPU usage, memory consumption, and response times, Elasticsearch helps detect anomalies and performance degradation early. Coupled with Kibana for data visualization, it offers comprehensive dashboards, enabling operations teams to monitor and react to changes swiftly.

```
application_cpu_percent: 45.3
application_memory_used: 1024MB
response_time: 120ms
```

Content Management Systems (CMS)

Content Management Systems leverage Elasticsearch to provide advanced search functionalities and ensure scalability. Whether it's a blog, news site, or documentation portal, Elasticsearch can index vast amounts of textual content, making it easily searchable and retrievable. Features such as faceted search and relevance scoring further refine the search process, offering users precise and prioritized content.

```
PUT /blog_posts/_doc/1
{
  "title": "Introduction to Elasticsearch",
  "body": "Elasticsearch is a distributed search and analytics engine...",
  "author": "John Doe",
  "tags": ["Elasticsearch", "Search Engine", "Analytics"],
  "published_date": "2023-10-01"
```

```
}
```

Geospatial Data Analysis

Elasticsearch's capability to handle geospatial data makes it invaluable for applications involving location-based services. Whether it's mapping user activities, tracking delivery fleets, or providing geofencing services, Elasticsearch efficiently indexes and queries geospatial data. The geo-point and geo-shape data types, along with geospatial queries, empower developers to implement sophisticated geolocation functionalities.

```
POST /locations/_search
{
  "query": {
    "geo_distance": {
      "distance": "50km",
      "location": {
        "lat": 40.7128,
        "lon": -74.0060
      }
    }
  }
}
```

Security Information and Event Management (SIEM)

Elasticsearch is also extensively used in Security Information and Event Management (SIEM) systems. By collecting and analyzing security-related data from multiple sources, such as firewalls, intrusion detection systems, and antivirus software, Elasticsearch helps in detecting and mitigating security threats. The high-speed indexing and querying capabilities ensure that security incidents are swiftly identified and addressed.

```
PUT /security_events/_doc/1
{
  "@timestamp": "2023-10-01T14:12:12",
  "event_type": "login_attempt",
  "username": "john_doe",
  "status": "failure",
  "ip_address": "192.168.1.100"
}
```

The versatility and efficiency of Elasticsearch across these various use cases underscore its position as a pivotal tool in data management and analytics. Its ability to handle large volumes of heterogeneous data types accurately and promptly makes it indispensable for modern enterprises striving to harness the power of their data.

1.6 Installing and Running Elasticsearch

Elasticsearch can be installed on various operating systems, including Windows, Linux, and macOS. This section details the steps required to install and run Elasticsearch on these operating systems. We will cover downloading the Elasticsearch distribution, unzipping the package, configuring essential settings, and starting the server. Following these steps will result in a functioning Elasticsearch instance on your local machine.

Step 1: Downloading Elasticsearch

The official Elasticsearch download page provides distributions suitable for different platforms. Visit https://www.elastic.co/downloads/elasticsearch and select the appropriate version for your operating system. Elasticsearch is distributed as a tar.gz archive for Unix-like systems and a zip archive for Windows systems.

Step 2: Installation on Linux and macOS

For Unix-like systems, follow these steps:

1. Open a terminal window.
2. Download the tar.gz archive using wget or curl. For example:

```
wget https://artifacts.elastic.co/downloads/elasticsearch/elasticsearch-<version
    >-linux-x86_64.tar.gz
```

   Alternatively, you can use curl:

```
curl -L -O https://artifacts.elastic.co/downloads/elasticsearch/elasticsearch-<
    version>-linux-x86_64.tar.gz
```

3. Extract the contents of the downloaded archive:

```
tar -xzf elasticsearch-<version>-linux-x86_64.tar.gz
```

4. Navigate to the Elasticsearch directory:

```
cd elasticsearch-<version>/
```

Installation on Windows

For Windows systems, follow these steps:

1. Download the zip archive from the Elasticsearch download page.
2. Unzip the downloaded file using an extraction tool like WinRAR or 7-Zip.

Step 3: Basic Configuration

Before running Elasticsearch, a minimal configuration is recommended to specify paths for data, logs, and ensure no configuration conflicts occur.

1. Open the Elasticsearch configuration file located at:

```
<install_path>/config/elasticsearch.yml
```

2. Set the path.data and path.logs to appropriate directories:

```
path.data: /path/to/data
path.logs: /path/to/logs
```

It's recommended to use absolute paths.

Step 4: Running Elasticsearch

To run Elasticsearch, use the following commands depending on your operating system:

For Linux and macOS:

1. Ensure you are in the Elasticsearch directory.
2. Run Elasticsearch using:

```
./bin/elasticsearch
```

The startup process can take a few moments. Once Elasticsearch is up and running, the terminal will display an output indicating successful startup.

For Windows:

1. Open a command prompt and navigate to the Elasticsearch directory.
2. Run Elasticsearch using:

```
.\bin\elasticsearch.bat
```

The process will display logs in the command prompt window soon after Elasticsearch starts.

```
[2023-10-01T12:00:00,000][INFO ][o.e.n.Node               ] [node-1] starting ...
...
[2023-10-01T12:00:03,456][INFO ][o.e.n.Node               ] [node-1] started
```

To verify that Elasticsearch is successfully running, open a web browser and navigate to http://localhost:9200. You should see a JSON response similar to:


```
{
  "name" : "node-1",
  "cluster_name" : "elasticsearch",
  "cluster_uuid" : "Xc-ETfeIQDaBEpkxH4wz5w",
  "version" : {
    "number" : "8.0.0",
    "build_flavor" : "default",
    "build_type" : "tar",
    "build_hash" : "8b1f5d5",
    "build_date" : "2023-10-01T12:34:56.789456Z",
    "build_snapshot" : false,
    "lucene_version" : "9.0.0",
    "minimum_wire_compatibility_version" : "7.10.0",
    "minimum_index_compatibility_version" : "7.0.0"
  },
  "tagline" : "You Know, for Search"
}
```


If the JSON response is returned, Elasticsearch is active and ready to accept requests.

Finally, it is advantageous to review the logs stored in the specified log directory to monitor the server's activities and troubleshoot any potential issues. The logs provide insight into the operational status and any incidents that may require attention.

1.7 Basic Terminology and Concepts

Elasticsearch encompasses a range of terms and concepts that are essential for understanding its functionality and effective utilization. This section aims to provide a comprehensive understanding of these fundamental ideas.

Cluster: A cluster in Elasticsearch is a collection of one or more nodes (servers) that together holds the entire data and provides federated indexing and search capabilities. Each cluster is identified by a unique name, which defaults to "elasticsearch" but can be customized. Clusters enable horizontal scalability by allowing data and workload to be distributed across multiple nodes.

Node: A node is a single server that is part of a cluster. It stores data and participates in the cluster's indexing and search capabilities. Each node is assigned a unique identifier and is identified by its name, which can be automatically generated or customized. Nodes can play various roles within a cluster, such as:

- **Master Node**: Responsible for cluster-wide management and administrative tasks, such as creating or deleting indices, tracking which nodes are part of the cluster, and deciding where shards should be allocated.
- **Data Node**: Stores data and performs data-related operations like CRUD (Create, Read, Update, Delete) and search operations.
- **Ingest Node**: Preprocesses documents before the actual indexing happens. For instance, it can enrich documents by adding additional data, remove fields for compliance, or extract information from log files.
- **Coordinating Node**: Acts as a query router, handling search requests, gathering results from other nodes, and returning the final result to the client. Any node that is not a master, ingest, or data node, automatically assumes the role of a coordinating node.

Index: An index is a collection of documents that share similar characteristics. For instance, an e-commerce application might have one index for products, one for customer data, and another for orders. Each index is identified by a unique name, which is used to refer to that index when performing indexing, search, update, and delete operations.

Document: A document is a basic unit of information that can be indexed. It is a JSON object (JavaScript Object Notation) that contains one or more fields, where each field has a name and a value. The value can be a single value or a list of values, and can include strings, numbers, dates, or even other JSON objects.

Shard: Elasticsearch provides the ability to subdivide an index into multiple pieces called shards. Each shard is an instance of a Lucene index, which can be stored on any node in a cluster. Shards allow Elasticsearch to horizontally split/scale your content volume and distribute documents across the cluster. There are two types of shards:

- **Primary Shard**: Each document you index is stored in a primary shard.

- **Replica Shard**: Copies of the primary shards that serve as failover mechanisms to prevent data loss and ensure high availability.

The number of primary shards is specified at index creation and cannot be changed thereafter, but the number of replicas can be adjusted dynamically.

Mapping: A mapping is the process of defining how documents and their fields are stored and indexed. This includes specifying data types (e.g., string, integer, date) and how fields should be indexed and stored. Tracking the structure of the documents ensures Elasticsearch effectively performs search and indexing operations.

Analyzer: An analyzer in Elasticsearch is used to convert a field's text into its indexed tokens or terms. It defines the preprocessing required for text, such as tokenization, stemming, and removing stop words. Custom analyzers can be implemented to handle complex text-processing requirements.

Query DSL (Domain Specific Language): Elasticsearch uses Query DSL, a JSON-based query language, to power the search capabilities. It allows for constructing comprehensive and sophisticated queries to extract relevant information. Common types of queries include:

- **Match Query**: Searches for documents that match a provided text.
- **Range Query**: Finds documents with numeric or date fields that fall within specific ranges.
- **Term Query**: Searches for documents that contain the exact term in a specified field.

Aggregation: Aggregations in Elasticsearch are used to compute and extract statistical and summary information from the data. They serve analytics purposes by enabling complex calculations like averages, sums, min/max values, and counts to be performed and grouped by specific criteria.

Here is a sample of how to define and use some of the key elements in Elasticsearch via JSON configurations:

```
PUT /ecommerce
{
  "settings": {
    "number_of_shards": 3,
```

```
    "number_of_replicas": 1
  },
  "mappings": {
    "properties": {
      "product_id": { "type": "integer" },
      "name": { "type": "text" },
      "price": { "type": "float" },
      "created_at": { "type": "date" }
    }
  }
}
```

This JSON request creates an index named “ecommerce” with 3 primary shards and 1 replica for each shard. It includes a mapping for product_id as an integer, name as text, price as a float, and created_at as a date field.

```
POST /ecommerce/_doc/1
{
  "product_id": 101,
  "name": "Elasticsearch Guidebook",
  "price": 45.99,
  "created_at": "2023-10-01"
}
```

This example shows how to insert a document into the “ecommerce” index. The JSON document includes fields product_id, name, price, and created_at, each with relevant data.

Preparing efficient queries and maintaining an optimized indexing strategy is key to leveraging Elasticsearch’s full capabilities. The concepts of clusters, nodes, indices, documents, shards, mapping, analyzers, Query DSL, and aggregations form the backbone of how data is managed, queried, and analyzed within Elasticsearch. The intricate interplay between these elements ensures robust performance and scalability for a wide range of search and analytics use cases.

1.8 Understanding the Elasticsearch Ecosystem

Elasticsearch exists within a versatile and extensive ecosystem designed to enhance its search and analytics capabilities. This ecosystem comprises several integral components, each complementing Elasticsearch to address varied functionality emphatically and efficiently.

The key components of the Elasticsearch ecosystem include:

- Elasticsearch itself
- Kibana
- Logstash
- Beats
- Elasticsearch Clients
- Elastic Cloud

Elasticsearch: At the core of the ecosystem is Elasticsearch, the search engine built on Apache Lucene. It is designed for horizontal scaling, near real-time search, and supports complex querying functionality. Elasticsearch's distributed architecture ensures high availability and fault tolerance, distributing data across multiple nodes and balancing the search load.

Kibana: Kibana provides visualization capabilities for data stored in Elasticsearch. It allows users to create and share dynamic dashboards that depict real-time data. By visualizing data trends and patterns, Kibana aids in significant insight discovery. For example, the following command can be used to install Kibana:

```
curl -L -O https://artifacts.elastic.co/downloads/kibana/kibana-7.10.2-linux-x86_64.tar.
    gz
tar -xzf kibana-7.10.2-linux-x86_64.tar.gz
cd kibana-7.10.2-linux-x86_64/
./bin/kibana
```

The output to verify the successful start of Kibana might look like:

```
[INFO ][listening][server][http] http://localhost:5601
[INFO ][status][plugin] Kibana is now available
```

Logstash: Logstash serves as the data processing pipeline, capable of ingesting data from various sources simultaneously. It processes data through its filter plugins which can transform and enhance each event prior to pushing it into Elasticsearch. A basic Logstash configuration looks like this:

```
input {
  file {
    path => "/var/log/syslog"
    start_position => "beginning"
  }
}

filter {
  grok {
    match => { "message" => "%{SYSLOGLINE}" }
```

```
  }
  date {
    match => [ "timestamp" , "MMM d HH:mm:ss", "MMM dd HH:mm:ss" ]
  }
}

output {
  elasticsearch {
    hosts => ["localhost:9200"]
    index => "syslog-%{+YYYY.MM.dd}"
  }
}
```

Logstash processes events as they come and pushes them to the configured Elasticsearch index 'syslog-

Beats: Beats are lightweight, single-purpose data shippers designed to send data from edge machines to Logstash or Elasticsearch. There are several types of Beats, each tailored to specific types of data:

- Filebeat - For forwarding and centralizing log files.
- Metricbeat - For collecting metrics from the operating system and from services running on the server.
- Packetbeat - For capturing network traffic data.
- Winlogbeat - For shipping Windows Event logs.
- Heartbeat - For monitoring uptime by pinging services.

Elasticsearch Clients: Elasticsearch supports various programming languages through clients that provide rich APIs for interacting with Elasticsearch clusters. Commonly used clients include the Java Client, Python Client (elasticsearch-py), and JavaScript Client (elasticsearch-js). These clients simplify the integration of Elasticsearch into diverse application environments.

For example, using the Python client to index a document might look like:

```
from elasticsearch import Elasticsearch
es = Elasticsearch(["localhost:9200"])

# Index a document
es.index(index="test_index", id=1, body={"user": "kimchy", "message": "Hello World"
    })
```

Elastic Cloud: Elastic Cloud offers Elasticsearch, Kibana, and the entire suite of Elastic Stack services in a cloud environment managed by Elastic.co. It eliminates the need for infrastructure management, providing scalability, security updates, and monitoring tools. Utilizing Elastic Cloud allows users to leverage the full power of Elasticsearch without the operational overhead.

Together, these components deliver a comprehensive and modular framework capable of addressing a wide array of search, logging, and analytics needs in various application domains. This modularity and integrative capability underpin Elasticsearch's strength and popularity in dealing with large volumes of heterogeneous data efficiently.

1.9 Community and Support Resources

Elasticsearch's vast and active community plays a critical role in its development, support, and dissemination of knowledge. This section describes the various community and support resources available for both beginners and advanced users to help them effectively utilize Elasticsearch.

The Elasticsearch project is under the stewardship of Elastic, the company behind the software. Elastic offers several support channels and resources that are accessible through their official website. These resources range from comprehensive documentation and forums to professional support services and training programs.

- **Official Documentation**: The starting point for understanding Elasticsearch is the official documentation, which provides extensive coverage on all aspects of the software, including installation, configuration, API usage, and advanced features. The documentation is meticulously maintained and continuously updated to reflect changes in newer versions. Users can access this at https://www.elastic.co/guide/en/elasticsearch/reference/current/index.html.
- **Elastic Forum**: Elastic maintains an official forum where users can ask questions, share knowledge, and discuss various Elasticsearch topics. The forum is frequented by both community users and Elastic employees, which ensures that inquiries are promptly addressed. It's a valuable resource for troubleshooting and staying updated with best practices. The forum can be found at https://discuss.elastic.co/.
- **GitHub Repository**: Elasticsearch is hosted on GitHub, which serves as the platform for its source code and issue tracking. The

GitHub repository is an excellent resource for developers looking to contribute to the project or follow its development. Users can report bugs, request features, and review code changes. The Elasticsearch repository is accessible at https://github.com/elastic/elasticsearch.

- **Stack Overflow**: The Elasticsearch tag on Stack Overflow is highly active, with numerous questions and answers provided by the community. Stack Overflow is beneficial for finding solutions to common problems and learning through the experiences of others. It also offers the advantage of community voting, which helps surface the most useful answers. Users can explore Elasticsearch-related questions at https://stackoverflow.com/questions/tagged/elasticsearch.

- **Subscription and Professional Support**: Elastic offers subscription-based support services that provide users with direct access to Elastic engineers and consultants. This support includes features such as technical support, guidance on best practices, and access to advanced tools and services. These subscriptions are suitable for enterprises and mission-critical applications where guaranteed support and service levels are necessary. Information on these services can be found at https://www.elastic.co/subscriptions.

- **Meetups and Conferences**: The Elasticsearch community organizes various meetups and conferences worldwide. These events provide opportunities for users to network, collaborate, and learn from each other. Notable events include the ElasticON conference, which is Elastic's official global conference that features talks, workshops, and presentations from users and Elastic engineers. Local meetups are also regularly held and can be found through platforms like Meetup.com or via the Elastic website at https://www.elastic.co/elasticon.

- **Online Courses and Training**: Elastic offers a range of online courses and training programs. These resources are designed to help users at all levels, from beginners to advanced practitioners. The training includes on-demand courses, instructor-led virtual classrooms, and in-person workshops. Topics covered range from basic Elasticsearch operations to advanced topics like security and scaling. More information on available courses can be found at https://www.elastic.co/training.

- **Books and Tutorials**: Numerous books and online tutorials are available that cover various aspects of Elasticsearch. These resources range from introductory material to deep dives into specific features or use cases. Notable books include "Elasticsearch: The Definitive Guide" by Clinton Gormley and Zachary Tong, and "Elasticsearch in Action" by Radu Gheorghe, Lee Hinman, and Roy Russo. These books provide additional perspectives and practical insights that complement the official documentation.

- **Community Blogs and Articles**: Many community members and organizations publish blogs and articles on Elasticsearch. These resources often provide practical insights, case studies, and tutorials that can help users implement and optimize their Elasticsearch deployments. Some popular blog platforms include Medium, Dev.to, and company-specific blogs like those from Qbox or Compose.

Engaging with the Elasticsearch community and leveraging these resources can significantly enhance a user's capability to effectively work with the software. Additionally, feedback and contributions from the community help drive the continuous improvement and innovation of Elasticsearch.

1.10 Hands-On: Your First Elasticsearch Query

To effectively use Elasticsearch, it is crucial to understand how to interact with it through queries. This section guides you through executing a basic search query, providing foundational knowledge for more advanced querying.

Before starting, ensure that Elasticsearch is up and running on your system. You should be familiar with its installation and basic setup from the previous sections. We recommend using tools like cURL or a REST client such as Postman to interact with Elasticsearch, as they provide a convenient way to execute HTTP requests.

Indexing a Document

The first step in querying Elasticsearch is to have data indexed within it. Let us index a sample document for this purpose. A document in

Elasticsearch is a JSON object that represents the basic unit of information.

Execute the following cURL command to create an index named test_-index and index a sample document:

```
curl -X POST "localhost:9200/test_index/_doc/1" -H 'Content-Type: application/json'
      -d'
{
  "title": "Elasticsearch Basics",
  "author": "John Doe",
  "content": "Elasticsearch is a highly scalable open-source full-text search and
      analytics engine."
}'
```

This command sends a POST request to the Elasticsearch server running on localhost at port 9200. The JSON payload contains fields such as title, author, and content. The -H flag specifies the content type of the request.

Verify that the document has been indexed by executing the following:

```
curl -X GET "localhost:9200/test_index/_doc/1"
```

If successful, the output should resemble:

```
{
  "_index" : "test_index",
  "_type" : "_doc",
  "_id" : "1",
  "_version" : 1,
  "found" : true,
  "_source" : {
    "title" : "Elasticsearch Basics",
    "author" : "John Doe",
    "content" : "Elasticsearch is a highly scalable open-source full-text search and analytics engine."
  }
}
```

Searching the Indexed Document

Now that we have a document indexed, let us perform a basic search query using Elasticsearch's _search endpoint. The most fundamental query is the match_all query, which returns all documents in the index.

```
curl -X GET "localhost:9200/test_index/_search" -H 'Content-Type: application/json'
      -d'
{
  "query": {
    "match_all": {}
  }
}'
```

The match_all query is versatile as it retrieves all documents from the specified index. However, more practical queries typically involve searching for specific criteria. To find documents containing specific terms, use the match query:

```
curl -X GET "localhost:9200/test_index/_search" -H 'Content-Type: application/json'
    -d'
{
  "query": {
    "match": {
      "content": "scalable"
    }
  }
}'
```

This query searches for documents where the content field contains the term "scalable". The output will show documents that match this criterion.


```
{
  "took" : 10,
  "timed_out" : false,
  "_shards" : {
    "total" : 5,
    "successful" : 5,
    "skipped" : 0,
    "failed" : 0
  },
  "hits" : {
    "total" : {
      "value" : 1,
      "relation" : "eq"
    },
    "max_score" : 0.2876821,
    "hits" : [
      {
        "_index" : "test_index",
        "_type" : "_doc",
        "_id" : "1",
        "_score" : 0.2876821,
        "_source" : {
          "title" : "Elasticsearch Basics",
          "author" : "John Doe",
          "content" : "Elasticsearch is a highly scalable open-source full-text search and analytics engine."
        }
      }
    ]
  }
}
```


Filtering and Combining Queries

For more refined search capabilities, Elasticsearch allows for complex queries by combining multiple conditions using bool queries. bool queries support several operators such as must, should, and filter.

To create a query that finds documents containing the word "scalable" in the content field and authored by "John Doe", use the following:

```
curl -X GET "localhost:9200/test_index/_search" -H 'Content-Type: application/json'
    -d'
{
  "query": {
    "bool": {
      "must": [
        { "match": { "content": "scalable" }},
        { "match": { "author": "John Doe" }}
```

```
      ]
    }
  }
}'
```

This query uses the bool query with multiple must conditions. Each term within the must array must be satisfied for a document to match the query.

Sorting and Pagination

Search results can be sorted and paginated for more effective data handling. To sort by the title field in ascending order, include the sort parameter:

```
curl -X GET "localhost:9200/test_index/_search" -H 'Content-Type: application/json'
    -d'
{
  "query": {
    "match_all": {}
  },
  "sort": [
    { "title": "asc" }
  ]
}'
```

Paginating results involves specifying the from and size parameters. These parameters define the starting point and number of results to return, respectively. For example, to fetch the first 10 documents:

```
curl -X GET "localhost:9200/test_index/_search" -H 'Content-Type: application/json'
    -d'
{
  "query": {
    "match_all": {}
  },
  "from": 0,
  "size": 10
}'
```

Retrieving Specific Fields

If only specific fields from the documents are required, use the _source parameter. This narrows down the response to include only the specified fields.

For instance, to retrieve only the title and author fields:

```
curl -X GET "localhost:9200/test_index/_search" -H 'Content-Type: application/json'
    -d'
{
  "_source": ["title", "author"],
  "query": {
    "match_all": {}
  }
```

```
}'
```

Adding More Documents

Finally, let us index a few more documents to enhance the dataset. Execute:

```
curl -X POST "localhost:9200/test_index/_doc/2" -H 'Content-Type: application/json'
     -d'
{
  "title": "Advanced Elasticsearch",
  "author": "Jane Smith",
  "content": "This document dives deeper into Elasticsearch functionalities."
}'
```

```
curl -X POST "localhost:9200/test_index/_doc/3" -H 'Content-Type: application/json'
     -d'
{
  "title": "Elasticsearch Use Cases",
  "author": "John Doe",
  "content": "Exploring various use cases of Elasticsearch in real-world scenarios."
}'
```

These commands index additional documents, expanding the dataset.

Executing these fundamental operations helps in beginning to understand and leverage Elasticsearch's powerful querying capabilities. Advanced queries, aggregations, and performance tuning can build upon these basics, enabling the handling of more sophisticated data retrieval requirements.

Chapter 2

Setting Up Your Elasticsearch Environment

This chapter covers the essentials of preparing and installing Elasticsearch on various operating systems, including Windows, macOS, and Linux. It provides step-by-step guidance on starting and stopping the Elasticsearch service, configuring basic settings, and understanding the directory layout. Additionally, it introduces Kibana setup and connectivity, as well as key configuration files, ensuring you can verify and optimize your Elasticsearch installation effectively.

2.1 System Requirements and Prerequisites

To ensure a smooth and effective setup of Elasticsearch, several system requirements and prerequisites must be met. This section delineates these requirements and necessary preparation steps, spanning hardware specifications, software dependencies, network configuration, and permissions, within various operating systems.

Hardware Specifications: For the optimal performance of Elasticsearch, the hardware specifications of your system are crucial. Minimum and recommended specifications are detailed below:

- **Minimum Specifications:**
  - **RAM:** 4 GB (8 GB is highly recommended)
  - **CPU:** 2 cores (4 or more cores are recommended)
  - **Disk Space:** 20 GB free space
- **Recommended Specifications:**
  - **RAM:** 8 GB
  - **CPU:** 4 cores or more
  - **Disk Space:** 100 GB or more, with SSDs preferred for improved performance

Elasticsearch performance is heavily dependent on the amount of available memory and the number of CPU cores. Insufficient resources might lead to slower indexing and search performance, potentially degrading the user experience.

Software Dependencies: Elasticsearch requires Java Development Kit (JDK) as it is a Java-based application. Specifically, Elasticsearch 7.x versions require JDK 8 or 11. Ensure the correct version of the JDK is installed on your system:

```
$ java -version
```

This command should return the installed Java version. If Java is not installed or the version is incorrect, download and install the appropriate version from the official Oracle or OpenJDK website.

Network Configuration: Elasticsearch communicates over HTTP and requires network ports to be appropriately configured. The default port for Elasticsearch is 9200 for HTTP communication, and 9300 for internode communication:

- **HTTP API port:** 9200
- **Transport layer port:** 9300

Ensure these ports are open and accessible in your firewall settings. On Linux-based systems, use the following commands to allow these ports:

```
$ sudo ufw allow 9200/tcp
$ sudo ufw allow 9300/tcp
```

On macOS and Windows, configure the firewall settings through their respective utilities to permit traffic on these ports.

Permissions: Running Elasticsearch requires specific user permissions to access system-level resources. It is recommended to run Elasticsearch as a non-root user to enhance security. Create a dedicated user for Elasticsearch:

```
$ sudo adduser elasticsearch
```

Grant this user the necessary permissions to access and modify the relevant directories and files.

Operating System-Specific Notes: Installation steps may vary slightly across different operating systems.

- **Windows:** Ensure you have administrative permissions to install programs and configure network settings. The installation package is typically in a ZIP format, which needs to be extracted and configured.
- **macOS:** You may need to adjust your system's security settings to install applications from identified developers, as well as configure the firewall to allow communication on Elasticsearch-specific ports.
- **Linux:** Different Linux distributions may have varied package managers (e.g., APT for Ubuntu, YUM for CentOS). Use the package manager appropriate for your distribution or opt for the generic tar.gz package.

Environment Variables: Set up necessary environment variables to facilitate the Elasticsearch operation:

```
$ export JAVA_HOME=/path/to/your/java
```

Ensure the path to Java binaries is correctly specified in your system's PATH environment variable.

Attention to these detailed system requirements and pre-requisites will lay a solid foundation for a seamless Elasticsearch setup, preventing avoidable errors and performance bottlenecks.

2.2 Installing Elasticsearch on Windows

This section elucidates the process of installing Elasticsearch on Windows operating systems, ensuring you accomplish a successful setup for subsequent configurations and operations. The installation process requires adherence to specific steps that encompass downloading the software, extracting the files, and initiating the Elasticsearch service. Each step will be systematically described to guarantee clarity and completeness.

First, ensure that your system meets the minimum requirements specified in the "System Requirements and Pre-requisites" section of this chapter. Elasticsearch requires a Java Development Kit (JDK) installation, preferably OpenJDK or Oracle JDK version 8 or later. Verify your current Java version by executing:

```
java -version
```

If Java is not installed or the version is outdated, download and install the latest version of OpenJDK from the official website.

- **Step 1: Downloading Elasticsearch**

Visit the official Elasticsearch download page at https://www.elastic.co/downloads/elasticsearch. Choose the Windows version, ensuring you select the appropriate architecture (32-bit or 64-bit) according to your system specifications. The download usually comes in a ZIP archive.

- **Step 2: Extracting the Files**

Locate the downloaded ZIP file, typically named elasticsearch-{version}.zip. Extract the contents to a desired installation directory. For example, extract it to C:\Elasticsearch for ease of access. Ensure the extraction preserves the directory structure of the ZIP file.

- **Step 3: Configuring Elasticsearch**

Within the extracted files, navigate to the config directory. Here, you'll find vital configuration files such as elasticsearch.yml, jvm.options, and log4j2.properties. For a basic setup, you might not need to alter these files significantly, but ensuring proper memory allocation in jvm.options aligns with your system's capabilities is recommended.

Open config\elasticsearch.yml in a text editor (e.g., Notepad). Modify settings as required, but for most basic installations, no changes are needed to start Elasticsearch. For instance, you might want to configure network settings or cluster names for more advanced setups.

Sample content of elasticsearch.yml might look like this:

```
cluster.name: my-application
node.name: node-1
path.data: C:\Elasticsearch\data
path.logs: C:\Elasticsearch\logs
network.host: 127.0.0.1
http.port: 9200
discovery.seed_hosts: ["127.0.0.1", "[::1]"]
cluster.initial_master_nodes: ["node-1"]
```

These settings ensure that Elasticsearch stores data in the C:\Elasticsearch\data directory and logs in the C:\Elasticsearch\logs directory. The network configuration binds the service to localhost.

- **Step 4: Starting and Stopping Elasticsearch**

To start Elasticsearch, open a Command Prompt window in administrator mode. Navigate to the bin directory of your Elasticsearch installation, and execute the following command:

```
elasticsearch.bat
```

The server will begin booting, and diagnostic information will appear on the Command Prompt screen. Successful startup is indicated by a message similar to:

```
[INFO ][o.e.n.Node ] [node-1] started
```

You can now open your web browser and navigate to http://localhost:9200. If Elasticsearch is running correctly, you should see a JSON response displaying cluster information.

To stop the Elasticsearch service, simply press Ctrl + C in the Command Prompt window where Elasticsearch is running. Alternatively, you can set up Elasticsearch as a Windows service for easier management.

- **Step 5: Setting Up Elasticsearch as a Windows Service**

For flexibility, especially in a production environment, Elasticsearch can be installed as a Windows service. This requires the elasticsearch-service.bat script found in the bin directory. Execute the following command in Command Prompt (running as Administrator):

```
elasticsearch-service.bat install
```

This command installs Elasticsearch as a service. To start the service, use:

```
elasticsearch-service.bat start
```

To stop the service, use:

```
elasticsearch-service.bat stop
```

And to remove the service:

```
elasticsearch-service.bat remove
```

It is prudent to verify the service's successful installation through the Windows Services app (services.msc), where you can also configure the startup type and other service properties.

By adhering to these steps and verifying each phase's successful completion, a robust Elasticsearch setup on a Windows system is ensconced, facilitating subsequent configurations and operational functionalities.

2.3 Installing Elasticsearch on macOS

To install Elasticsearch on macOS, you can utilize either the Homebrew package manager or manually install the software by downloading it from the official Elasticsearch website. Both methods are reliable; however, using Homebrew simplifies the installation process. The following steps detail each approach, providing comprehensive, meticulous instructions to ensure a successful setup.

Using Homebrew

Homebrew is a popular package manager for macOS that simplifies the installation of software. To install Elasticsearch using Homebrew, follow these steps:

- **Ensure Homebrew is Installed**: Open the Terminal application and check if Homebrew is already installed by running:

```
brew -v
```

If Homebrew is not installed, you can install it by executing the following command:

```
/bin/bash -c "$(curl -fsSL https://raw.githubusercontent.com/Homebrew/install
    /HEAD/install.sh)"
```

- **Install Elasticsearch**: Once Homebrew is installed and updated, you can proceed with the Elasticsearch installation by typing:

```
brew tap elastic/tap
brew install elastic/tap/elasticsearch-full
```

- **Start Elasticsearch**: After the installation completes, you can start the Elasticsearch service by running:

```
brew services start elastic/tap/elasticsearch-full
```

To stop the Elasticsearch service, you can use:

```
brew services stop elastic/tap/elasticsearch-full
```

Verifying the Installation

To verify that Elasticsearch is running correctly, you can query the Elasticsearch HTTP interface. Open Terminal and run:

```
curl -X GET "localhost:9200/"
```

The expected response should resemble:

```
{
  "name" : "your-computer-name",
  "cluster_name" : "elasticsearch",
  "cluster_uuid" : "some-uuid",
  "version" : {
    "number" : "7.10.0",
    "build_flavor" : "default",
    "build_type" : "tar",
    "build_hash" : "some-hash",
    "build_date" : "2020-11-17T00:00:00.000Z",
    "build_snapshot" : false,
    "lucene_version" : "8.7.0",
    "minimum_wire_compatibility_version" : "6.8.0",
    "minimum_index_compatibility_version" : "6.0.0"
  },
  "tagline" : "You Know, for Search"
}
```

Manual Installation

For users who prefer not to use Homebrew, manual installation is also straightforward. The steps include downloading, extracting, and configuring Elasticsearch as follows:

- **Download the Elasticsearch zip file**: Navigate to the official Elasticsearch download page (https://www.elastic.co/downloads/elasticsearch) and download the latest macOS zip file.

- **Extract the Archive**: Open the Terminal and navigate to the directory where the zip file was downloaded. Extract the contents using:

```
unzip elasticsearch-7.10.0-darwin-x86_64.zip
```

- **Move Elasticsearch to an Appropriate Directory**: It is recommended to move the extracted directory to /usr/local. Run:

```
sudo mv elasticsearch-7.10.0 /usr/local/elasticsearch
```

- **Start Elasticsearch**: To start Elasticsearch, navigate to the bin directory and run the elasticsearch executable:

```
cd /usr/local/elasticsearch/bin
./elasticsearch
```

  To run Elasticsearch in the background, use:

```
./elasticsearch -d
```

Verifying the Installation

Similar to the verification process with Homebrew, you can check if Elasticsearch is running by querying the HTTP interface. In Terminal, run:

```
curl -X GET "localhost:9200/"
```

The response should be:

```
{
  "name" : "your-computer-name",
  "cluster_name" : "elasticsearch",
  "cluster_uuid" : "some-uuid",
  "version" : {
    "number" : "7.10.0",
    "build_flavor" : "default",
    "build_type" : "tar",
    "build_hash" : "some-hash",
    "build_date" : "2020-11-17T00:00:00.000Z",
    "build_snapshot" : false,
    "lucene_version" : "8.7.0",
    "minimum_wire_compatibility_version" : "6.8.0",
    "minimum_index_compatibility_version" : "6.0.0"
  },
  "tagline" : "You Know, for Search"
}
```

Completing these installation steps ensures Elasticsearch is properly configured on macOS. Always refer to official documentation for updates or changes in installation procedures.

2.4 Installing Elasticsearch on Linux

Installation of Elasticsearch on a Linux system requires careful attention to the selection of appropriate package formats, commands, and configuration steps. Following, we provide a detailed explanation of the installation process for Elasticsearch on popular Linux distributions like Debian-based distributions (e.g., Ubuntu) and Red Hat-based distributions (e.g., CentOS).

The installation process can be divided into three main steps: importing the Elasticsearch public GPG key, adding the Elasticsearch repository to the package manager, and finally, installing the Elasticsearch package.

Importing the Elasticsearch Public GPG Key

Before installing Elasticsearch from its repository, it is essential to ensure the authenticity of the packages. Importing the Elasticsearch public GPG key achieves this.

```
wget -qO - https://artifacts.elastic.co/GPG-KEY-elasticsearch | sudo apt-key add -
```

This command downloads the GPG key and automatically adds it to the system's list of trusted keys using the 'apt-key add' command for Debian-based systems.

For Red Hat-based systems:

```
rpm --import https://artifacts.elastic.co/GPG-KEY-elasticsearch
```

The 'rpm –import' command performs a similar function, integrating the GPG key into the RPM key database.

Adding the Elasticsearch Repository

Once the GPG key is added, the next step involves adding the Elasticsearch repository to the system's package manager.

For Debian-based systems (e.g., Ubuntu), create a file named 'elastic-7.x.list' in the '/etc/apt/sources.list.d/' directory:

```
echo "deb https://artifacts.elastic.co/packages/7.x/apt stable main" | sudo tee -a /etc/
    apt/sources.list.d/elastic-7.x.list
```

Update the package list to include the newly added repository:

```
sudo apt-get update
```

For Red Hat-based systems (e.g., CentOS), create a new repository configuration file named 'elasticsearch.repo' under '/etc/yum.repos.d/':

```
sudo tee /etc/yum.repos.d/elasticsearch.repo <<- 'EOF'
[elasticsearch-7.x]
name=Elasticsearch repository for 7.x packages
baseurl=https://artifacts.elastic.co/packages/7.x/yum
gpgcheck=1
gpgkey=https://artifacts.elastic.co/GPG-KEY-elasticsearch
enabled=1
autorefresh=1
type=rpm-md
EOF
```

This command block uses 'tee' to create the file, appending the repository configuration to it.

Installing Elasticsearch Package

With the Elasticsearch repository added, the package installation process is straightforward using the package manager.

For Debian-based systems, install Elasticsearch with the following command:

```
sudo apt-get install elasticsearch
```

For Red Hat-based systems, use yum to perform the installation:

```
sudo yum install elasticsearch
```

Configuring Elasticsearch to Start Automatically

Post-installation, configure Elasticsearch to start automatically when the system boots.

Enable and start the Elasticsearch service on Debian-based systems using systemd:

```
sudo systemctl enable elasticsearch
sudo systemctl start elasticsearch
```

Similarly, on Red Hat-based systems:

```
sudo systemctl enable elasticsearch
sudo systemctl start elasticsearch
```

These commands ensure that Elasticsearch will automatically start with the system by enabling the service via systemd and then starting it.

Verifying the Installation

After starting Elasticsearch, it is crucial to verify whether the installation was successful. Use the following command to check the status of the Elasticsearch service:

```
sudo systemctl status elasticsearch
```

A successful installation will show Elasticsearch as active (running). Additionally, verify Elasticsearch is running by performing an HTTP request to the localhost on port 9200:

```
curl -X GET "localhost:9200/"
```

The output should be a JSON response with the cluster information, confirming that Elasticsearch is running correctly.


```
{
  "name" : "your_node_name",
  "cluster_name" : "elasticsearch",
  "cluster_uuid" : "XXXXXXXXXXXXXX",
  "version" : {
    "number" : "7.x.x",
    "build_flavor" : "default",
    "build_type" : "deb/rpm",
    "build_hash" : "XXXXXXXXXXXXXXXXXXXX",
    "build_date" : "YYYY-MM-DDTHH:MM:SS.SSSZ",
    "build_snapshot" : false,
    "lucene_version" : "8.x.x",
    "minimum_wire_compatibility_version" : "6.x.x",
    "minimum_index_compatibility_version" : "6.x.x"
  },
  "tagline" : "You Know, for Search"
}
```


This response validates that Elasticsearch is operational and configured correctly on your Linux system.

2.5 Starting and Stopping the Elasticsearch Service

Initiating and halting the Elasticsearch service is fundamental to managing your Elasticsearch environment. Proper control over these processes ensures that the service is available when needed and conserves system resources when it is not. This section will delineate the precise commands and methods for starting and stopping Elasticsearch across different operating systems.

To begin with, Elasticsearch can be started by directly executing the Elasticsearch binary. For users who have installed Elasticsearch using package managers, such as 'apt' or 'yum', it is also possible to manage the service through 'systemd' or 'service' commands. The following examples illustrate these methods for Windows, macOS, and Linux systems.

- **Windows:** On Windows systems, Elasticsearch can be started from the Command Prompt or PowerShell. Navigate to the 'bin' directory of the Elasticsearch installation and execute the 'elasticsearch.bat' file. This script will launch the service in the foreground.

```
cd C:\Program Files\Elasticsearch\bin
elasticsearch.bat
```

  To stop the Elasticsearch service, simply close the Command Prompt window or terminate the process from the Task Manager.

- **macOS and Linux:** On macOS and Linux systems, the process is quite similar. Navigate to the 'bin' directory of the Elasticsearch installation and start the Elasticsearch service by executing the 'elasticsearch' script.

```
cd /usr/local/elasticsearch/bin
./elasticsearch
```

  To stop Elasticsearch, you can use the 'Ctrl+C' key combination in the terminal where the process is running.

- **Using systemd:** To start the Elasticsearch service, use the following command:

```
sudo systemctl start elasticsearch
```

  To stop the service, the command is:

```
sudo systemctl stop elasticsearch
```

Moreover, if you need to restart Elasticsearch, which is often necessary after configuration changes, the command is:

```
sudo systemctl restart elasticsearch
```

To enable Elasticsearch to start automatically upon system boot, use:

```
sudo systemctl enable elasticsearch
```

Conversely, to disable the automatic start upon boot:

```
sudo systemctl disable elasticsearch
```

- **Using service:** For systems that utilize the older 'init.d' system (common on older distributions), the 'service' command is used.

  To start Elasticsearch:

  ```
  sudo service elasticsearch start
  ```

  To stop it:

  ```
  sudo service elasticsearch stop
  ```

  To restart the service:

  ```
  sudo service elasticsearch restart
  ```

- **Verifying Service Status:** To ensure that the Elasticsearch service is running correctly, you can check its status with the 'systemctl' or 'service' commands.

  Using 'systemctl':

  ```
  sudo systemctl status elasticsearch
  ```

  Using 'service':

  ```
  sudo service elasticsearch status
  ```

  These commands will provide you with information about the Elasticsearch process, confirming whether it is active and running without issues.

By mastering these commands and understanding the operational behaviors of the Elasticsearch service, administrators can efficiently manage their Elasticsearch instances. This ensures high availability and optimal performance of the Elasticsearch environment.

2.6 Basic Configuration Settings

Configuring Elasticsearch correctly is critical for optimizing its performance and ensuring it operates reliably under various workloads. This section delves into essential configuration settings that determine how Elasticsearch behaves during indexing and querying operations, cluster management, and other key functions.

elasticsearch.yml

The primary configuration file, elasticsearch.yml, is located in the config directory of your Elasticsearch installation. This file specifies most of Elasticsearch's settings. Editing this file allows for customization of node-specific configurations as well as cluster-wide settings.

A typical entry in elasticsearch.yml might look like the following:

```
cluster.name: my-application
node.name: node-1
path.data: /var/lib/elasticsearch
path.logs: /var/log/elasticsearch
network.host: 192.168.0.1
http.port: 9200
```

Each configuration parameter is straightforward:

- cluster.name sets the name of your cluster. This name is used to identify the cluster in logs and monitoring tools.
- node.name defines the name of the node. This helps in distinguishing logs from different nodes.
- path.data specifies the directory where Elasticsearch stores data. Ensure this path has sufficient storage and is on a fast disk.
- path.logs designates the directory for storing log files. Monitoring log files can help in diagnosing issues.
- network.host determines the network interfaces on which Elasticsearch listens. Configuring this properly ensures that Elasticsearch is accessible on the desired network.

- http.port sets the port on which Elasticsearch serves HTTP requests. The default is 9200, but this can be changed to avoid conflicts or accommodate security requirements.

Cluster and Node Settings

Cluster and node settings are vital for the proper functioning and management of Elasticsearch clusters:

- discovery.seed_hosts is an array of addresses used to seed the discovery process of new nodes. This setting can include IP addresses or hostnames of existing nodes in the cluster.

```
discovery.seed_hosts: ["192.168.0.1", "192.168.0.2"]
```

- cluster.initial_master_nodes is an array of node names or IDs to elect the initial master nodes during cluster bootstrapping. This setting is used only during the initial cluster formation.

```
cluster.initial_master_nodes: ["node-1", "node-2"]
```

Memory Settings

Optimizing memory usage is crucial for Elasticsearch performance. The Java Virtual Machine (JVM) settings are configured in jvm.options. Key settings include:

- -Xms and -Xmx settings define the minimum and maximum heap sizes for the JVM. It's recommended to set these to the same value to prevent heap resizing, which can be costly. Generally, 50% of the available memory should be allocated to the heap, not exceeding 32GB.

```
-Xms16g
-Xmx16g
```

- -XX:+UseG1GC enables the G1 Garbage Collector, which is recommended for Elasticsearch.

```
-XX:+UseG1GC
```

Thread Pools

Thread pools in Elasticsearch manage the execution of different types of operations. Proper configuration of these pools ensures efficient resource utilization.

- thread_pool.search.size configures the number of threads in the search thread pool.
- thread_pool.index.size configures the number of threads in the indexing thread pool.

```
thread_pool.search.size: 15
thread_pool.index.size: 10
```

Index Settings

Index management is facilitated by settings specified during index creation or updated dynamically. Essential settings include:

- index.number_of_shards defines the number of primary shards. This setting cannot be changed after index creation.
- index.number_of_replicas specifies the number of replica shards for each primary shard.

```
PUT /my_index
{
  "settings": {
    "index": {
      "number_of_shards": 3,
      "number_of_replicas": 2
    }
  }
}
```

Security Settings

Securing your Elasticsearch cluster is paramount. Some essential settings include:

- xpack.security.enabled enables or disables security features.
- xpack.security.transport.ssl.enabled enables SSL/TLS for node-to-node communication.

```
xpack.security.enabled: true
xpack.security.transport.ssl.enabled: true
```

Properly adjusting these fundamental configuration settings tailors Elasticsearch to the specific needs of your environment, ensuring optimal performance, reliability, and security.

2.7 Elasticsearch Directory Layout

A comprehensive understanding of the Elasticsearch directory layout is crucial to efficiently manage, configure, and troubleshoot your Elasticsearch installation. This section details the various directories and their purposes within the Elasticsearch installation directory, typically referred to as ES_HOME.

Upon a successful installation of Elasticsearch, the primary directory structure within ES_HOME is organized as follows:

```
ES_HOME/
  bin/
  config/
  data/
  jdk/
  lib/
  logs/
  modules/
  plugins/
  tmp/
```

- **bin/**

  The bin/ directory contains executable files that manage Elasticsearch operations. These scripts are useful for starting, stopping, and managing the Elasticsearch node from the command line:

  ```
  ES_HOME/bin/elasticsearch
  ES_HOME/bin/elasticsearch-plugin
  ES_HOME/bin/elasticsearch-keystore
  ES_HOME/bin/elasticsearch-certutil
  ```

  The elasticsearch command starts the Elasticsearch server, while elasticsearch-plugin manages the installation and removal of plugins. The elasticsearch-keystore is used to manage secure settings, and elasticsearch-certutil assists in generating SSL/TLS certificates.

- **config/**

  The config/ directory is essential for configuring the Elasticsearch node. It contains the elasticsearch.yml file, which houses the primary configuration settings, and other important configuration files:

  ```
  ES_HOME/config/elasticsearch.yml
  ES_HOME/config/jvm.options
  ES_HOME/config/log4j2.properties
  ES_HOME/config/users
  ES_HOME/config/users_roles
  ```

The elasticsearch.yml file is the main configuration file where you define settings such as cluster name, node name, paths to directories, and network settings. The jvm.options file contains JVM-specific options that influence Elasticsearch's runtime behavior. The log4j2.properties file manages logging settings, including log levels and output destinations. User authentication and roles are configured in the users and users_roles files, respectively.

- **data/**

  The data/ directory is where all indexed data is stored by default. Each index is organized into a separate subdirectory here, maintaining the index's data shards:

  ES_HOME/data/nodes/0/indices/

  The path structure inside the data/ directory reflects the configuration of the Elasticsearch node's data paths.

- **jdk/**

  The jdk/ directory includes the pre-packaged Java Development Kit (JDK) that Elasticsearch uses. This ensures that Elasticsearch uses a compatible version of Java, providing consistency across different environments.

- **lib/**

  The lib/ directory contains the core libraries and dependencies required by Elasticsearch:

  ES_HOME/lib/elasticsearch-<version>.jar

  These jar files include the essential components that Elasticsearch depends on to function properly.

- **logs/**

  The logs/ directory stores log files generated by Elasticsearch. This directory is crucial for monitoring the health and activity of the Elasticsearch instance:

  ES_HOME/logs/<cluster-name>.log
  ES_HOME/logs/gc.log

  Logs include general operational logs, garbage collection logs, and any errors or anomalies occurring within the Elasticsearch processes.

- **modules/**

The modules/ directory contains built-in modules that come with Elasticsearch. Modules can include various features ranging from different types of analysis engines to specialized functionality:

ES_HOME/modules/ingest-common/
ES_HOME/modules/lang-mustache/

These are integral parts of Elasticsearch and extend its capabilities without requiring additional plugins.

- **plugins/**

  The plugins/ directory holds installed plugins. Plugins enhance or add new features to Elasticsearch, such as additional analysis plugins, repository plugins for snapshot and restore, and more:

  ES_HOME/plugins/analysis-phonetic/
  ES_HOME/plugins/repository-s3/

  Each plugin is typically isolated in its subdirectory, containing all related files and resources.

- **tmp/**

  The tmp/ directory is used for temporary files by Elasticsearch. These are typically transient files, necessary for the functioning of certain processes or during specific tasks like snapshotting:

  ES_HOME/tmp/

  During troubleshooting or setting up the environment, it's crucial to understand each of these directories and their significance. Proper navigation and manipulation of these directories ensure efficient management and fine-tuning of your Elasticsearch instance.

2.8 Setting Up Kibana and Connecting to Elasticsearch

Kibana is an open-source data visualization and exploration tool that allows you to interact with your Elasticsearch data through charts and graphs. Setting up Kibana and connecting it to Elasticsearch involves several critical steps, including downloading, installing, configuring, and starting the Kibana service. This section provides detailed instructions to ensure that Kibana is set up correctly and connected to your Elasticsearch instance.

First, download the appropriate Kibana version that matches your Elasticsearch version from the official Elastic website:

```
wget https://artifacts.elastic.co/downloads/kibana/kibana-7.10.0-linux-x86_64.tar.gz
```

Extract the downloaded archive:

```
tar -xzf kibana-7.10.0-linux-x86_64.tar.gz
cd kibana-7.10.0-linux-x86_64/
```

Kibana's configuration file, kibana.yml, is located in the config directory within the Kibana home directory. To connect Kibana to your Elasticsearch instance, you need to edit this file to specify the Elasticsearch endpoint. Open kibana.yml in a text editor:

```
nano config/kibana.yml
```

Locate the following settings in the kibana.yml configuration file and adjust them as needed:

```
# The URL of the Elasticsearch instance to use for all your queries.
elasticsearch.hosts: ["http://localhost:9200"]

# The port where Kibana server will listen
server.port: 5601

# The hostname where Kibana will be accessed
server.host: "localhost"
```

Make sure that the elasticsearch.hosts setting points to the correct URL of your Elasticsearch instance. If Elasticsearch is running on a different host or port, update the value accordingly.

After saving the changes to kibana.yml, start the Kibana service by running:

```
./bin/kibana
```

The console should display log messages indicating that Kibana is starting. Upon successful startup, these logs can be seen:

```
log [13:00:00.000] [info][status][plugin:kibana@7.10.0] Status changed from uninitialized to green - Ready
log [13:00:00.001] [info][status][plugin:elasticsearch@7.10.0] Status changed from yellow to green - Ready
log [13:00:00.002] [info][listening] Server running at http://localhost:5601
```

Next, confirm that Kibana is connected to Elasticsearch by navigating to http://localhost:5601 in a web browser. The Kibana user interface should load, and you may be prompted to create an index pattern to start exploring your data. An index pattern defines which indices you want to explore and must match at least one index present in Elasticsearch.

To create an index pattern, follow these steps:

- Navigate to the "Management" tab in the Kibana interface.
- Click on "Index Patterns" under the "Kibana" section.
- Click the "Create index pattern" button.
- Enter the name of one of your indices, or use a wildcard (*) to match multiple indices, then click "Next step".
- Select the time field (if applicable) to be used for time-based data and click "Create index pattern".

After creating an index pattern, you can start using Kibana's Discover, Visualize, and Dashboard features to interact with and visualize your Elasticsearch data.

Ensure that both Elasticsearch and Kibana are running properly. Monitoring their logs for any errors can provide insights into potential issues:

```
tail -f logs/kibana.log
```

If Kibana does not start or fails to display correctly, common issues include mismatched versions of Elasticsearch and Kibana or incorrect Elasticsearch endpoint URL in the kibana.yml file. Ensure both services are compatible and correctly configured.

By following these steps, Kibana will be set up and connected to Elasticsearch, enabling a powerful interface for data analysis and visualization.

2.9 Understanding Elasticsearch Configuration Files

Elasticsearch relies on several configuration files to manage vital settings and runtime behaviors. These files include elasticsearch.yml, jvm.options, log4j2.properties, and log4shell.properties. Thorough understanding of these configuration files is essential to optimize performance, ensure security, and maintain stability.

The primary configuration file for Elasticsearch is elasticsearch.yml. This file contains key settings, including node configuration, cluster configuration, network settings, and path settings. The configuration is in

YAML format, which requires careful adherence to syntax rules such as indentation. Below is an example of a minimal elasticsearch.yml configuration:

```
cluster.name: my-cluster
node.name: node-1
path.data: /var/lib/elasticsearch
path.logs: /var/log/elasticsearch
network.host: 0.0.0.0
discovery.seed_hosts: ["host1", "host2"]
cluster.initial_master_nodes: ["node-1", "node-2"]
```

Each setting is self-explanatory:

- cluster.name: Name of the cluster to which this node belongs.
- node.name: Unique identifier for the node within the cluster.
- path.data: Directory where index data is stored.
- path.logs: Directory where log files are stored.
- network.host: IP address or hostname where Elasticsearch listens for incoming connections.
- discovery.seed_hosts: List of nodes used to discover the cluster.
- cluster.initial_master_nodes: List of master-eligible nodes used for cluster bootstrapping.

The jvm.options file configures JVM settings impacting Elasticsearch's operation, such as heap size and garbage collection (GC) settings. Below is an example of setting the initial and maximum heap size in jvm.options:

```
-Xms2g
-Xmx2g
```

This example sets both the initial and maximum heap size to 2 GB. It is crucial that these settings are equal to prevent Elasticsearch from performance degradation due to dynamically adjusting heap size during runtime.

Another vital configuration file is log4j2.properties, which manages logging configuration. Effective logging configuration aids in troubleshooting and monitoring. Elasticsearch uses the Log4j 2 framework for logging. A basic section of a log4j2.properties file might look as follows:

```
status = error
name = Elasticsearch
appender.console.type = Console
appender.console.name = console
appender.console.layout.type = PatternLayout
appender.console.layout.pattern = [%d{ISO8601}][%-5p][%-25c] %marker%m%n
rootLogger.level = info
rootLogger.appenderRef.console.ref = console
```

Key aspects illustrated above:

- Logging at the info level is specified.
- Console output is chosen as the logging destination.
- A pattern layout determines the format of log messages.

Elasticsearch developers must also be aware of the log4shell.properties file, which is essential for mitigations against vulnerabilities like Log4Shell. Typically, this file is pre-configured by Elasticsearch developers and does not require frequent modifications from end-users.

For dynamic changes, using the _cluster/settings API provides convenience without server restarts. As an example, to update the number of replicas dynamically:

```
PUT /_cluster/settings
{
  "persistent": {
    "index.number_of_replicas": 2
  }
}
```

In this context, the configuration is applied at the cluster level and persists across node restarts.

Comprehending and manipulating these files correctly ensures the Elasticsearch cluster operates optimally, safeguarding it from preventable issues while enabling performance tuning tailored to specific use-cases.

2.10 Hands-On: Verifying Your Installation

Once you have installed Elasticsearch and set up Kibana, it is essential to verify that the installation is working correctly. This involves ensuring that the Elasticsearch service is running, able to process requests, and that Kibana can successfully connect to your Elasticsearch instance. The verification process includes using command-line tools to send HTTP requests to Elasticsearch's RESTful API, examining logs, and confirming cluster health.

To begin, ensure your Elasticsearch service is running. Open a terminal or command prompt and navigate to the Elasticsearch directory. Use the following command to start the Elasticsearch service:

```
bin/elasticsearch
```

You should see output indicating that the service has started successfully. To confirm that Elasticsearch is running, you can send an HTTP GET request to the root endpoint using the curl command:

```
curl -X GET "localhost:9200/"
```

The expected response should be similar to the following JSON structure:

```
{
  "name" : "node-1",
  "cluster_name" : "elasticsearch",
  "cluster_uuid" : "nMCvH_rgSraLjax0boBXFw",
  "version" : {
    "number" : "8.0.0",
    "build_flavor" : "default",
    "build_type" : "tar",
    "build_hash" : "8e03099",
    "build_date" : "2022-09-29T06:49:26.902226046Z",
    "build_snapshot" : false,
    "lucene_version" : "9.0.0"
  },
  "tagline" : "You Know, for Search"
}
```

The values for name, cluster_name, cluster_uuid, and version may vary depending on your specific installation and configuration. The presence of these key-value pairs indicates that Elasticsearch is running properly.

Next, to check if your Elasticsearch cluster is healthy, execute the following command:

```
curl -X GET "localhost:9200/_cluster/health?pretty"
```

This command checks the cluster's health and returns a response similar to:

```
{
  "cluster_name" : "elasticsearch",
  "status" : "green",
  "timed_out" : false,
  "number_of_nodes" : 1,
  "number_of_data_nodes" : 1,
  "active_primary_shards" : 1,
  "active_shards" : 1,
  "relocating_shards" : 0,
  "initializing_shards" : 0,
  "unassigned_shards" : 0,
  "delayed_unassigned_shards" : 0,
  "number_of_pending_tasks" : 0,
  "number_of_in_flight_fetch" : 0,
  "task_max_waiting_in_queue_millis" : 0,
  "active_shards_percent_as_number" : 100.0
}
```


The status field should ideally be green, indicating that all primary and replica shards are active and operational. A yellow status means that primary shards are active but some or all replica shards are unassigned, while red indicates that some primary shards are unassigned.

After confirming Elasticsearch's health, verify that Kibana is properly connected to the Elasticsearch instance. Ensure that the Kibana service is running by navigating to the Kibana directory and starting the service:

```
bin/kibana
```

Open your web browser and navigate to http://localhost:5601. You should see the Kibana welcome screen if the connection to Elasticsearch is successful. Once Kibana is open, you can navigate to the "Dev Tools" section to issue queries directly to Elasticsearch using the Console.

For instance, execute a simple GET request within the Kibana Console to confirm connectivity:

```
GET /
```

This should return the same JSON structure received earlier when using the curl command. Additionally, you can check the cluster health from within Kibana by executing:

```
GET _cluster/health
```

Both commands should yield similar responses to those produced via the command-line interface, thus confirming that Kibana is connected and able to communicate with Elasticsearch.

If any issues are encountered during these steps, check the Elasticsearch and Kibana logs for error messages. Elasticsearch logs can be found in the logs directory within the Elasticsearch installation folder:

```
logs/elasticsearch.log
```

Kibana logs can be found in the logs directory within the Kibana installation folder:

```
logs/kibana.log
```

Review these log files for errors or warnings that provide clues about potential issues. Common problems include port conflicts, insufficient memory allocation, and network configuration issues, which can often be resolved by adjusting the relevant settings in elasticsearch.yml or kibana.yml configuration files.

Following these steps ensures that your Elasticsearch and Kibana installations are functioning correctly, providing a solid foundation for further development and exploration within the Elastic Stack ecosystem.

Chapter 3

Elasticsearch Core Concepts

This chapter delves into the fundamental concepts of Elasticsearch, including its document model, index structures, and the roles of shards and replicas within a cluster. It explains the architecture of nodes and clusters, the significance of mappings and analyzers, and the document lifecycle from indexing to deletion. Additionally, it introduces full-text search principles and relevance scoring, providing a solid foundation for understanding Elasticsearch's core functionalities.

3.1 The Elasticsearch Document Model

Elasticsearch, at its core, is built around the concept of a document model. Unlike traditional relational databases that operate with rows and tables, Elasticsearch utilizes JSON (JavaScript Object Notation) documents to store data. This approach allows for greater flexibility and scalability, catering to a wide array of use cases from search engines to real-time analytics.

A document in Elasticsearch is a structured data unit represented in JSON format. It consists of fields, with each field having associated data, differing in types such as strings, integers, or arrays. Documents contain the actual data one intends to search and analyze using Elasticsearch.

```
{
    "id": "1",
    "title": "Introduction to Elasticsearch",
    "author": "John Doe",
    "publication_year": 2023,
    "genres": ["Technology", "Search Engine"],
    "available": true,
    "description": "A comprehensive guide to learning Elasticsearch."
}
```

The above document represents a sample book entry, illustrating various data types—string, integer, boolean, and array—supported by Elasticsearch.

Each document is stored within an index, which serves as a collection that holds similar documents. The structure is akin to a database in relational database paradigms. An index is identified by a unique name and contains documents of a consistent schema.

- **Indexing Documents**

When a document is indexed, it undergoes analysis and transformation processes, potentially involving tokenization, filtering, and normalization, before being stored. This preparation enhances the efficiency and effectiveness of search operations.

To index a document, one can utilize the Elasticsearch RESTful API. For example, to index the sample document above in an index named books, the following command is used:

```
curl -X PUT "localhost:9200/books/_doc/1" -H 'Content-Type: application/json' -d'
{
    "id": "1",
    "title": "Introduction to Elasticsearch",
    "author": "John Doe",
    "publication_year": 2023,
    "genres": ["Technology", "Search Engine"],
    "available": true,
    "description": "A comprehensive guide to learning Elasticsearch."
}
'
```

Here, the endpoint /books/_doc/1 signifies that the document is indexed in the books index with a unique identifier of 1. The HTTP method PUT is employed to create or update the document.

- **Retrieving Documents**

Retrieval operations, such as fetching a document by its ID, are essential to the document model. Elasticsearch provides a straightforward API for this purpose:

```
curl -X GET "localhost:9200/books/_doc/1"
```

The response yields the requested document, encoded in JSON:

```
{
    "_index": "books",
    "_type": "_doc",
    "_id": "1",
    "_version": 1,
    "_seq_no": 0,
    "_primary_term": 1,
    "found": true,
    "_source": {
        "id": "1",
        "title": "Introduction to Elasticsearch",
        "author": "John Doe",
        "publication_year": 2023,
        "genres": ["Technology", "Search Engine"],
        "available": true,
        "description": "A comprehensive guide to learning Elasticsearch."
    }
}
```

- **Updating and Deleting Documents**

Documents can also be updated or deleted using the corresponding Elasticsearch API calls. Updating involves modifying certain fields while maintaining the document's identity:

```
curl -X POST "localhost:9200/books/_update/1" -H 'Content-Type: application/json' -
    d'
{
    "doc": {
        "available": false
    }
}
'
```

The response indicates the update was successful, marking the document as not available while preserving its other data.

Deleting a document simplifies the index management process, ensuring irrelevant or obsolete data is removed:

```
curl -X DELETE "localhost:9200/books/_doc/1"
```

This command permanently removes the document with ID 1 from the books index.

- **Document Relationships and Nested Structures**

Elasticsearch supports nested document structures to depict complex relationships within a single document:

```
{
    "id": "2",
    "title": "Advanced Elasticsearch Queries",
    "author": {
        "first_name": "Jane",
        "last_name": "Smith"
    },
    "publication_year": 2022,
    "genres": ["Technology"],
    "available": true,
    "chapters": [
        {
            "title": "Chapter 1",
            "summary": "Introduction to advanced querying"
        },
        {
            "title": "Chapter 2",
            "summary": "Improving search relevance"
        }
    ]
}
```

The nested structure in the above example enables the encapsulation of related entities within a single document, enhancing search capabilities and data integrity.

Understanding the Elasticsearch document model is crucial for effectively leveraging the platform's full potential. Adopting a document-oriented approach facilitates scalable and flexible data handling, contributing to robust search and analytics solutions.

3.2 Indexes and Types in Elasticsearch

In Elasticsearch, an index is a collection of documents that share similar characteristics. The index is the primary container that allows Elasticsearch to store, search, and manage these documents efficiently. Each index is identified by a unique name, which is used to reference the index when performing operations such as searching or indexing new documents.

An index in Elasticsearch is akin to a database in a traditional relational database management system (RDBMS). Within each index, documents are stored and can be retrieved using a variety of search queries. These documents must follow a schema defined by mappings, which specify the data types and structure of each field within the documents.

An example of creating an index in Elasticsearch is provided below:

```
PUT /my_index
{
  "settings": {
    "number_of_shards": 3,
    "number_of_replicas": 2
  }
}
```

In this example, an index named my_index is created with custom settings specifying 3 primary shards and 2 replica shards for each primary shard. The primary shards are responsible for storing the actual data, while the replicas provide fault tolerance and high availability.

Types in Elasticsearch were historically used to categorize documents that share a common set of fields within an index. However, since Elasticsearch 6.0, the concept of multiple types within a single index has been deprecated and eventually removed in version 7.0. This shift was made to simplify the data model and enhance scalability and performance.

Prior to this change, one could define multiple types within an index as shown below:

```
PUT /my_index
{
  "mappings": {
    "type1": {
      "properties": {
        "field1": { "type": "text" }
      }
    },
    "type2": {
      "properties": {
        "field2": { "type": "integer" }
      }
    }
  }
}
```

In the above example, my_index contains two types, type1 and type2, each with different fields. Although this feature was useful for categorizing documents, it introduced complexity and potential conflicts, especially with name collisions and management overhead.

With the removal of types, each index now contains documents that are implicitly of a single type, and all document mappings are defined at the root level. This simplification is illustrated in the following example:

```
PUT /my_index
{
  "mappings": {
```

```
    "properties": {
      "field1": { "type": "text" },
      "field2": { "type": "integer" }
    }
  }
}
```

In this modern approach, the my_index index has a single mapping at the root level, defining all necessary fields directly within the properties object. This approach reduces ambiguity and ensures consistent usage patterns across all Elasticsearch indices.

Searching for documents within an index can be achieved using a variety of queries. Below is an example of a simple search query:

```
GET /my_index/_search
{
  "query": {
    "match": {
      "field1": "search_text"
    }
  }
}
```

This search query performs a match query on field1, looking for documents containing the term search_text. Elasticsearch provides a rich query DSL (Domain Specific Language) that allows users to construct complex search queries, enabling advanced full-text search capabilities.

Efficient indexing and searching in Elasticsearch are achieved through the use of inverted indices, which allow quick lookups of terms and their associated documents. The process of creating these inverted indices involves tokenization, where text fields are broken down into individual terms, followed by the construction of data structures that map these terms to document IDs.

Inverted indices support fast retrieval and relevance scoring, which are crucial aspects of Elasticsearch's search functionality. This ensures that users receive accurate and timely search results based on their queries.

In summary, indexes and their mappings are fundamental to the organization and retrieval of documents within Elasticsearch. The elimination of multiple types within an index has streamlined the data model, making it easier to design, manage, and scale Elasticsearch clusters.

3.3 Understanding Shards and Replicas

In Elasticsearch, efficient data storage and high availability are facilitated by the concepts of shards and replicas. These mechanisms enable distribution of data across multiple nodes, enhancing both performance and fault tolerance. To comprehend their roles fully, we will explore how shards and replicas function within an Elasticsearch cluster.

A shard is the fundamental unit of storage in Elasticsearch. Each index is divided into a set of smaller units called primary shards. By default, an index has five primary shards, though this is configurable at the time of index creation. Shards empower Elasticsearch to horizontally partition data, which means that each shard can be hosted on different nodes in a cluster. This promotes parallel processing of queries, as the workload can be distributed, improving search and indexing performance.

Replicas, on the other hand, are copies of the primary shards. The main purpose of replicas is to ensure data redundancy and high availability. In the event of node failure, replicas serve as backups that can be used to recover lost primary shards. Elasticsearch allows the configuration of the number of replica shards per primary shard. For instance, with a replication factor of one, each primary shard will have one replica, effectively doubling the storage requirement.

```
PUT /my_index
{
  "settings": {
    "index": {
      "number_of_shards": 3,
      "number_of_replicas": 2
    }
  }
}
```

In the example above, the "number_of_shards" parameter is set to three, resulting in three primary shards for the index my_index. The "number_of_replicas" parameter is set to two, indicating that each primary shard will have two replica shards. Thus, a total of nine shards will be created (3 primary shards + 6 replica shards).

When an index is created, Elasticsearch will attempt to evenly balance the primary and replica shards across the available nodes in the cluster. This balancing is crucial for optimal resource utilization and fault tolerance. If the cluster has fewer nodes than the total number of shards, some nodes will host multiple shards, which could potentially lead to hotspots and degraded performance.

Shard allocation awareness and settings allow further control over shard distribution across the cluster. These settings ensure that shards are spread out according to specific criteria, such as hardware characteristics, data centers, or zones, enhancing fault isolation.

```
PUT /_cluster/settings
{
  "persistent": {
    "cluster.routing.allocation.awareness.attributes": "rack_id"
  }
}
```

In the code snippet above, shard allocation awareness is configured based on the "rack_id" attribute. Elasticsearch will try to distribute both primary and replica shards in such a way that they do not reside on the same rack, improving data redundancy.

Replica shards are not only crucial for data redundancy but also contribute to search performance. Query requests can be served by both primary and replica shards, allowing Elasticsearch to distribute the query load and respond more quickly. When a node containing a primary shard fails, one of its replicas can be promoted to act as the new primary shard, ensuring continued data availability and integrity.

Table 3.1: Cluster Health Status

Key	Value
cluster_name	elasticsearch
status	green
number_of_nodes	5
number_of_data_nodes	5
active_primary_shards	15
active_shards	30
relocating_shards	0
initializing_shards	0
unassigned_shards	0
delayed_unassigned_shards	0
number_of_pending_tasks	0
number_of_in_flight_fetch	0
task_max_waiting_in_queue_millis	0
active_shards_percent_as_number	100.0

The output above, retrieved from the /_cluster/health endpoint, indicates a healthy cluster ("status": "green") with 15 primary shards and 15 replicas (30 total active shards), demonstrating successful distribution across the nodes.

Understanding how Elasticsearch utilizes shards and replicas to distribute data efficiently and ensure high availability is fundamental for optimizing cluster configuration and performance. Adhering to these principles is critical for managing large data volumes and ensuring robust, high-performing search and indexing operations.

3.4 Nodes and Clusters in Elasticsearch

Elasticsearch is designed to be distributed, allowing it to process large volumes of data rapidly across numerous nodes. Understanding the architecture of nodes and clusters is pivotal for designing scalable and fault-tolerant search infrastructures.

A **node** in Elasticsearch is a single, operational unit in the Elasticsearch ecosystem. It represents a single instance of Elasticsearch and maintains part of the data as well as handles certain portions of the indexing and search requests. Nodes can be started in standalone mode or joined to form clusters, providing the backbone for distributed data storage and processing.

Node Types and Roles

In Elasticsearch, nodes have different roles based on the tasks they perform. The main types of nodes include:

- **Master Node**: This node is responsible for cluster-wide management functions such as creating or deleting an index and tracking which nodes are part of the cluster. A resilient cluster setup typically includes three or more dedicated master nodes to ensure high availability.

- **Data Node**: These nodes store data and execute data-related operations such as CRUD (Create, Read, Update, Delete), search, and aggregation. Depending on the deployment requirements, data nodes often possess a higher memory and disk space allocation.

- **Ingest Node**: This node is responsible for preprocessing documents before the actual indexing process, using ingest pipelines. This can include various transformations such as enriching data or removing unwanted fields.

- **Coordinating Node**: Though all nodes can act as a coordinating node by default, a dedicated coordinating node is responsible for distributing search and indexing requests across the cluster and consolidating the results. These nodes enhance performance under high traffic conditions.

Cluster Formation and Management

A **cluster** in Elasticsearch is a collection of one or more nodes that together store and distribute data while providing federated search capabilities across all nodes. Each cluster is identified by a unique name, which is crucial as nodes use this identifier to join the cluster.

Cluster management encompasses the following key aspects:

Cluster State

The cluster state is a data structure maintained by the Elasticsearch cluster. This structure includes information about the cluster-wide settings, the state of indices, the location of shards, and other metadata necessary for the cluster's operation. All data and master nodes hold a copy of the cluster state, but only master-eligible nodes can elect a master node to manage and update this state.

Discovery and Coordination

Nodes in Elasticsearch utilize a discovery mechanism to find each other and join a cluster. The `zen-disco` module orchestrates this process. By default, Elasticsearch uses unicast or multicast for node discovery within a network. The master node orchestrates the coordination of tasks among all nodes by maintaining the cluster state and ensuring synchronization.

Sharding and Replication

The concepts of shards and replicas are closely interrelated with the structure of nodes and clusters. For clarity:

- **Shards**: A shard is a basic unit of storage in Elasticsearch. Every index is subdivided into multiple primary shards, and each shard can reside on different data nodes. This partitioning enables the distribution and parallel processing of data across the cluster.

- **Replicas**: Replicas are copies of the primary shards. They provide redundancy and high availability. When a primary shard fails, a replica shard can quickly replace it, ensuring consistency and fault tolerance. Replication also aids in load balancing as search requests can be served by both primary and replica shards.

Node Communication and Failover

Nodes communicate with each other using a mechanism based on the Transport layer, which typically relies on TCP. This communication ensures coordinated operations, efficient distribution of tasks, and quick failover in case of node failures.

If a node fails:

- The master node updates the cluster state, marking the failed node offline.
- Data contained in the offline node's primary shards is restored from the replicas present in other nodes.
- Services running on the failed node are redistributed to maintain performance and availability.

Configuring Nodes and Clusters

An efficient Elasticsearch cluster hinges on optimal configuration. Key settings include:

```
# Elasticsearch YAML configuration
node.name: node-1
cluster.name: my_elasticsearch_cluster

# Designate node roles
node.master: true
node.data: true
node.ingest: false

# Discovery settings for unicast discovery
discovery.seed_hosts: ["host1", "host2"]
cluster.initial_master_nodes: ["node-1", "node-2", "node-3"]

# Network host and port configuration
network.host: 0.0.0.0
http.port: 9200
transport.port: 9300
```

Example: Creating a Cluster

Assuming we have three nodes (node-1, node-2, and node-3), the configuration for node-1 might look as follows:

```
node.name: node-1
cluster.name: my_elasticsearch_cluster
node.master: true
node.data: true
network.host: "192.168.1.10"
discovery.seed_hosts: ["192.168.1.10", "192.168.1.11", "192.168.1.12"]
cluster.initial_master_nodes: ["node-1", "node-2", "node-3"]
```

For node-2 and node-3, similar configurations would be made with respective IP addresses and node names. When the nodes are started, they will form a single Elasticsearch cluster named my_elasticsearch_cluster.

Practical Considerations

Scalability

Adding new nodes to a cluster scales horizontally by distributing the data and workload across more nodes. Elasticsearch's architecture supports seamless addition of nodes, which can be integrated into the existing framework without the necessity of downtime or significant reconfiguration.

Fault Tolerance

Elasticsearch's use of sharding and replication inherently provides fault tolerance. By configuring an appropriate number of replica shards, clusters can handle node failures without data loss. A robust cluster setup includes multiple master-eligible nodes ensuring master node election continuity even when one or more nodes fail.

Performance Optimization

Optimizing performance in an Elasticsearch cluster involves tuning:

- Resource allocation (CPU, memory, and disk I/O).
- Search and indexing rate limits.
- Number and size of indices and shards.
- Network settings to reduce latency.

Regular monitoring and adjustments based on workload patterns are necessary to maintain optimal cluster performance.

An in-depth understanding of nodes and clusters forms the foundation for leveraging Elasticsearch's full capabilities. The correct configuration and management of nodes and clusters ensure a balance between performance, scalability, and resilience, ultimately determining the efficiency and reliability of the Elasticsearch deployment.

3.5 Mapping and Analyzers

Mapping and analyzers are critical components in Elasticsearch that play pivotal roles in the indexing and search processes. Understanding these concepts deeply is essential for leveraging the full potential of Elasticsearch.

Mapping is akin to defining the schema for a database. In Elasticsearch, a mapping is used to define how a document and its fields are stored and indexed. A mapping can control how Elasticsearch dynamically identifies and interprets the structure and data types of the fields in a document, including defining custom configurations for various types of fields.

An analyzer, on the other hand, is a text processing tool that Elasticsearch uses to transform text into a format suitable for search and indexing. This transformation involves multiple steps, including character filtering, tokenization, and token filtering.

To elaborate, let us dissect these concepts further, beginning with mapping.

Mapping in Elasticsearch

Mappings determine the data type for each field (such as strings, numbers, dates, etc.) and how those fields should be indexed and stored. They provide an opportunity to specify settings to control analysis, term vectors, and other field operations. For example, a string field can be mapped as either full-text or keyword, optimizing it for searching or aggregations respectively.

Consider a sample mapping for a blog type document:

```
{
  "mappings": {
    "properties": {
      "title": {
        "type": "text",
        "analyzer": "standard"
      },
      "author": {
        "type": "keyword"
      },
      "date": {
        "type": "date"
      },
      "content": {
        "type": "text",
        "analyzer": "english"
      }
    }
```

```
  }
}
```

In this example, the title and content fields are analyzed text fields suitable for full-text search. The author field is a keyword field, useful for structured search and aggregations. The date field is explicitly typed as a date, allowing Elasticsearch to understand and optimize queries involving date ranges.

Mappings can also include various metadata such as settings for the specific analyzer used on text fields, norms, index options, and other custom behaviors.

Custom Analyzers

Analyzers break text down into tokens or terms and then apply a series of operations to transform these tokens for indexing. Custom analyzers can be built by combining standard or custom tokenizers and token filters.

A custom analyzer configuration might look like the following:

```
{
  "settings": {
    "analysis": {
      "analyzer": {
        "my_custom_analyzer": {
          "type": "custom",
          "tokenizer": "standard",
          "filter": ["lowercase", "porter_stem"]
        }
      }
    }
  }
}
```

In this scenario, the my_custom_analyzer uses the standard tokenizer to break text into words, applies the lowercase filter to convert all tokens to lowercase, and then uses the porter_stem filter to apply stemming, ensuring that related words are indexed as the same token.

Field Analysis Process

The field analysis process is executed at both indexing and search times. When a document is indexed, its analyzed fields undergo processing based on the specified analyzers, and the generated terms are stored in an inverted index. Similarly, when a search query is executed, the terms within the query undergo the same analysis process.

For example, assume we have the content field analyzed with my_custom_analyzer:

```
PUT /my_index/_doc/1
{
  "content": "Running is fun"
}

GET /my_index/_analyze
{
  "analyzer": "my_custom_analyzer",
  "text": "Running is fun"
}
```

The analysis of the text "Running is fun" with a standard tokenizer, followed by lowercase and porter_stem filters would yield tokens like run, is, fun which are stored in the index and used during search processes.

Built-in Analyzers

Elasticsearch includes several built-in analyzers that serve common text processing needs:

- **standard**: The default analyzer, which tokenizes text on word boundaries, considers punctuation, and lowercases terms.
- **simple**: Tokenizes text based on non-letter characters and converts tokens to lowercase.
- **whitespace**: Simply tokenizes text based on whitespace characters and doesn't modify case.
- **stop**: Similar to the simple analyzer but removes common English stop words.
- **keyword**: Treats the entire input text as a single token.

Effective use of mappings and analyzers can optimize the performance and relevance of search results. Crafting the correct schema and analysis pipeline is crucial to ensure data is indexed and queried accurately and efficiently. By leveraging the power of custom and built-in analyzers, one can cater to a diverse set of search requirements and enhance the functionality of an Elasticsearch deployment.

3.6 Document Lifecycle: Indexing, Updating, and Deleting

In Elasticsearch, the document lifecycle is pivotal for maintaining and manipulating data within an index. This section discusses the processes involved in indexing, updating, and deleting documents, elucidating the intrinsic operations and methodologies that facilitate these tasks.

The lifecycle of a document in Elasticsearch can be visualized as a series of states: creation (indexing), modification (updating), and removal (deleting). Understanding these states is essential for optimizing performance and ensuring data integrity within an Elasticsearch cluster.

Indexing a Document

Indexing is the initial process of adding a document to an Elasticsearch index. When a document is indexed, it is converted into a search-friendly format and stored in one of the index's shards. To illustrate, consider the following example:

```
PUT /my_index/_doc/1
{
  "title": "Elasticsearch Basics",
  "author": "John Doe",
  "publish_date": "2023-09-01",
  "content": "This is a beginner's guide to Elasticsearch."
}
```

In this example, a document is being indexed into the `my_index` index under the type `_doc` with an ID of 1. The indexing request uses the HTTP verb `PUT`, which is idempotent, meaning subsequent requests with the same payload will not create duplicates.

Upon successful indexing, Elasticsearch performs the following operations:

- **Parsing and Mapping**: The document is parsed, and Elasticsearch determines the appropriate mappings for the fields based on predefined settings or dynamic mapping rules.
- **Tokenization and Analysis**: Text fields undergo analysis, where they are tokenized and transformed into terms by analyzers. This step is critical for full-text search capabilities.
- **Storage**: The analyzed terms and original document are stored within the index. Elasticsearch distributes these documents across the shards based on the document ID and a hashing algorithm.

Updating a Document

Updating a document in Elasticsearch requires a different approach compared to traditional database systems. Instead of modifying the existing document directly, Elasticsearch internally marks the old document as deleted and indexes a new version with the changes. Consider the following update request:

```
POST /my_index/_update/1
{
  "doc": {
    "title": "Elasticsearch Advanced"
  }
}
```

In this example, the document with ID 1 in `my_index` had its `title` field updated. Elasticsearch executes the update by:

- **Retrieving** the existing document.
- **Applying** the update to the document.
- **Reindexing** the updated document as a new version.
- **Marking** the previous version as deleted for future cleanup by the background merge process.

Additionally, the `_update` endpoint supports scripting for more complex modifications:

```
POST /my_index/_update/1
{
  "script": {
    "source": "ctx._source.views += params.increment",
    "lang": "painless",
    "params": {
      "increment": 1
    }
  }
}
```

Here, the document field `views` is incremented by 1 via a script written in Elasticsearch's scripting language, Painless. This method is efficient for partial updates, reducing overhead compared to traditional update operations.

Deleting a Document

Deleting a document removes it from the index. Like updates, deletions are logical. Elasticsearch marks the document as deleted, and the document physically remains in the index until segment merging happens. To delete the previously mentioned document, you would use:

```
DELETE /my_index/_doc/1
```

The deletion request marks the document with ID 1 for deletion in the my_index index. The document is no longer searchable immediately after the deletion operation. However, the underlying data persists in the filesystem until Elasticsearch triggers a segment merge, reclaiming the storage space occupied by the deleted document.

Impact of Document Lifecycle Operations on Performance

Each operation within the document lifecycle has implications on the performance and behavior of an Elasticsearch cluster:

- **Indexing**: High indexing rates increase I/O operations and consume CPU resources for parsing and analysis. Optimizing index settings and choosing appropriate analyzers can mitigate these costs.

- **Updating**: Frequent updates result in multiple versions of documents, increasing the index size until segment merges clean up obsolete versions. Using partial updates and scripting judiciously can minimize these impacts.

- **Deleting**: Bulk deletions may lead to expensive background merge operations. Utilizing the delete_by_query API for batch deletions can streamline this process when needed.

```
POST /my_index/_delete_by_query
{
  "query": {
    "match": {
      "author": "John Doe"
    }
  }
}
```

The above command removes all documents authored by "John Doe" from the my_index index. This bulk operation is efficient for large-scale deletions compared to individual delete requests.

Each phase in the document lifecycle — from indexing to deletion — is integral to maintaining Elasticsearch's performance and ensuring data consistency. Understanding these operations and their underlying mechanisms empowers users to optimize their Elasticsearch clusters effectively.

```
{
  "took": 30,
  "timed_out": false,
  "total": 2,
  "deleted": 2,
  "batches": 1,
  "version_conflicts": 0,
  "noops": 0,
  "retries": {
    "bulk": 0,
    "search": 0
  },
  "throttled_millis": 0,
  "requests_per_second": -1,
  "throttled_until_millis": 0,
  "failures": []
}
```


3.7 Full-Text Search Concepts

Elasticsearch is deeply rooted in the principles of full-text search, which is the foundational technology behind searching extensive text data efficiently and effectively. Full-text search revolves around analyzing and indexing textual content to facilitate rapid searches based on relevant matches. Here, we explore the core components and methodologies that enable these capabilities in Elasticsearch, providing a comprehensive understanding of its search mechanics.

Text Analysis and Tokenization

Text analysis is a critical step in full-text search, where raw text is processed and transformed into a format suitable for indexing. This involves breaking down the text into individual units, or tokens, through a process called tokenization. Tokens often correspond to words or terms, but depending on the language and the specific requirements, tokenization can also involve more sophisticated rules.

Elasticsearch uses analyzers to perform text analysis. An analyzer can be defined as a combination of one tokenizer and zero or more token filters. A typical analyzer performs the following steps:

- **Character Filters:** These preprocess the text to remove unwanted characters or transform it in some way. Examples include removing HTML tags or replacing certain characters.
- **Tokenizer:** This divides the text into individual terms or tokens. For instance, the standard tokenizer splits text at word boundaries, removing punctuation and unnecessary whitespace.

- **Token Filters:** These refine the tokens further by modifying or removing some tokens. Common filters include lowercasing, stop word removal, stemming, and synonym expansion.

The following code snippet demonstrates how to configure and test a custom analyzer in Elasticsearch:

```
PUT /my_index
{
  "settings": {
    "analysis": {
      "char_filter": {
        "html_strip": {
          "type": "html_strip"
        }
      },
      "tokenizer": {
        "standard": {
          "type": "standard"
        }
      },
      "filter": {
        "lowercase": {
          "type": "lowercase"
        },
        "asciifolding": {
          "type": "asciifolding"
        },
        "stop": {
          "type": "stop",
          "stopwords": ["and", "is", "the"]
        }
      },
      "analyzer": {
        "custom_analyzer": {
          "type": "custom",
          "char_filter": ["html_strip"],
          "tokenizer": "standard",
          "filter": ["lowercase", "asciifolding", "stop"]
        }
      }
    }
  }
}
```

This analyzer performs HTML stripping, tokenization with the standard tokenizer, and then applies lowercase, ASCII folding, and stop word filters.

Inverted Index Structure

The heart of Elasticsearch's full-text search capabilities lies in its use of an inverted index. Unlike traditional databases using B-trees or other structures for data retrieval, an inverted index is optimized for search operations involving large volumes of text data.

An inverted index maps terms to their locations in a set of documents. At a high level, it consists of:

- **Terms:** The smallest units derived from tokenization.
- **Postings List:** Lists of document references where each term appears.

Consider an example dataset with documents:

```
Doc1: "Elasticsearch is a distributed, RESTful search engine."
Doc2: "A search engine can index massive amounts of data."
```

The inverted index will construct entries for significant terms:

```
Term: Elasticsearch -> [Doc1]
Term: search -> [Doc1, Doc2]
Term: engine -> [Doc1, Doc2]
```

This allows Elasticsearch to quickly identify documents containing specific search terms and rank them based on relevance.

Relevance and Scoring

Elasticsearch uses sophisticated algorithms to determine the relevance of documents in relation to a given query. The most significant of these algorithms is the *Term Frequency-Inverse Document Frequency (TF-IDF)* scoring formula, which considers both the frequency of terms within a document and their rarity across all documents.

The **formula for TF-IDF** is expressed as:

$$\text{TF-IDF} = \left(\frac{\text{Term Frequency}}{\text{Document Length}} \right) \times \log \left(\frac{\text{Total Number of Documents}}{\text{Document Frequency}} \right)$$

This ensures that terms frequently appearing in few documents (thus highly relevant) are weighted more heavily than common terms present in many documents.

Additionally, Elasticsearch introduces enhancements like **BM25** (Best Matching 25), which improves upon standard TF-IDF by considering term saturation, document length normalization, and other factors to further refine relevance scoring.

Query Parsing and Matching

When a search query is issued, Elasticsearch utilizes query parsers to interpret and execute the query. There are different types of queries relative to full-text search:

- **Match Query:** The most common full-text query, which analyzes the target field's text and performs a search.

```
GET /my_index/_search
{
  "query": {
    "match": {
      "content": "search engine"
    }
  }
}
```

- **Multi-Match Query:** Extended from a match query, it searches multiple fields.

```
GET /my_index/_search
{
  "query": {
    "multi_match": {
      "query": "search engine",
      "fields": ["title", "description"]
    }
  }
}
```

The output for the match query might look like:

```
{
  "hits": {
    "total": 2,
    "hits": [
      {
        "_index": "my_index",
        "_id": "1",
        "_score": 0.75,
        "_source": {
          "content": "Elasticsearch is a distributed, RESTful search engine."
        }
      },
      {
        "_index": "my_index",
        "_id": "2",
        "_score": 0.65,
        "_source": {
          "content": "A search engine can index massive amounts of data."
        }
      }
    ]
  }
}
```

Understanding full-text search concepts is pivotal for leveraging Elasticsearch's strengths. Knowledge of analyzers, inverted index structures, relevance scoring, and effective query parsing and matching empowers users to harness Elasticsearch for complex and highly efficient search operations.

3.8 Understanding Relevance and Scoring

Relevance and scoring are central to the functionality of Elasticsearch when performing full-text searches. These mechanisms determine how well each document in the index matches the query, and subsequently, how they are ordered in the search results.

When a search query is executed, Elasticsearch calculates a relevance score for every document that matches the query. This score is used to rank documents, ensuring that the most relevant documents appear at the top of the search results.

The primary component used in scoring is the term frequency-inverse document frequency (TF-IDF) model, though Elasticsearch also supports more advanced models like BM25.

- **Term Frequency (TF):** This metric captures the frequency of a term within a document. The idea is that terms appearing more frequently in a document might be more relevant to the document's content. Mathematically, this can be represented as:

  $$\text{TF}(t, d) = \frac{\text{count}(t, d)}{\text{max count in document}},$$

  where count(t, d) is the number of occurrences of term t in document d.

- **Inverse Document Frequency (IDF):** While TF measures within-document importance, IDF measures term importance across many documents. It determines the uniqueness of the term across the entire index. The IDF score can be calculated as:

  $$\text{IDF}(t) = \log\left(\frac{N}{\text{doc count}(t)}\right),$$

  where N is the total number of documents in the corpus and doc count(t) is the number of documents containing the term t.

- **TF-IDF:** Combining TF and IDF scores gives a better measure of the term's relevance. The TF-IDF score is computed as:

  $$\text{TF-IDF}(t, d) = \text{TF}(t, d) \times \text{IDF}(t).$$

In Elasticsearch, scoring calculation also accounts for field length and other normalization factors to ensure relevance accurately reflects the intent behind user queries.

- **BM25:** While the TF-IDF model provides a strong foundation for text relevance, BM25 improves upon it by incorporating term saturation and document length normalization. BM25 uses the formula:

$$\text{score}(q,d) = \sum_{t \in q} \text{IDF}(t) \cdot \frac{\text{TF}(t,d) \cdot (k_1 + 1)}{\text{TF}(t,d) + k_1(1 - b + b \cdot \frac{|d|}{\text{avgdl}})},$$

  where k_1 and b are parameters that control term frequency saturation and length normalization respectively, $|d|$ is the length of the current document, and avgdl is the average document length in the corpus.

In practice, Elasticsearch uses a variant called Okapi BM25 as the default similarity algorithm. This model is generally regarded as providing better relevance scoring by adjusting the influence of term frequency.

- **Practical Scoring Example:** Consider an Elasticsearch index with three documents about computer science. For a query searching for "machine learning," Elasticsearch calculates a relevance score for each document based on the term presence and frequency.

  Below is an example of how to execute such a query in Elasticsearch:

```
{
  "query": {
    "match": {
      "content": "machine learning"
    }
  }
}
```

When these results are returned, you can see the relevance score for each document. Assume three documents returned with IDs 1, 2, and 3. The scores might be represented in the result as:

The document with the highest score (ID 1) is deemed the most relevant to the query "machine learning".

Index	ID	Score	Title
cs-papers	1	1.573879	Introduction to Machine Learning
cs-papers	2	1.150387	Advanced Machine Learning Algorithms
cs-papers	3	0.897134	Applications of Machine Learning in Data Science

Table 3.2: Relevance Scores for Documents

Understanding and effectively utilizing Elasticsearch's relevance scoring requires a combination of theoretical knowledge and practical experience. While default configurations of scoring models work for general purposes, tuning these parameters to fit specific use cases can yield better search results.

Score customization can be further refined by using function score queries, where functions such as script score, decay, field value factor, and weight are used to influence the final score dynamically. This fine-tuning ensures that search results align more closely with the specific requirements and contextual relevance dictated by the use case.

3.9 Hands-On: Creating Your First Index

Creating an index in Elasticsearch is a straightforward process that involves a series of API calls to configure the index settings, mappings, and optionally, include some initial data. This section will guide you through the process of creating your first index step-by-step, ensuring that you understand the necessary concepts and commands involved.

To begin, ensure that your Elasticsearch instance is up and running. You can use RESTful API calls via tools such as curl, or more sophisticated methods such as using Kibana's Dev Tools console or an Elasticsearch client in a programming language like Python or Java.

The primary command to create an index is the PUT request to the /index_name endpoint. Here's an example of how you can create an index named my_first_index with minimal configuration:

```
curl -X PUT "localhost:9200/my_first_index"
```

This command creates an index with default settings. However, for most use cases, you will want to define specific settings and mappings. Let's proceed by creating an index with custom settings, including the number of shards and replicas.

- **Custom Index Settings**

  The settings for an index include the number of shards and replicas. By default, Elasticsearch creates five primary shards and one replica for each index. In our example, we will explicitly set these parameters to control the behavior of our index.

```
curl -X PUT "localhost:9200/my_custom_index" -H 'Content-Type: application
    /json' -d'
{
  "settings": {
    "index": {
      "number_of_shards": 3,
      "number_of_replicas": 2
    }
  }
}
'
```

  In this configuration, the index my_custom_index is created with three primary shards and two replicas per shard. The Content-Type: application/json header informs the server that the request body contains JSON data.

- **Defining Mappings**

  Mappings define the structure of the documents in an index. They specify how data fields are analyzed and indexed. Let's define a mapping for a hypothetical document with fields such as title, author, and publish_date.

```
curl -X PUT "localhost:9200/my_custom_index" -H 'Content-Type: application
    /json' -d'
{
  "settings": {
    "number_of_shards": 3,
    "number_of_replicas": 2
  },
  "mappings": {
    "properties": {
      "title": {
        "type": "text"
      },
      "author": {
        "type": "keyword"
      },
      "publish_date": {
        "type": "date"
      }
    }
  }
}
'
```

In this example, the title field is defined as text, which means it will be analyzed and tokenized to support full-text search capabilities. The author field is defined as keyword, suitable for exact matches and aggregations, while the publish_date field is defined as date, supporting date operations.

- **Indexing Documents**

  After creating the index with the desired settings and mappings, we can index documents into it. The following example demonstrates how to index a document into my_custom_index:

```
curl -X POST "localhost:9200/my_custom_index/_doc/1" -H 'Content-Type:
     application/json' -d'
{
  "title": "Elasticsearch Guidebook",
  "author": "John Doe",
  "publish_date": "2023-01-01"
}
'
```

  The above command indexes a document with title, author, and publish_date fields into the index my_custom_index. The document is assigned an ID of 1. Elasticsearch automatically indexes the document, making it searchable based on the mappings defined earlier.

- **Retrieving Documents**

  To verify that our document has been successfully indexed, we can retrieve it using a GET request:

```
curl -X GET "localhost:9200/my_custom_index/_doc/1"
```

  The server's response should display the indexed document, confirming its presence in the index.

```
{
  "_index": "my_custom_index",
  "_type": "_doc",
  "_id": "1",
  "_version": 1,
  "_seq_no": 0,
  "_primary_term": 1,
  "found": true,
  "_source": {
    "title": "Elasticsearch Guidebook",
    "author": "John Doe",
    "publish_date": "2023-01-01"
  }
}
```

- **Updating Documents**

If updates are required, you can update an existing document using the _update endpoint, which partially executes updates on the existing document without replacing it entirely:

```
curl -X POST "localhost:9200/my_custom_index/_update/1" -H 'Content-
    Type: application/json' -d'
{
  "doc": {
    "title": "Advanced Elasticsearch Guidebook"
  }
}
'
```

This command updates the title of the document with ID 1.

- **Deleting Documents**

  Finally, you may need to delete a document. The DELETE request can be used as follows:

```
curl -X DELETE "localhost:9200/my_custom_index/_doc/1"
```

  This command deletes the document with ID 1 from the index my_custom_index.

By following these steps, you have created an index, defined settings and mappings, and indexed, retrieved, updated, and deleted documents. This foundational knowledge will facilitate deeper exploration of Elasticsearch's powerful full-text search and analytics capabilities.

3.10 Troubleshooting Common Issues

In any system as complex as Elasticsearch, issues are inevitable. This section outlines some of the most common problems one might encounter, along with practical solutions, maintaining a detailed and systematic approach.

Cluster State Issues and Split Brain Situations

Split-brain problems occur when the cluster state becomes inconsistent, often due to network partitions. This complication can lead to data loss or corruption.

```
curl -X GET "localhost:9200/_cluster/health"
```

Monitor cluster health regularly. An appropriate configuration ensures that a master node is always available to maintain the cluster state.

Use the discovery.zen.minimum_master_nodes setting to prevent split-brain:

```
discovery.zen.minimum_master_nodes: 2
```

Slow Queries and Performance Degradation

Diagnosing slow queries involves multiple factors, including inefficient mappings, poor index structures, and inadequate hardware resources.

```
curl -X GET "localhost:9200/my_index/_search?pretty" -H 'Content-Type: application
    /json' -d'
{
  "profile": true,
  "query": {
    "match": {
      "message": "search term"
    }
  }
}'
```

Profiling identifies bottlenecks in query processing. To optimize, ensure that mappings and analyzers are correctly defined. Additionally, configuring caches can ameliorate performance:

```
indices.queries.cache.size: 10%
indices.fielddata.cache.size: 15%
```

Shard Allocation Failures

Shard allocation issues can emerge due to insufficient disk space, incorrect configurations, or network problems. Investigate the allocation state:

```
curl -X GET "localhost:9200/_cluster/allocation/explain"
```

Based on this analysis, actions such as relocating shards or increasing disk space can resolve the problem.

Index Corruption and Data Recovery

Index corruption might be caused by hardware failures or software bugs. To ensure data recoverability, regularly back up indices using snapshot and restore APIs.

```
curl -X PUT "localhost:9200/_snapshot/my_backup/snapshot_1?wait_for_completion
    =true"
```

```
curl -X POST "localhost:9200/_snapshot/my_backup/snapshot_1/_restore"
```

Snapshots should be stored in a reliable repository to safeguard against data loss.

Cluster Formation Failures

If nodes fail to join the cluster, ensure network configurations and settings are correct. Common issues include wrong IP addresses or incorrect port settings.

```
journalctl -u elasticsearch
```

Check logs for errors and verify that all nodes have consistent configurations. Correctly setting the network.host attribute can resolve many formation issues:

```
network.host: 0.0.0.0
```

Insufficient Memory and Out of Memory Errors

Elasticsearch requires sufficient memory. Out of memory errors can be mitigated by properly configuring the heap size:

```
-Xms4g
-Xmx4g
```

It's crucial to set the min and max heap size to the same value to prevent the JVM from resizing the heap dynamically, which impairs performance.

High CPU Usage

High CPU usage often correlates with complex queries, indexing operations, or inadequate thread pool configurations. Monitoring thread pools can identify the sources of CPU spikes:

```
curl -X GET "localhost:9200/_cat/thread_pool?v"
```

Optimizing thread pool settings or scaling the hardware appropriately can alleviate high CPU usage.

Networking Issues

Inter-node communication problems must be swiftly identified to maintain cluster health. Ensuring that firewalls, security groups, and network settings are configured correctly is vital.

```
curl -X GET "localhost:9200/_cat/nodes?v"
```

Investigate logs for connection refusals or timeouts and rectify any configuration inconsistencies.

Document Indexing Failures

Failures in document indexing can result from mapping issues, large bulk requests, or inappropriate settings. Analyzing failed indexing attempts provides insight:

```
curl -X GET "localhost:9200/_bulk_endpoint/_search?scroll=1m" -H 'Content-Type:
      application/json' -d'
{
  "query": {
    "match_all": {}
  }
}'
```

Adjusting the bulk request size or correcting mappings can resolve such issues. Ensure the mappings align with the document structure and validate before indexing.

This systematic and detailed approach ensures a thorough understanding of troubleshooting facets in Elasticsearch, improving cluster health and efficiency.

Chapter 4

Indexing and Managing Data

This chapter focuses on the processes involved in preparing, indexing, and managing data within Elasticsearch. It covers defining schemas and mappings, utilizing the REST API for data operations, and performing bulk indexing tasks. Additionally, it addresses updating and deleting documents, handling partial updates and upserts, and optimizing indexing performance. Practical guidance on using ingest nodes and pipelines, managing index templates, and real-world data indexing examples is also provided.

4.1 Preparing Data for Indexing

Before data can be effectively indexed within Elasticsearch, it must be properly prepared. This involves a series of steps aimed at ensuring data consistency, defining clear structures, and managing data types for optimal search and indexing performance. Preparing data for indexing is crucial as it sets the foundation for subsequent operations such as querying and analysis.

- **Data Cleansing:** Data cleansing is the initial step in the preparation process. It involves identifying and rectifying errors in the data to ensure accuracy and consistency. Typical errors include missing values, duplicate entries, and erroneous records. Handling these issues helps in maintaining the integrity of the dataset.

Here is a Python script demonstrating basic data cleansing using Pandas:

```
import pandas as pd

# Load dataset
data = pd.read_csv('dataset.csv')

# Remove duplicate rows
data = data.drop_duplicates()

# Fill missing values
data = data.fillna('UNKNOWN')

# Save the cleaned dataset
data.to_csv('cleaned_dataset.csv', index=False)
```

In this script, the dataset is loaded, duplicate rows are removed, and missing values are filled with a placeholder ('UNKNOWN'). Finally, the cleaned data is saved to a new file.

- **Data Transformation:** Transformation involves converting data into a format suitable for indexing. This may include normalizing data, converting data types, and ensuring all text is in a consistent format, such as lowercase. For example, dates may need to be standardized to a common format like ISO 8601.

The following Python script demonstrates transforming a dataset into an Elasticsearch-compatible format:

```
import pandas as pd

# Load cleaned dataset
data = pd.read_csv('cleaned_dataset.csv')

# Normalize text data to lowercase
data['text_column'] = data['text_column'].str.lower()

# Convert date column to ISO 8601 format
data['date_column'] = pd.to_datetime(data['date_column']).dt.strftime('%Y-%m-%dT
    %H:%M:%SZ')

# Save the transformed dataset
data.to_csv('transformed_dataset.csv', index=False)
```

Here, text and date columns are standardized to ensure uniformity, which helps in maintaining consistency during indexing.

- **Defining Data Structure:** Establishing a well-defined data structure is essential for effective indexing. This involves creating a clear schema that outlines the data types and structures of the various fields within the documents to be indexed. Elasticsearch supports a variety of field data types: text, keyword, date, long, double, boolean, and more.

A detailed mapping file in JSON format can be defined as follows:

```
{
  "mappings": {
    "properties": {
      "title": { "type": "text" },
      "author": { "type": "keyword" },
      "publication_date": { "type": "date" },
      "price": { "type": "double" },
      "in_stock": { "type": "boolean" }
    }
  }
}
```

This schema specifies that the title field is analyzed as text, author is stored as a keyword, publication_date is treated as a date, price is a double, and in_stock is a boolean.

- **Data Validation:** Validation is a critical step to ensure that the data conforms to the defined schema. It helps in catching inconsistencies and errors before they are indexed. This includes validation of data types, formats, and checking for any constraints.

For instance, the following Python snippet validates date formatting:

```
import pandas as pd

# Load transformed dataset
data = pd.read_csv('transformed_dataset.csv')

# Validate date format
def validate_date_format(date_str):
    try:
        pd.to_datetime(date_str, format='%Y-%m-%dT%H:%M:%SZ')
        return True
    except ValueError:
        return False

data['valid_date'] = data['date_column'].apply(validate_date_format)

# Filter out invalid dates
valid_data = data[data['valid_date'] == True]

# Save validated dataset
valid_data.to_csv('validated_dataset.csv', index=False)
```

This script uses Pandas to apply a date validation function, retaining only the records with valid date formats and saving the validated dataset.

- **Indexing Format Conversion:** The final preparation step involves converting the validated dataset into a format suitable for Elasticsearch indexing. Typically, this involves converting the dataset into JSON, which Elasticsearch natively understands and processes efficiently.

Here is an example of converting a CSV file to JSON format for indexing:

```
import pandas as pd
import json

# Load validated dataset
data = pd.read_csv('validated_dataset.csv')

# Convert to JSON format
data_json = data.to_json(orient='records', lines=True)

# Save JSON to file
with open('data.json', 'w') as file:
    file.write(data_json)
```

In this example, the validated dataset is read and converted to JSON format using the Pandas library, and then it is written to a file in JSON lines format, which is well-suited for bulk indexing in Elasticsearch.

Proper preparation of data for indexing enhances the downstream operations performed within Elasticsearch, ensuring efficient and accurate data access and manipulation.

4.2 Defining Schemas and Mappings

Defining schemas and mappings is a fundamental step in the process of indexing and managing data within Elasticsearch. Understanding how to tailor mappings to your data is essential for optimizing searching and indexing performance, as well as ensuring the correctness of data retrieval operations. The schema, or mapping, defines the structure of the documents stored within an index and specifies how each field in the document is stored and indexed.

Elasticsearch mappings define the data types of each field, such as text, keyword, numerical types, date, and others, along with optional attributes like analyzers, norms, and term vectors. When a new index is created, Elasticsearch dynamically creates mappings unless explicitly provided by the user. While dynamic mapping is useful for quick prototyping, it is recommended to define explicit mappings in production environments to maintain control over how your data is indexed and searched.

A mapping can be defined explicitly during index creation using the REST API. Below is an example of defining a mapping for an index to store a collection of blog posts.

```
PUT /blogs
{
  "mappings": {
    "properties": {
      "title": {
        "type": "text",
        "analyzer": "standard"
      },
      "author": {
        "type": "keyword"
      },
      "content": {
        "type": "text",
        "analyzer": "english"
      },
      "publish_date": {
        "type": "date"
      },
      "views": {
        "type": "integer"
      },
      "tags": {
        "type": "keyword"
      }
    }
  }
}
```

This mapping specifies various fields along with their respective data types. The ‘title‘ and ‘content‘ fields are stored as text with different analyzers. ‘author‘ and ‘tags‘ fields are of type ‘keyword‘, indicating they should not be analyzed. The ‘publish_date‘ field is stored as a ‘date‘ and ‘views‘ as an ‘integer‘.

- The distinction between ‘text‘ and ‘keyword‘ types is crucial. ‘text‘ fields are analyzed to support full-text search, where the field content is tokenized into individual terms. Analyzers can be defined and customized. In the example above, the ‘content‘ field uses the ‘english‘ analyzer, which applies English-specific text analysis.

- The ‘keyword‘ type is used for structured data that should not be analyzed, making it suitable for exact match queries. For instance, filtering articles by author or matching tags exactly should use the ‘keyword‘ type.

- Numerical and date fields enable range queries and sorting. Integer types are used for whole numbers, while various floating-point types can store decimal numbers. Date fields support a variety of date formats and can be used in time-based queries, aggregation, and sorting.

- Custom analyzers can be defined to fine-tune the text analysis process. An analyzer consists of a tokenizer and zero or more token filters. Below is an example of a custom analyzer:

```
PUT /blogs
{
  "settings": {
    "analysis": {
      "analyzer": {
        "my_custom_analyzer": {
          "type": "custom",
          "tokenizer": "standard",
          "filter": ["lowercase", "asciifolding"]
        }
      }
    }
  },
  "mappings": {
    "properties": {
      "content": {
        "type": "text",
        "analyzer": "my_custom_analyzer"
      }
    }
  }
}
```

This custom analyzer, ‘my_custom_analyzer‘, uses the standard tokenizer and includes two filters: ‘lowercase‘ and ‘asciifolding‘. It can be applied to the ‘content‘ field by specifying it in the field’s settings within the ‘mappings‘.

- Handling complex JSON structures in documents often requires nested and object types. The ‘object‘ type is suitable for single-level nested objects, while the ‘nested‘ type is needed for arrays of objects to support accurate querying.

```
PUT /ecommerce
{
  "mappings": {
    "properties": {
      "customer": {
        "type": "object",
        "properties": {
          "name": { "type": "text" },
          "age": { "type": "integer"},
          "address": {
            "type": "object",
            "properties": {
              "street": { "type": "text" },
              "city": { "type": "keyword" }
            }
          }
        }
      },
      "order_items": {
        "type": "nested",
        "properties": {
          "product_name": { "type": "text" },
          "quantity": { "type": "integer" }
        }
      }
    }
  }
}
```

In this example, 'customer' is an object containing nested properties, while 'order_items' is a nested field, allowing for more sophisticated query capabilities on arrays of objects.

Accurately defining schemas and mappings in Elasticsearch ensures efficient storage, retrieval, and querying of data. Understanding these concepts and effectively applying them is integral for the effective use of Elasticsearch in various applications.

4.3 Indexing Data with the REST API

Indexing data in Elasticsearch is a fundamental operation that involves storing documents in an index to enable efficient searching and retrieval. Utilizing the REST API for indexing allows flexible, language-agnostic interactions with Elasticsearch. This section details the process of indexing data with the REST API, concentrating on techniques and strategies to ensure successful data operations.

To index a document, the HTTP PUT method is employed. This method is used to create a new document or update an existing document by specifying a unique document identifier. Below is a sample command to index a document:

```
PUT /my_index/_doc/1
{
  "field1": "value1",
  "field2": "value2"
}
```

This command indexes a document into the my_index index with a document ID of 1. The request body contains the document to be indexed in JSON format.

In scenarios where it is preferable not to specify a document ID, the POST method can be used. Elasticsearch will automatically generate a document ID:

```
POST /my_index/_doc
{
  "field1": "value1",
  "field2": "value2"
}
```

When the above command executes, Elasticsearch responds with a unique document ID:

```
{
  "_index" : "my_index",
  "_type" : "_doc",
  "_id" : "generated_id",
  "_version" : 1,
  "result" : "created",
  "_shards" : {
    "total" : 2,
    "successful" : 1,
    "failed" : 0
  },
  "_seq_no" : 0,
  "_primary_term" : 1
}
```

For creating indices with dynamic mapping, Elasticsearch uses the default mappings unless explicitly defined. If control over document structure and field types is necessary, pre-defining the index mappings is advisable, as discussed in the *Defining Schemas and Mappings* section.

When indexing documents, a vital consideration is data consistency during index updates. Elasticsearch uses versioning to ensure consistency. Each document comprises a _version field that increments with every update. Conflict handling occurs through optimistic concurrency control if multiple processes attempt to update the same document simultaneously. An update operation succeeds only if the document's current version matches the specified version.

Example of an update that addresses version control:

```
PUT /my_index/_doc/1?if_seq_no=35&if_primary_term=2
{
  "field1": "new_value1",
  "field2": "new_value2"
}
```

In the presence of a version conflict, Elasticsearch returns a 409 Conflict status code.

The indexing process involves more than merely storing data. Parameters specified in indexing requests can control the behavior of Elasticsearch:

- refresh: Immediately makes the indexed document available for search by refreshing the index. Usage: PUT /my_index/_doc/1?refresh=true

- routing: Directs the document to a specific shard, enhancing write throughput. Usage: PUT /my_index/_doc/1?routing=user_1

- pipeline: Ingests pipelines parameters for processing documents before indexing. Usage: PUT /my_index/_doc/1?pipeline=my_pipeline

An understanding of the bulk indexing operation is crucial when handling large volumes of data. The _bulk API optimizes for performance by reducing the number of network round-trips and server-side indexing workload. A bulk request encapsulates multiple methods like index, update, or delete:

```
POST /_bulk
{ "index" : { "_index" : "my_index", "_id" : "1" } }
{ "field1" : "value1", "field2" : "value2" }
{ "index" : { "_index" : "my_index", "_id" : "2" } }
{ "field1" : "value3", "field2" : "value4" }
```

The response provides the status and potential errors for each operation:

```
{
  "took" : 30,
  "errors" : false,
  "items" : [
    {
      "index" : {
        "_index" : "my_index",
        "_type" : "_doc",
        "_id" : "1",
        "_version" : 1,
        "result" : "created",
        "_shards" : {
          "total" : 2,
          "successful" : 1,
          "failed" : 0
        },
        "status" : 201
      }
    },
    {
      "index" : {
        "_index" : "my_index",
        "_type" : "_doc",
        "_id" : "2",
        "_version" : 1,
        "result" : "created",
        "_shards" : {
          "total" : 2,
          "successful" : 1,
          "failed" : 0
        },
        "status" : 201
      }
    }
  ]
}
```

Correctly managing indexed data using these operations and parameters ensures robust performance and data integrity. Understanding these mechanisms is integral for proficiently managing Elasticsearch data through its REST API.

4.4 Bulk Indexing Operations

Bulk indexing operations in Elasticsearch provide a means to increase throughput and efficiency by batching multiple indexing requests into a single API call. This capability is indispensable for applications dealing with large volumes of data where performance considerations are paramount.

Elasticsearch's _bulk API supports indexing, updating, and deleting multiple documents in one request, minimizing network overhead and optimizing resource utilization on the server side.

To perform a bulk indexing operation, you must structure the request body in a specific format. Each line in the request corresponds to a single operation, starting with a metadata line that indicates the action (e.g., index, update, delete) and followed, when applicable, by the source data of the document to index or update. Line breaks separate different operations.

Below is an example of how to use the _bulk endpoint to index multiple documents:

```
POST /_bulk
{ "index" : { "_index" : "books", "_id" : "1" } }
{ "title" : "Elasticsearch Basics", "author" : "John Doe", "year" : 2020 }
{ "index" : { "_index" : "books", "_id" : "2" } }
{ "title" : "Advanced Elasticsearch", "author" : "Jane Smith", "year" : 2021 }
{ "index" : { "_index" : "books", "_id" : "3" } }
{ "title" : "Mastering Elasticsearch", "author" : "Alice Brown", "year" : 2022 }
```

In this example:

- The first line specifies an index action for a document with ID 1 in the books index.
- The second line provides the document source for the first index action.
- The process repeats for additional documents with IDs 2 and 3.

The response from Elasticsearch indicates the outcome of each action.

```
{
  "took" : 30,
  "errors" : false,
  "items" : [
    {
      "index" : {
        "_index" : "books",
        "_id" : "1",
        "_version" : 1,
        "result" : "created",
        "_shards" : {
          "total" : 2,
          "successful" : 1,
          "failed" : 0
        },
        "status" : 201
      }
    },
    {
      "index" : {
        "_index" : "books",
        "_id" : "2",
        "_version" : 1,
        "result" : "created",
        "_shards" : {
          "total" : 2,
          "successful" : 1,
          "failed" : 0
        },
        "status" : 201
      }
    },
    {
      "index" : {
        "_index" : "books",
        "_id" : "3",
        "_version" : 1,
        "result" : "created",
        "_shards" : {
          "total" : 2,
          "successful" : 1,
          "failed" : 0
        },
        "status" : 201
      }
    }
  ]
}
```


You can also include update and delete operations in a bulk request, as shown below:

```
POST /_bulk
{ "update" : { "_id" : "1", "_index" : "books" } }
{ "doc" : {"title" : "Elasticsearch Basics", "year" : 2021} }
{ "delete": { "_index" : "books", "_id" : "3" } }
```

In this instance:

- The first operation is an update, modifying the document with ID

1 to change the year to 2021.

- The second operation is a delete, removing the document with ID 3 from the books index.

The response reflects the changes made by the update and delete operations:


```
{
  "took" : 20,
  "errors" : false,
  "items" : [
    {
      "update" : {
        "_index" : "books",
        "_id" : "1",
        "_version" : 2,
        "result" : "updated",
        "_shards" : {
          "total" : 2,
          "successful" : 1,
          "failed" : 0
        },
        "status" : 200
      }
    },
    {
      "delete" : {
        "_index" : "books",
        "_id" : "3",
        "_version" : 2,
        "result" : "deleted",
        "_shards" : {
          "total" : 2,
          "successful" : 1,
          "failed" : 0
        },
        "status" : 200
      }
    }
  ]
}
```


To handle large data sets, consider splitting the bulk request into manageable chunks. Large bulk requests can exhaust memory or server resources, causing failures or performance degradation. Best practice recommends limiting bulk requests to a size that your environment can handle efficiently. For example, requests containing a few megabytes of data or a few thousand actions provide a good balance between performance and resource utilization.

Using the Python client for Elasticsearch, you can implement bulk operations conveniently. The helpers.bulk module simplifies the process. Here's an example:

```
from elasticsearch import Elasticsearch, helpers
```

```
es = Elasticsearch()

actions = [
    { "_op_type": "index", "_index": "books", "_id": "1",
      "_source": { "title": "Elasticsearch Basics", "author": "John Doe", "year": 2020
          }},
    { "_op_type": "index", "_index": "books", "_id": "2",
      "_source": { "title": "Advanced Elasticsearch", "author": "Jane Smith", "year":
          2021 }},
    { "_op_type": "index", "_index": "books", "_id": "3",
      "_source": { "title": "Mastering Elasticsearch", "author": "Alice Brown", "year":
          2022 }}
]

helpers.bulk(es, actions)
```

In this Python script:

- An Elasticsearch client instance is initialized.
- A list of actions is defined, where each action corresponds to an index operation with document data.
- The helpers.bulk function executes the bulk request.

Bulk indexing operations enhance the scalability and performance of Elasticsearch deployments by reducing the overhead associated with multiple individual requests. Applying bulk operations judiciously can significantly optimize data ingestion processes, paving the way for efficient data management within the Elasticsearch ecosystem.

4.5 Updating and Deleting Documents

Updating and deleting documents in Elasticsearch require a thorough understanding of how the system manages data changes without compromising performance and consistency. Unlike traditional relational databases, Elasticsearch uses a different strategy to handle document updates and deletions due to its distributed and schema-free nature.

Document Updates: When a document requires updating, Elasticsearch does not alter the existing document. Instead, it performs a *reindexing* operation. The existing document is marked as deleted, and a new version of the document is indexed. This mechanism ensures that searches are not interrupted and index consistency is maintained. The reindexing process creates a new document with an incremented version number, thereby preserving the historical state of the document.

To update a document, a POST request can be made to the /index_-name/_update/document_id endpoint. The partial document containing the changes is specified within the request body.

```
POST /my_index/_update/1
{
  "doc": {
    "field1": "new_value",
    "field2": "updated_value"
  }
}
```

In this example, the fields field1 and field2 of the document with document_id 1 in my_index are updated to new values. The _update API ensures atomicity of the update process.

Elasticsearch also supports scripting within the update request. This allows for modifications to be made based on the document's existing state. The script is supplied via the script field in the request:

```
POST /my_index/_update/1
{
  "script": {
    "inline": "ctx._source.field1 += params.additional",
    "lang": "painless",
    "params": {
      "additional": " updated"
    }
  }
}
```

Here, the value of field1 is appended with " updated". The Painless scripting language is used for its efficiency and security.

Deleting Documents: Deleting a document in Elasticsearch efficiently involves marking it as deleted rather than physically removing it immediately. This is known as a *soft delete*. Physical deletion occurs later during the segment merging process, ensuring optimized data management and performance.

A document can be deleted by issuing a DELETE request to the /index_name/_doc/document_id endpoint:

```
DELETE /my_index/_doc/1
```

This command deletes the document with document_id 1 from my_-index. A successful response confirms the deletion.

Bulk Updates and Deletions: For bulk operations, Elasticsearch provides the _bulk API, enabling multiple update and delete actions in a single request. The request body consists of action lines followed by data lines, separated by newline characters.

```
POST /my_index/_bulk
{"update":{"_id":"1"}}
{"doc":{"field1":"new_value"}}
{"delete":{"_id":"2"}}
```

In the bulk request above, the first action updates the document with document_id 1, while the second action deletes the document with document_id 2. Each action and its corresponding document representation are separated by newline characters.

Bulk operations are particularly useful for significant data modifications as they reduce the number of network round-trips, thereby improving performance. It is important to handle bulk responses efficiently, assessing individual actions' statuses to ensure successful execution and appropriate error handling.

Concurrency Control: Elasticsearch employs Optimistic Concurrency Control (OCC) to handle concurrent document modifications. Each document update or delete operation can include a version parameter to ensure the operation is performed only if the provided version matches the document's current version. This prevents lost updates caused by simultaneous changes.

```
POST /my_index/_update/1?version=2
{
  "doc": {
    "field1": "attempted_value"
  }
}
```

If the provided version parameter (version=2) does not match the document's current version, the update fails, ensuring data integrity.

Understanding updating and deleting documents within Elasticsearch is integral to managing data effectively. Proper usage of the provided APIs and mechanisms facilitates maintaining consistent and reliable data stores in a distributed environment.

4.6 Handling Partial Updates and Upserts

Elasticsearch provides robust mechanisms for handling partial updates and upserts, which are essential for efficient document management in large datasets. Partial updates allow for modifying specific fields within a document without needing to reindex the entire document. Upserts, on the other hand, combine the functionality of updating a document if it exists or inserting a new document if it does not.

Partial updates are facilitated by the _update API, which enables only the specified fields to be modified. This is achieved through a script or a partial document, rendering the process more resource-efficient than a full reindexing. Below is an example of using a partial document for updating.

```
POST /index_name/_update/document_id
{
  "doc": {
    "field_to_update": "new_value",
    "another_field": "another_value"
  }
}
```

In this example, the doc parameter is used to specify the fields and their new values. Elasticsearch updates these fields in the existing document identified by document_id within the specified index_name. Only the fields mentioned under doc are altered, leaving the rest of the document intact.

For more complex updates, a script can be used to manipulate the document. Scripting allows for conditional logic and arithmetic operations during updates:

```
POST /index_name/_update/document_id
{
  "script": {
    "source": "ctx._source.field_name += params.increment",
    "lang": "painless",
    "params": {
      "increment": 5
    }
  }
}
```

In this script, the field_name value is incremented by 5. The source code is written in the painless scripting language, which is optimized for performance and security within Elasticsearch.

An upsert operation updates an existing document if it exists; otherwise, it creates a new document. This is especially useful in scenarios where the presence of a document cannot be guaranteed. To perform an upsert, include the upsert field in the update request:

```
POST /index_name/_update/document_id
{
  "scripted_upsert": true,
  "script": {
    "source": "ctx._source.count = params.count",
```

```
    "lang": "painless",
    "params": {
      "count": 1
    }
  },
  "upsert": {
    "count": 0
  }
}
```

In this example, the script field updates the count field. The upsert field provides the initial structure of the document should it not exist, setting count to 0. The scripted_upsert flag ensures that the script is executed during the creation of new documents.

Partial updates and upserts are essential in various scenarios:

- Reducing Indexing Overhead: Updating only necessary fields minimizes the load on the system and improves performance.
- Handling Dynamic Data: Upserts are particularly useful for logs or sensor data where the presence of a document is unpredictable.
- Efficient Resource Utilization: By avoiding complete reindexing, resources such as CPU and disk I/O are conserved.

Consider the following practical example where partial updates and upserts could be used:

```
POST /user_activity/_update/user_id
{
  "script": {
    "source": "ctx._source.login_count += 1",
    "lang": "painless"
  },
  "upsert": {
    "login_count": 1
  }
}
```

This example increments the login_count each time a user logs in. If the user document does not exist, an initial login_count of 1 is set.

Concurrency issues can arise during partial updates and upserts, especially in distributed systems. Elasticsearch uses versioning to manage concurrent updates. Each document has a version number, which increments with every update. By specifying the version in the update request, conflicts can be detected and managed.

```
POST /index_name/_update/document_id?version=2
{
```

```
  "doc": {
    "field_to_update": "new_value"
  }
}
```

This versioned update only executes if the document's current version matches the specified version, preventing stale data writes.

Best practices for handling partial updates and upserts include:

- Optimize Scripts: Ensure scripts are optimized for performance. Complex scripts can impact indexing speed.
- Use Versioning: Employ versioning to handle concurrent update scenarios and avoid data inconsistencies.
- Monitor Performance: Regularly monitor the performance of update operations to identify bottlenecks.
- Test Thoroughly: Test update and upsert logic in your development environment to ensure correctness before deploying to production.

Understanding and implementing partial updates and upserts efficiently ensures that Elasticsearch operates optimally, providing reliability and performance in handling large volumes of data.

4.7 Using Ingest Nodes and Pipelines

Ingest nodes and pipelines are a critical feature in Elasticsearch that allow for pre-processing of documents before they are indexed. This functionality provides a mechanism to transform and enrich data at ingestion time without the need for an external processing system. Ingest nodes act as intermediaries that can modify document content while pipelines define sequences of processors to apply to documents.

An ingest node is a special type of Elasticsearch node that can perform data transformations. When a document is submitted for indexing, it can be routed through one or more ingest pipelines. Each pipeline consists of multiple processors that modify the document in some way. For example, a pipeline can be configured to add geo-location data based on an IP address or to reformat date strings into a standard format.

To illustrate this process, we start by defining an ingest pipeline. Below is a detailed example that demonstrates how to create a pipeline which adds fields, removes fields, and updates existing fields.

First, we create an ingest pipeline that will:

- Convert dates from one format to another.
- Add a new field indicating the ingestion time.
- Remove unnecessary fields.

The following LaTeX and JSON code define such a pipeline:

```
PUT _ingest/pipeline/my_pipeline
{
  "description": "A pipeline to transform documents",
  "processors": [
    {
      "date": {
        "field": "timestamp",
        "target_field": "timestamp",
        "formats": ["dd/MM/yyyy HH:mm:ss", "ISO8601"],
        "timezone": "UTC"
      }
    },
    {
      "set": {
        "field": "ingestion_time",
        "value": "{{_ingest.timestamp}}"
      }
    },
    {
      "remove": {
        "field": "field_to_remove"
      }
    }
  ]
}
```

In this example:

- The date processor is used to unify date formats. It converts the timestamp field from multiple specified formats to a single target format.
- The set processor adds a new field ingestion_time to the document, capturing the time at which the document was processed by the pipeline.
- The remove processor deletes a field that is not needed for indexing.

Once the pipeline is set up, documents can be indexed through it. Using the following LaTeX and JSON code example, we index a document using this ingest pipeline:

```
PUT my_index/_doc/my_id?pipeline=my_pipeline
{
  "timestamp": "23/09/2023 10:24:00",
  "message": "This is a test document",
  "field_to_remove": "This field will be removed"
}
```

After running the above request, Elasticsearch will return an ingestion timestamp and confirm that the field_to_remove has been deleted. Below is an example of a document after processing via the pipeline:

```
{
  "_index": "my_index",
  "_type": "_doc",
  "_id": "my_id",
  "_version": 1,
  "found": true,
  "_source": {
    "timestamp": "2023-09-23T10:24:00.000Z",
    "message": "This is a test document",
    "ingestion_time": "2023-09-23T10:24:05.123Z"
  }
}
```

Ingest pipelines can include a variety of processors, enabling complex data transformations:

- grok for parsing and extracting structured fields from arbitrary text.
- geoip to enrich documents with geographical data from IP addresses.
- script to execute custom scripts for advanced transformations.
- json for decoding JSON strings.

Complex pipelines can be designed by chaining multiple processors together. For instance, the following pipeline both enriches documents with geographical information and extracts structured fields from log messages using grok patterns:

```
PUT _ingest/pipeline/complex_pipeline
{
  "description": "A complex pipeline for log processing",
  "processors": [
    {
      "grok": {
        "field": "message",
        "patterns": ["%{COMMONAPACHELOG}"]
      }
```

```
    },
    {
      "geoip": {
        "field": "clientip"
      }
    },
    {
      "set": {
        "field": "ingestion_time",
        "value": "{{_ingest.timestamp}}"
      }
    }
  ]
}
```

Documents processed through this pipeline are expected to have log entries in the common Apache log format. The grok processor extracts structured fields such as clientip, response, and bytes. The geoip processor then enriches this document with geographical data based on the extracted clientip. Finally, a set processor adds an ingestion timestamp.

Indexing a document through this complex pipeline is similar to the simpler example provided earlier:

```
PUT logs/_doc/log1?pipeline=complex_pipeline
{
  "message": "127.0.0.1 - frank [10/Oct/2000:13:55:36 -0700] \"GET /apache_pb.gif
      HTTP/1.0\" 200 2326"
}
```

The resulting document will be considerably enriched with additional fields extracted and generated by the pipeline:

```
{
  "_index": "logs",
  "_type": "_doc",
  "_id": "log1",
  "_version": 1,
  "found": true,
  "_source": {
    "message": "127.0.0.1 - frank [10/Oct/2000:13:55:36 -0700] \"GET /apache_pb.gif HTTP/1.0\" 200 2326",
    "clientip": "127.0.0.1",
    "ident": "frank",
    "auth": "frank",
    "timestamp": "2000-10-10T20:55:36.000Z",
    "verb": "GET",
    "request": "/apache_pb.gif",
    "httpversion": "1.0",
    "response": "200",
    "bytes": "2326",
    "geoip": {
      "continent_name": "North America",
      "country_name": "United States",
      "region_name": "California",
      "city_name": "Los Angeles",
      "latitude": 34.0522,
      "longitude": -118.2437
    },
    "ingestion_time": "2023-09-23T10:25:00.456Z"
  }
}
```

The utility of ingest processors lies in their ability to operate directly within Elasticsearch, reducing dependencies on external processing frameworks and simplifying data workflows. This ensures that all data modifications are centralized, versioned, and applied consistently during index time.

By mastering ingest pipelines, users can significantly enhance the preparation and enrichment of their data, optimizing it for more effective search and analysis within Elasticsearch.

4.8 Optimizing Indexing Performance

Optimizing indexing performance in Elasticsearch involves various strategies and configurations that can significantly enhance the speed and efficiency of indexing operations. This is crucial for applications requiring large-scale data ingestion and real-time search capabilities. Understanding and implementing these optimizations can lead to substantial performance gains.

Several key factors influence indexing performance: hardware configuration, Elasticsearch settings, index design, data processing techniques, and network considerations.

Firstly, hardware configuration is fundamental. Adequate memory (RAM) ensures that Elasticsearch can utilize file system caches, reducing disk I/O. Fast disks, preferably SSDs, improve write performance. Properly configured compute resources ensure that CPU is not a bottleneck during indexing operations. Network bandwidth and latency can also impact performance, particularly in distributed clusters.

- **Memory (RAM)**: Having sufficient memory to hold the working set of data and indices in the filesystem cache is critical. Aim to allocate 50% of the physical memory to the JVM heap, while leaving the rest for the filesystem cache.
- **Disk**:
  - Use fast disks such as SSDs.
  - Ensure adequate disk I/O throughput to handle write operations and merge activities.
- **CPU**: More cores can parallelize the indexing process, but ensure CPU is not the primary bottleneck.

- **Network**: High throughput and low latency networks reduce the overhead of distributed operations.

Elasticsearch settings play a pivotal role in tuning performance. Adjusting these configurations depending on the indexing workload can yield improved results. Key settings include:

refresh_interval: This setting controls how often Elasticsearch makes indexed documents available for search. During heavy indexing periods, consider increasing the refresh_interval to reduce the refresh overhead.

```
PUT /my_index/_settings
{
  "refresh_interval": "30s"
}
```

number_of_replicas: Setting the number of replicas to 0 during the initial bulk indexing phase reduces the overall indexing time. After indexing, you can increase replicas to ensure data redundancy.

```
PUT /my_index/_settings
{
  "number_of_replicas": 0
}
```

index.translog.durability: Setting this to async during heavy indexing periods can improve performance, but it comes with a trade-off in resilience.

```
PUT /my_index/_settings
{
  "index.translog.durability": "async"
}
```

Index design is another critical factor. Properly designed indices enhance performance and scalability. Considerations include:

- **Sharding Strategy**: Allocate an appropriate number of primary shards based on expected data size and query patterns. Too few shards can limit parallelism, while too many shards can lead to inefficient resource usage.
- **Mapping Design**: Define explicit mappings with proper data types, and disable features like norms, _all field, or unnecessary _source storage when not needed.
- **Optimized Field Types**: Utilize field types that minimize storage

and processing overhead. For example, use keyword fields for exact matches and text fields for full-text search.

Data processing techniques can also boost indexing speed. Preprocessing data outside Elasticsearch to reduce transformation work during indexing can significantly enhance throughput. Techniques include:

- **Bulk Indexing**: Employ the bulk API to minimize the overhead associated with individual index operations.
- **Routing**: Use custom routing to direct related data to the same shard, reducing cross-shard coordination.

```
POST /_bulk
{ "index" : { "_index" : "my_index", "_id" : "1" } }
{ "field1" : "value1", "field2" : "value2" }
{ "index" : { "_index" : "my_index", "_id" : "2" } }
{ "field1" : "value3", "field2" : "value4" }
```

Network considerations include optimizing communication between Elasticsearch nodes and data sources. Ensuring low-latency, high-throughput network connections can drastically reduce indexing time in a distributed setup.

By combining optimized hardware configurations, fine-tuned Elasticsearch settings, strategic index design, efficient data processing techniques, and reliable network setups, you can achieve high-performing indexing operations in Elasticsearch. These optimizations contribute to a responsive and efficient search infrastructure capable of handling large-scale data ingestion with ease.

4.9 Managing Index Templates

Index templates in Elasticsearch are critical configurations that allow users to define settings and mappings for indices that match a certain pattern. This facilitates the simplification and standardization of index creation, ensuring consistency and reducing the risk of human error.

Index templates are defined using JSON and can be managed via the Elasticsearch REST API. They can specify settings, mappings, and aliases that should be applied to newly created indices that match a given pattern. Below, we discuss the key components and operations involved in managing index templates.

For instance, let's consider an example where we need to create an index template for log data that follows a specific naming convention like 'logs-*'. The configuration of this template would include:

- Settings: Define various index settings such as the number of primary shards, replicas, refresh interval, etc.
- Mappings: Specify the field types, analyzers, and other properties to ensure that the data is indexed in an optimized manner.
- Aliases: Define aliases for indices, providing a level of abstraction and convenience in accessing these indices.

Here is an example of an index template that could be used for log data:

```
PUT _index_template/logs_template
{
  "index_patterns": ["logs-*"],
  "template": {
    "settings": {
      "number_of_shards": 1,
      "number_of_replicas": 1,
      "refresh_interval": "5s"
    },
    "mappings": {
      "properties": {
        "timestamp": {
          "type": "date"
        },
        "message": {
          "type": "text"
        },
        "log_level": {
          "type": "keyword"
        },
        "request_id": {
          "type": "keyword"
        }
      }
    },
    "aliases": {
      "current_logs": {}
    }
  }
}
```

To explain the components:

- index_patterns: An array of wildcard patterns. Any new index whose name matches one of these patterns will have this template applied.
- settings: In this example, we set the number of primary shards to 1, replicas to 1, and a refresh interval of 5 seconds.

- mappings: Defines the data structure. In this case, timestamp is defined as a date, message as a text field, log_level and request_id as keyword fields.
- aliases: An alias current_logs is applied, which will allow future queries to use this alias rather than the specific index name.

To retrieve a list of all index templates:

```
GET _index_template
```

To retrieve a specific index template:

```
GET _index_template/logs_template
```

This way, the details of the logs_template can be reviewed and verified.

To update an existing index template, you issue another PUT request with the same name and the new configuration. For example, to change the refresh_interval setting:

```
PUT _index_template/logs_template
{
  "index_patterns": ["logs-*"],
  "template": {
    "settings": {
      "number_of_shards": 1,
      "number_of_replicas": 1,
      "refresh_interval": "10s" // Updated refresh interval
    },
    "mappings": {
      "properties": {
        "timestamp": {
          "type": "date"
        },
        "message": {
          "type": "text"
        },
        "log_level": {
          "type": "keyword"
        },
        "request_id": {
          "type": "keyword"
        }
      }
    },
    "aliases": {
      "current_logs": {}
    }
  }
}
```

This effectively overwrites the existing template with the new settings.

To delete an index template, use the DELETE method:

```
DELETE _index_template/logs_template
```

This removes the template from the cluster and will not affect existing indices but will prevent the template from being applied to new indices.

By leveraging index templates, you can maintain consistency across your indices, streamline index management, and ensure optimal performance settings are applied.

4.10 Hands-On: Real-world Data Indexing Examples

This section demonstrates the practical application of indexing data into Elasticsearch using real-world examples. We will walk through the process of preparing data, defining appropriate mappings, and executing indexing operations using both single document and bulk indexing methods.

To begin with, let's define a sample dataset. We will use a fictional e-commerce dataset consisting of product information. This dataset contains the following fields:

- id: A unique identifier for each product
- name: The name of the product
- description: A brief description of the product
- price: The price of the product
- categories: A list of categories to which the product belongs
- stock_quantity: The quantity of the product available in stock
- release_date: The release date of the product

First, we structure the data in JSON format for a single product entry. An example JSON document might look like the following:

```
{
    "id": "p12345",
    "name": "Sample Product",
    "description": "A detailed description of the sample product.",
    "price": 19.99,
    "categories": ["electronics", "gadgets"],
    "stock_quantity": 150,
```

```
    "release_date": "2023-01-15"
}
```

Next, we need to define the mapping for the Elasticsearch index that will store these product documents. Mapping helps Elasticsearch understand the structure of the data and the data types for each field. Here, we choose appropriate data types for each field in the mapping:

```
PUT /products
{
    "mappings": {
        "properties": {
            "id": { "type": "keyword" },
            "name": { "type": "text" },
            "description": { "type": "text" },
            "price": { "type": "float" },
            "categories": { "type": "keyword" },
            "stock_quantity": { "type": "integer" },
            "release_date": { "type": "date", "format": "yyyy-MM-dd" }
        }
    }
}
```

To index a single product document, we can use the following cURL command:

```
curl -X PUT "localhost:9200/products/_doc/p12345" -H 'Content-Type: application/
    json' -d'
{
    "id": "p12345",
    "name": "Sample Product",
    "description": "A detailed description of the sample product.",
    "price": 19.99,
    "categories": ["electronics", "gadgets"],
    "stock_quantity": 150,
    "release_date": "2023-01-15"
}
'
```

For bulk indexing operations, we need to format our data to be compatible with the Elasticsearch bulk API. Below is an example of how to structure multiple product documents for bulk indexing:

```
{ "index": { "_index": "products", "_id": "p12346" } }
{ "id": "p12346", "name": "Another Product", "description": "Description of another
    product.", "price": 29.99, "categories": ["electronics"], "stock_quantity": 75, "
    release_date": "2022-12-10" }
{ "index": { "_index": "products", "_id": "p12347" } }
{ "id": "p12347", "name": "Yet Another Product", "description": "Description of yet
    another product.", "price": 39.99, "categories": ["home appliances"], "
    stock_quantity": 200, "release_date": "2023-02-20" }
```

To perform the bulk indexing using a cURL command, we save the above JSON data to a file named bulk_data.json and execute the following command:

```
curl -X POST "localhost:9200/_bulk" -H 'Content-Type: application/json' --data-
    binary @bulk_data.json
```

The output of the bulk indexing operation will provide detailed information about the success or failure of each indexed document:


```
{
  "took" : 123,
  "errors" : false,
  "items" : [
    {
      "index" : {
        "_index" : "products",
        "_type" : "_doc",
        "_id" : "p12346",
        "_version" : 1,
        "result" : "created",
        "_shards" : {
          "total" : 2,
          "successful" : 2,
          "failed" : 0
        },
        "status" : 201
      }
    },
    {
      "index" : {
        "_index" : "products",
        "_type" : "_doc",
        "_id" : "p12347",
        "_version" : 1,
        "result" : "created",
        "_shards" : {
          "total" : 2,
          "successful" : 2,
          "failed" : 0
        },
        "status" : 201
      }
    }
  ]
}
```


If correctly performed, the bulk indexing command will insert multiple product documents into the products index efficiently. This method is highly beneficial when dealing with large datasets that need to be ingested into Elasticsearch.

These examples illustrate how to leverage the REST API for indexing both individual and bulk data in a practical, real-world scenario. Attention to matching data types and using appropriate REST endpoints ensures efficient data operations within Elasticsearch.

Chapter 5

Search and Query Functions

This chapter examines Elasticsearch's search and query capabilities, including the query DSL, match and multi-match queries, and term and range queries. It explains advanced techniques such as boolean queries, full-text search methods, and the essentials of sorting and pagination. Additionally, it covers highlighting search results and understanding search relevance, culminating in practical guidance on crafting complex and efficient queries.

5.1 Introduction to Elasticsearch Queries

In Elasticsearch, querying is a fundamental operation that facilitates extracting and analyzing data from the indexed documents. Elasticsearch provides a robust and versatile Query Domain Specific Language (DSL) tailored for constructing various queries to retrieve specific data subsets. This section delves into the core principles underlying Elasticsearch queries, offering a comprehensive understanding of how to effectively leverage the querying capabilities.

At its core, the query DSL allows users to structure their search logic clearly and concisely. The DSL is JSON-based, enabling the combination of multiple query types to perform intricate searches. These queries are broadly categorized into two types: leaf queries and compound queries. Leaf queries target specific field values, whereas compound queries combine multiple queries to form complex search criteria.

The simplest form of a query in Elasticsearch is a match query, designed to search for documents matching specified criteria. Below is a basic example to illustrate its implementation:

```
{
  "query": {
    "match": {
      "message": "Elasticsearch"
    }
  }
}
```

This query searches for documents where the message field contains the term Elasticsearch.

Elasticsearch also provides the multi-match query, an extension of the match query, enabling search across multiple fields. This is particularly useful when the query term could reside in different fields within the documents. An example is provided below:

```
{
  "query": {
    "multi_match": {
      "query": "Elasticsearch",
      "fields": ["title", "content", "tags"]
    }
  }
}
```

Here, the query searches for the term Elasticsearch across the title, content, and tags fields, enhancing the search coverage and precision.

Another prominent query type is the term query, which is more precise in targeting exact terms rather than analyzed text. Term queries match exact terms and are often used for structured data such as dates, numbers, and tags. Below is an exemplary term query targeting documents with a specific status:

```
{
  "query": {
    "term": {
      "status": "active"
    }
  }
}
```

This query retrieves documents where the status field precisely matches active, emphasizing its use in non-analyzed terms.

For numerical and date ranges, range queries are indispensable. Such queries enable filtering documents based on the specified range criteria. Below is an example demonstrating a range query for filtering documents within a date range:

```
{
  "query": {
    "range": {
      "publish_date": {
        "gte": "2022-01-01",
        "lte": "2022-12-31"
      }
    }
  }
}
```

This query retrieves documents where the publish_date falls within the year 2022, making it particularly useful for temporal data filtering.

Compound queries empower the construction of complex search conditions by combining multiple query types. The boolean query (bool query) is a prime example, employing logical operators such as must, should, and must_not to define comprehensive search criteria. Below is an illustrative bool query combining multiple conditions:

```
{
  "query": {
    "bool": {
      "must": [
        {"match": {"title": "Elasticsearch"}},
        {"range": {"publish_date": {"gte": "2023-01-01"}}}
      ],
      "should": [
        {"term": {"status": "active"}}
      ],
      "must_not": [
        {"term": {"type": "deprecated"}}
      ]
    }
  }
}
```

In this query, documents must match the title as Elasticsearch and have a publish_date greater than or equal to 2023-01-01. Additionally, it should preferably have a status of active and must not be of type deprecated.

Understanding the construction and execution of these queries in Elasticsearch is pivotal for crafting efficient and effective search operations. Through these query types, one can build tailored search functionalities, yielding precise and relevant results aligned with the underlying dataset's structure and schema.

5.2 The Query DSL: An Overview

The Elasticsearch Query Domain-Specific Language (DSL) provides a powerful, flexible, and expressive syntax to define queries within the Elasticsearch environment. This DSL allows users to perform detailed searches and aggregations on their data, enabling precise control over how queries are executed and how results are returned. By utilizing the Query DSL, users can harness the full potential of Elasticsearch's search capabilities.

The Query DSL is expressed in JSON format, offering a structured way to specify queries. This structure facilitates the definition of complex queries by combining different query types in a clear and legible manner. Below is an example illustrating the basic structure of a DSL query:

```
{
  "query": {
    "match": {
      "title": "Elasticsearch"
    }
  }
}
```

In this example, the query is a simple match query, which looks for documents containing the term "Elasticsearch" in the "title" field.

There are two primary categories of queries in the Elasticsearch Query DSL:

- Leaf Queries: These operate on specific fields and produce individual relevance scores.
- Compound Queries: These wrap other queries, enabling the combination and customization of these queries.

Leaf Queries

Leaf queries comprise match, term, range, and other queries that operate directly on the data fields. These queries can be further divided into full-text queries and term-level queries. Full-text queries analyze the input text and are suitable for searching large sections of text, while term-level queries do not perform any text analysis, making them suitable for exact matches.

- *Match Query*: Searches analyzed full-text fields for the provided input.

- *Term Query*: Searches exact terms without analyzing the input.
- *Range Query*: Finds documents with values falling within a specified range.

```
{
  "query": {
    "range": {
      "date": {
        "gte": "2020-01-01",
        "lte": "2021-12-31"
      }
    }
  }
}
```

Compound Queries

Compound queries enable the combination of multiple leaf and other compound queries to construct more sophisticated queries. Key types include bool, dis_max, and constant_score queries.

- *Bool Query*: Combines multiple sub-queries using boolean logic (must, should, must_not, filter).
- *Dis_max Query*: Selects the single best-matching query result from multiple queries.
- *Constant_score Query*: Wraps a query and assigns it a constant score, ignoring the relevance score.

A common use of the bool query is to combine multiple queries to achieve a compound search criterion:

```
{
  "query": {
    "bool": {
      "must": [
        { "match": { "title": "Elasticsearch" }},
        { "range": { "date": { "gte": "2020-01-01" }}}
      ],
      "filter": [
        { "term": { "status": "published" }}
      ]
    }
  }
}
```

In this example, the query must match documents where the title contains "Elasticsearch" and the date is greater than or equal to "2020-01-01". Additionally, only documents with the status "published" are selected.

Function Score Queries

Function score queries provide the ability to modify the relevance scores of documents that satisfy a query. This is particularly useful for customizing the ranking of search results based on specific criteria.

```
{
  "query": {
    "function_score": {
      "query": { "match": { "title": "Elasticsearch" }},
      "boost": "5",
      "functions": [
        {
          "filter": { "match": { "category": "books" }},
          "weight": 2
        }
      ],
      "score_mode": "multiply",
      "boost_mode": "multiply"
    }
  }
}
```

In this example, documents matching the title "Elasticsearch" are boosted by 5, and documents categorized as "books" are further weighted by 2, with scores multiplied accordingly.

The Query DSL in Elasticsearch is highly versatile, accommodating a wide range of search requirements through its modular and composable syntax. Mastery of the Query DSL empowers users to craft precise and efficient queries, thereby making the most of Elasticsearch's powerful search capabilities.

5.3 Match and Multi-Match Queries

Match and multi-match queries are fundamental components of Elasticsearch's search functionality, enabling efficient full-text search capabilities. These types of queries allow users to perform flexible searches against text fields, and they adapt to the varying complexities of search needs, from simple text matching to more nuanced, multi-field searching. Understanding these queries is crucial for leveraging Elasticsearch's full-text search power.

The match query is designed to execute searches against a single field, employing Elasticsearch's text analysis capabilities to provide relevant results for text-based data. In contrast, the multi-match query extends this functionality by searching across multiple fields simultaneously, thus accommodating use cases where the desired search terms may span multiple text fields.

The basic structure of a match query in Elasticsearch is straightforward. The query matches the search term against the analyzed text in the specified field. The following example demonstrates a simple match query:

```
{
  "query": {
    "match": {
      "message": "elasticsearch"
    }
  }
}
```

In this example, the query searches for the term "elasticsearch" within the "message" field. The match query utilizes Elasticsearch's inverted index to efficiently locate documents that contain the search term, scoring them based on relevance metrics such as term frequency.

The match query also supports various options to fine-tune the search behavior. For instance, one can control the operator used for matching, such as "and" or "or", specify fuzziness for approximate matching, or define a minimum should match criterion. The following example showcases a match query with additional parameters:

```
{
  "query": {
    "match": {
      "message": {
        "query": "elasticsearch tutorial",
        "operator": "and",
        "fuzziness": "AUTO",
        "minimum_should_match": "75%"
      }
    }
  }
}
```

Here, the query searches for documents containing both "elasticsearch" and "tutorial" in the "message" field, allowing for fuzzy matching and requiring at least 75% of the terms to match.

Transitioning to multi-match queries, these allow multiple fields to be queried simultaneously, which is particularly useful when data is dispersed across various fields. The structure of a multi-match query is similar to the match query but includes multiple fields within the search criteria. The following example illustrates a multi-match query:

```
{
  "query": {
    "multi_match": {
```

```
      "query": "elasticsearch guide",
      "fields": ["title", "description", "content"]
    }
  }
}
```

In this case, the query looks for the terms “elasticsearch” and “guide” across the “title”, “description”, and “content” fields, scoring and ranking documents based on their relevance across these fields.

The multi-match query supports various types that adjust the scoring behavior to match different search requirements. These types include “best_fields”, “most_fields”, “cross_fields”, and “phrase”. Each type modifies how the query terms are processed and combined. For instance, “best_fields” selects the best scoring field, while “most_fields” considers combined scores from all fields. The following example shows a multi-match query utilizing the “most_fields” type:

```
{
  "query": {
    "multi_match": {
      "query": "elasticsearch guide",
      "fields": ["title", "description", "content"],
      "type": "most_fields"
    }
  }
}
```

This configuration searches “title”, “description”, and “content” fields, aggregating scores across all fields to provide a cumulative relevance score for each document.

Another important aspect of multi-match queries is the ability to apply different weights to fields, known as boosting. Boosting allows certain fields to influence the score more heavily, which is beneficial when certain fields are deemed more significant in the search context. The following example integrates boosting into the multi-match query:

```
{
  "query": {
    "multi_match": {
      "query": "elasticsearch guide",
      "fields": ["title^2", "description", "content"]
    }
  }
}
```

In this configuration, the “title” field is given twice the weight of the “description” and “content” fields, increasing its influence on the overall score.

Match and multi-match queries form the foundation for building powerful full-text search applications with Elasticsearch. By understanding their nuances and leveraging their capabilities, one can craft highly relevant and efficient search queries that meet a wide array of search needs.

5.4 Term and Range Queries

Term and range queries in Elasticsearch are essential for filtering data based on exact matches or numerical ranges. These queries can significantly enhance data retrieval efficiency and accuracy by narrowing down the search space to relevant documents.

Term Queries:

A term query finds documents containing exact terms in a specified field. This is particularly useful when searching for numeric fields, date fields, exact values, and identifiers like email addresses or user IDs. Unlike text fields, which are analyzed and tokenized, the term query does not perform any analysis on the search terms or the field values.

```
{
  "query": {
    "term": {
      "user.id": {
        "value": "12345"
      }
    }
  }
}
```

In this example, the query searches for documents where the ‘user.id‘ field has a value exactly equal to "12345".

Range Queries:

Range queries allow you to search for values within a specified range. They are particularly useful for date and numeric fields. Elasticsearch supports various range parameters such as ‘gte‘ (greater than or equal to), ‘lte‘ (less than or equal to), ‘gt‘ (greater than), and ‘lt‘ (less than).

```
{
  "query": {
    "range": {
      "timestamp": {
        "gte": "2021-01-01",
        "lte": "2021-12-31",
        "format": "yyyy-MM-dd"
      }
```

```
      }
    }
}
```

This query searches for documents with a 'timestamp' field that falls within the range of January 1, 2021, to December 31, 2021. The 'format' parameter ensures that the dates are correctly interpreted.

Understanding Range Parameters:

- gte (greater than or equal to): Includes the specified value in the results.
- lte (less than or equal to): Includes the specified value in the results.
- gt (greater than): Excludes the specified value from the results.
- lt (less than): Excludes the specified value from the results.

```
{
  "query": {
    "range": {
      "age": {
        "gt": 10,
        "lt": 20
      }
    }
  }
}
```

This query retrieves documents where the 'age' field is greater than 10 and less than 20, excluding the boundaries.

Combining Term and Range Queries:

Combining term and range queries in a single query can achieve more refined and complex search criteria. Below is an example using a boolean query to combine both types:

```
{
  "query": {
    "bool": {
      "must": [
        {
          "term": {
            "status": "active"
          }
        },
        {
          "range": {
            "created_at": {
              "gte": "2022-01-01",
```

```
            "lte": "2022-12-31",
            "format": "yyyy-MM-dd"
          }
        }
      }
    ]
  }
 }
}
```

This query filters documents that have the 'status' field set to "active" and a 'created_at' date within the year 2022.

Performance Considerations:

Using term and range queries impacts Elasticsearch's performance, especially with large datasets. Always ensure proper indexing of fields to improve query performance. Non-analyzed fields for term queries and optimized date formats for range queries can make a significant difference.

Additionally, Elasticsearch processes range queries on numeric fields efficiently by leveraging internal BKD trees. However, for fields with a wide range of unique values, consider the memory and CPU implications.

Outputs from executing these queries can be illustrated as follows:


```
{
  "hits" : {
    "total" : {
      "value" : 5,
      "relation" : "eq"
    },
    "max_score" : 1.0,
    "hits" : [
      {
        "_index" : "users",
        "_type" : "_doc",
        "_id" : "1",
        "_score" : 1.0,
        "_source" : {
          "user.id" : "12345",
          "name" : "John Doe"
        }
      }
    ]
  }
}
```


Term and range queries provide foundational capabilities that, when appropriately utilized, can significantly refine search results. They are integral in building structured and highly specific search functionalities within Elasticsearch.

5.5 Boolean Queries

In Elasticsearch, Boolean queries are a powerful and versatile tool that allows users to combine multiple criteria to fine-tune their search results. By leveraging Boolean logic, one can execute complex queries that encompass various conditions, enabling the retrieval of highly relevant data. Boolean queries consist of several types: must, must_not, should, and filter. Each of these contributes differently to the query logic and relevance calculation.

An itemized bullet point list identifies the clause types:

- A must clause indicates that the query must match the document for it to be included in the results. A document must meet all the criteria specified in the must clause.
- A must_not clause excludes documents that match the specified criteria from the search results. It is akin to a negation operator in Boolean logic.
- A should clause acts as a “soft must” clause. While documents matching the should clause do not need to satisfy all the criteria, documents matching more should clauses will be scored higher, thereby ranking higher in the results.
- A filter clause functions similarly to the must clause but differs in that it does not contribute to the scoring. Filters are often used for operations such as restricting search results by date ranges or categories where scoring is not essential.

The structure of a Boolean query in Elasticsearch follows specifics of query DSL (Domain Specific Language). It is formally constructed using the following format:

```
{
  "query": {
    "bool": {
      "must": [ ... ],
      "must_not": [ ... ],
      "should": [ ... ],
      "filter": [ ... ]
    }
  }
}
```

To illustrate the application of Boolean queries, consider an example where we search for documents that must have a title containing "Elasticsearch" but must not have a status of "draft". Additionally, the documents should preferably have a tag of "search", and we want to filter the results to only include documents last updated after 2020-01-01.

```
{
  "query": {
    "bool": {
      "must": [
        {
          "match": {
            "title": "Elasticsearch"
          }
        }
      ],
      "must_not": [
        {
          "term": {
            "status.keyword": "draft"
          }
        }
      ],
      "should": [
        {
          "term": {
            "tags": "search"
          }
        }
      ],
      "filter": [
        {
          "range": {
            "last_updated": {
              "gt": "2020-01-01"
            }
          }
        }
      ]
    }
  }
}
```

The must clause contains a match query which ensures that only documents with a title matching "Elasticsearch" are retrieved. The must_not clause employs a term query to exclude any documents with the status field equal to "draft". In the should clause, a term query specifies that documents with the tags field containing "search" are preferred but not mandatory. The filter clause uses a range query to restrict the results to documents updated after January 1, 2020.

These clauses can be nested and combined to form complex query logic. Below is an advanced example demonstrating a possible nested Boolean query:

```
{
  "query": {
    "bool": {
      "must": [
```

```
        {
          "bool": {
            "should": [
              {
                "match": {
                  "title": "Elasticsearch"
                }
              },
              {
                "match": {
                  "title": "Search Engine"
                }
              }
            ]
          }
        }
      ],
      "filter": [
        {
          "bool": {
            "must": [
              {
                "term": {
                  "category.keyword": "technology"
                }
              },
              {
                "range": {
                  "last_updated": {
                    "gte": "2021-01-01"
                  }
                }
              }
            ]
          }
        }
      ]
    }
  }
}
```

In this query, the top-level must clause contains another Boolean query, which specifies that the document's title should either be "Elasticsearch" or "Search Engine". The filter clause contains its own nested Boolean query requiring both the category to be "technology" and the last_updated date to be on or after January 1, 2021. This example showcases how Boolean queries can encapsulate complex, multi-layered conditions to retrieve precise and targeted search results.

Understanding how to effectively utilize Boolean queries is crucial for creating robust and efficient search mechanisms in Elasticsearch. By mastering the nuances of must, must_not, should, and filter clauses, one can leverage the full potential of Elasticsearch's querying capabilities to meet diverse search requirements.

5.6 Full-Text Search Techniques

Full-text search in Elasticsearch enables searching through large volumes of text-based data, leveraging its capability to analyze textual data and return relevant results. This functionality is powered by the full-text queries, which are designed to search text fields based on their analyzed tokens rather than their stored values.

Elasticsearch provides several full-text queries, each serving a specific purpose. The most prominent ones include the match, multi_match, query_string, and simple_query_string. These queries ensure that text searches are flexible and accurate, accommodating a variety of search needs.

```
{
  "query": {
    "match": {
      "message": "Elasticsearch full-text search"
    }
  }
}
```

The match query is the most commonly used full-text query and employs an analyzer to convert the input text into terms to be matched against the indexed documents. The example demonstrates a basic match query searching for the phrase "Elasticsearch full-text search" within the message field.

For scenarios where multiple fields need to be searched, the multi_match query is utilized. This query expands on the match query, allowing for simultaneous searching across multiple fields.

```
{
  "query": {
    "multi_match": {
      "query": "Elasticsearch guidebook",
      "fields": ["title", "content"]
    }
  }
}
```

In this example, the multi_match query searches for the term "Elasticsearch guidebook" in both the title and content fields. The multi_match query supports various types, such as best_fields, most_fields, or cross_fields, enhancing its versatility.

The query_string is another advanced full-text search technique. It offers the ability to perform complex queries using a query string with the Lucene query syntax. This is particularly useful for performing detailed searches where specific clauses and operators are required.

```
{
  "query": {
    "query_string": {
      "query": "(Elasticsearch AND guidebook) OR \"full-text search\"",
      "default_field": "content"
    }
  }
}
```

The above query searches the content field for documents that either match both "Elasticsearch" and "guidebook" or the exact phrase "full-text search". The query_string syntax provides extensive functionality, including wildcard searches, boosting terms, fuzzy matching, and proximity searches.

For simpler implementations where user input is directly used in the query, the simple_query_string query is ideal. It supports a subset of the Lucene query syntax and is designed to be error-tolerant, preventing parsing errors from user-generated queries.

```
{
  "query": {
    "simple_query_string": {
      "query": "Elasticsearch +guidebook | \"full-text search\"",
      "fields": ["title^5", "content"]
    }
  }
}
```

Here, the simple_query_string query searches for documents containing "Elasticsearch" and "guidebook" or the phrase "full-text search" in the title and content fields. The title field is given a boosting factor of 5, prioritizing matches in the title over the content.

Analyzers play a critical role in full-text searching. They process the text during both indexing and query time, affecting the terms that are stored and searched. An analyzer typically comprises a tokenizer and a sequence of token filters. The built-in standard analyzer, for example, tokenizes text using the Unicode Text Segmentation algorithm and applies filters like lowercase normalization and stop word removal.

Custom analyzers can be defined to suit specific needs:

```
{
  "settings": {
    "analysis": {
      "analyzer": {
        "custom_analyzer": {
          "type": "custom",
          "tokenizer": "standard",
          "filter": ["lowercase", "asciifolding"]
```

```
      }
    }
  }
 }
}
```

This custom analyzer uses the standard tokenizer and two filters: lowercase and asciifolding. The latter converts characters to their ASCII equivalents, which is useful for handling accented characters.

Additionally, Elasticsearch supports highlighting, providing emphasis on matching terms within search results. Highlighting enhances user experience by indicating which parts of the document matched the query.

```
{
  "query": {
    "match": {
      "content": "Elasticsearch guidebook"
    }
  },
  "highlight": {
    "fields": {
      "content": {}
    }
  }
}
```

The query highlights where "Elasticsearch guidebook" appears in the content field. The highlight results are included in the search response, allowing for clear presentation of matched terms.

Full-text search techniques in Elasticsearch provide powerful tools for retrieving and emphasizing relevant information from large text data sets. These techniques are integral to building effective search functionalities in various applications, from simple text searches to complex query string operations.

5.7 Sorting and Pagination

Sorting and pagination serve as essential tools in making the search results usable and navigable, especially when dealing with large datasets. Elasticsearch provides robust mechanisms to sort results on various fields and paginate through them efficiently. Understanding these functions is crucial for optimizing performance and ensuring relevant data is retrieved seamlessly.

Sorting in Elasticsearch is facilitated through the sort parameter. It can be used within any search query to order the results based on one or multiple fields. The syntax for sorting is straightforward and supports various data types like strings, numbers, and dates. Here is an example of a simple sorting command that arranges results in ascending order based on the timestamp field:

```
{
  "query": {
    "match_all": {}
  },
  "sort": [
    {
      "timestamp": {
        "order": "asc"
      }
    }
  ]
}
```

For more advanced sorting, Elasticsearch allows for multi-level sorting. This is particularly useful when there are ties in the primary sort field. The secondary fields can be used as tie-breakers. Below is an example where first the timestamp field is sorted in descending order, and within those results, the user_id field is sorted in ascending order:

```
{
  "query": {
    "match_all": {}
  },
  "sort": [
    {
      "timestamp": {
        "order": "desc"
      }
    },
    {
      "user_id": {
        "order": "asc"
      }
    }
  ]
}
```

Sorting supports several modes that can handle scenarios where arrays or multi-value fields are present in the documents. The mode parameter can take values like min, max, sum, avg, and median, determining how these values are considered in sorting. Here is an example demonstrating the avg mode:

```
{
  "query": {
    "match_all": {}
  },
  "sort": [
    {
```

```
        "ratings": {
          "order": "desc",
          "mode": "avg"
        }
      }
    ]
}
```

In addition to sorting, pagination plays a pivotal role in efficiently handling large datasets by breaking them into manageable chunks. Elasticsearch provides the from and size parameters to accomplish this. The from parameter specifies the starting point of the result set, while size defines the number of results to retrieve. Here is an example:

```
{
  "query": {
    "match_all": {}
  },
  "from": 10,
  "size": 5
}
```

This query skips the first 10 results and retrieves the next 5. While this method is simple to implement, it may lead to performance issues for very large result sets as the from value increases. This is because Elasticsearch needs to load and skip over a large number of records.

A more efficient way to handle deep pagination is by using the search_after parameter in conjunction with sorting. This method makes use of the values from the previous page of results as reference points to fetch the next set of results. This approach mitigates the performance drawbacks of high from values. Here is an example:

```
{
  "query": {
    "match_all": {}
  },
  "sort": [
    {
      "timestamp": {
        "order": "asc"
      }
    },
    {
      "unique_id": {
        "order": "asc"
      }
    }
  ],
  "size": 5,
  "search_after": [1599832992000, "doc1"]
}
```

In this example, search_after uses the last values of timestamp and unique_id from the previous page of results to fetch the next set.

For extensive data accumulation, Elasticsearch provides scroll and point-in-time (PIT) APIs for more controlled and large-scale pagination. The scroll API is suitable for extracting large datasets where each subsequent scroll request fetches the next batch of results. Here is an example using the scroll API:

```
{
  "scroll": "1m",
  "size": 100,
  "query": {
    "match_all": {}
  }
}
```

The initial scroll request establishes a context valid for 1 minute. Each subsequent scroll request retrieves the next batch of results until the context expires or all results are retrieved.

Understanding sorting and pagination facilitates the crafting of efficient queries while ensuring that users can navigate through large datasets seamlessly. Utilizing these mechanisms effectively can significantly enhance both the performance and the user experience of search applications.

5.8 Highlighting Search Results

Highlighting search results in Elasticsearch allows users to emphasize the relevant parts of the documents that match the search criteria. This feature is particularly useful for applications that require a display of query matches within a broader context, such as showing snippets of text or specific fields in a search result interface.

In Elasticsearch, the highlighting feature can be used in conjunction with various queries to mark the matching terms. The highlights are typically marked using HTML tags, which can be customized. This section will delve into the configuration options and implementation details of highlighting in Elasticsearch.

To utilize highlighting in a search request, you need to include a 'highlight' element in the query body. The 'highlight' element specifies the fields to be highlighted and various configuration settings, such as the pre-tags and post-tags used to wrap the highlighted text.

```
{
```

```
  "query": {
    "match": {
      "content": "Elasticsearch"
    }
  },
  "highlight": {
    "fields": {
      "content": {}
    }
  }
}
```

In this example, the query searches for the term ‘Elasticsearch‘ within the ‘content‘ field and highlights the matching terms. By default, Elasticsearch uses ‘<em>‘ and ‘</em>‘ tags to wrap the highlighted text. The response includes the original documents and additional fields with the highlighted fragments.

Customization of highlight tags can enhance readability or adapt to different HTML templates:

```
{
  "query": {
    "match": {
      "content": "Elasticsearch"
    }
  },
  "highlight": {
    "pre_tags": ["<strong>"],
    "post_tags": ["</strong>"],
    "fields": {
      "content": {}
    }
  }
}
```

Here, the highlighted text will be wrapped in ‘<strong>‘ tags instead of the default ‘<em>‘ tags, making the matches appear bold.

To further refine the highlighting behavior, several additional parameters can be used:

- **Fragment Size**: Controls the size of the text fragments where highlights are applied.
- **Number of Fragments**: Specifies the maximum number of fragments to return.
- **Fragmenter**: Determines how text is split into fragments. The default ‘simple‘ fragmenter can be replaced with ‘span‘ for higher precision.

Consider the following example illustrating these parameters:

```
{
  "query": {
    "match": {
      "content": "Elasticsearch"
    }
  },
  "highlight": {
    "order": "score",
    "highlight_query": {
      "bool": {
        "must": [
          {
            "match": {
              "content": "Elasticsearch"
            }
          }
        ],
        "filter": {
          "range": {
            "date": {
              "gte": "2020-01-01"
            }
          }
        }
      }
    },
    "fields": {
      "content": {
        "fragment_size": 150,
        "number_of_fragments": 3,
        "fragmenter": "span"
      }
    }
  }
}
```

In this query:

- order: The score value prioritizes fragments based on their relevance score.
- highlight_query: Allows specifying a custom query just for highlighting purposes, such as combining boolean and range queries.
- fragment_size: A fragment_size of 150 characters.
- number_of_fragments: Limits to three fragments.
- fragmenter: Uses the span fragmenter for more sophisticated fragment splitting.

Understanding the highlighted fragments in the response is crucial:

```
{
  "hits": {
    "total": 1,
```

```
    "hits": [
      {
        "_index": "my_index",
        "_type": "_doc",
        "_id": "1",
        "_score": 1.0,
        "_source": {
          "content": "A tutorial on Elasticsearch and its powerful search capabilities."
        },
        "highlight": {
          "content": [
            "A tutorial on <em>Elasticsearch</em> and its powerful search
                capabilities."
          ]
        }
      }
    ]
  }
}
```

In the response, the highlight field contains the highlighted fragments of the content field, with matching terms wrapped in '<em>' tags.

Highlighting boosts the user experience by providing direct visual feedback on where the search terms appear within the documents. Properly configuring highlighting ensures relevant sections of documents are prominently displayed, aiding users in quickly locating the information they need.

5.9 Understanding Search Relevance

Search relevance is a critical aspect of Elasticsearch, determining the quality and usefulness of search results presented to the user. The relevance score assigned to each document by Elasticsearch impacts the order in which search results are returned. This section delves into the underlying mechanics of relevance scoring, the factors that influence it, and the methods available to fine-tune it for optimal performance.

Elasticsearch employs the Okapi BM25 as its default relevance scoring algorithm. BM25 belongs to the family of probabilistic information retrieval models and is renowned for its effectiveness in ranking documents based on their relevance to a query. At its core, BM25 is built upon the concepts of term frequency and inverse document frequency, combined with a saturation function to handle document length normalization. The score for a document relative to a query is derived using these principles, yielding a non-negative score where a higher value indicates greater relevance.

$$\text{score}(q,d) = \sum_{t \in q} \text{IDF}(t) \cdot \frac{f(t,d) \cdot (k_1 + 1)}{f(t,d) + k_1 \cdot (1 - b + b \cdot \frac{|d|}{\text{avgdl}})}$$

In this equation:

- q denotes the query.
- d represents the document.
- t is a term within the query.
- f(t, d) is the frequency of term t in document d.
- k_1 is a positive tuning parameter that calibrates term frequency saturation.
- b is a scaling factor that adjusts the impact of document length.
- |d| is the length of document d.
- avgdl is the average document length across the corpus.

The term frequency component $\frac{f(t,d) \cdot (k_1+1)}{f(t,d)+k_1 \cdot (1-b+b \cdot \frac{|d|}{\text{avgdl}})}$ models the diminishing returns on term frequency by using a hyperbolic function to saturate the score. The document frequency parameter IDF(t) quantifies how common or rare a term is across all documents, reducing the influence of ubiquitous terms:

$$\text{IDF}(t) = \log\left(\frac{1 + N}{1 + n_t}\right) + 1$$

where N is the total number of documents in the corpus, and n_t is the number of documents containing the term t.

Elasticsearch uses a combination of factors to produce a relevance score for each document:

- Term Frequency (TF): Measures how often a term appears in a document. Higher term frequency generally correlates with higher relevance.
- Inverse Document Frequency (IDF): Assesses how common or rare a term is across all documents. Rare terms are given more weight than common terms.

- Field Length Normalization: Normalizes the term frequency score based on the length of the field to prevent bias towards longer documents.

- Query Term Boosting: Allows certain query terms to be manually given more importance, adjusting the weight of the terms in the relevance calculation.

By default, Elasticsearch computes a score for documents that match the query and uses the aforementioned factors to rank these documents. However, Elasticsearch also offers various ways to affect these scoring mechanisms, including custom scoring scripts, boosting specific fields, or even using different similarity algorithms if BM25 is not suitable for a particular use case.

Using the function_score query, one can customize how scores are computed by applying functions to modify the relevance scores of documents based on factors like field values or arbitrary custom scripts. Consider the following example:

```
{
  "query": {
    "function_score": {
      "query": {
        "match": {
          "description": "quick brown fox"
        }
      },
      "functions": [
        {
          "filter": { "term": { "category": "rare" } },
          "weight": 5
        },
        {
          "filter": { "term": { "category": "common" } },
          "weight": 1
        }
      ],
      "boost_mode": "multiply"
    }
  }
}
```

In this example, documents belonging to the category "rare" are given a significantly higher weight than those in the "common" category by multiplying their scores by 5 and 1 respectively. The boost_mode parameter specifies that the function scores should be multiplied with the original query scores.

Output from this query would be displayed as:

```
{
  "hits": {
    "total": 2,
    "max_score": 10.287682,
    "hits": [
      {
        "_index": "test",
        "_type": "doc",
        "_id": "1",
        "_score": 10.287682,
        "_source": { ... }
      },
      {
        "_index": "test",
        "_type": "doc",
        "_id": "2",
        "_score": 5.143841,
        "_source": { ... }
      }
    ]
  }
}
```

These results show how relevance scoring can be effectively manipulated to fit specific search contexts.

Understanding and fine-tuning search relevance in Elasticsearch is crucial for creating efficient and user-responsive search applications. By leveraging different scoring models and fine-tuning parameters, one can achieve highly tailored and relevant search results that enhance both user satisfaction and practical search utility.

5.10 Hands-On: Crafting Complex Queries

Interacting with Elasticsearch involves designing sophisticated queries that can handle a comprehensive range of search needs. The following provides an in-depth exploration into constructing and optimizing complex queries, leveraging the principles and functions previously discussed.

To begin, consider a common use case where a complex query retrieves data based on multiple criteria. This can involve combining various query types—such as boolean queries, term queries, and range queries—into a single, cohesive search request.

```
{
  "query": {
    "bool": {
      "must": [
        {
          "match": {
            "description": "Elasticsearch"
          }
```

```
        },
        {
          "range": {
            "timestamp": {
              "gte": "2023-01-01",
              "lte": "2023-12-31"
            }
          }
        }
      ],
      "filter": {
        "term": {
          "status": "published"
        }
      },
      "should": [
        {
          "match": {
            "author": "John Doe"
          }
        }
      ],
      "minimum_should_match": 1
    }
  }
}
```

In this query, a boolean query is used to encapsulate various conditions. The must clause requires all included conditions to be satisfied, while the filter provides an additional restriction that does not influence the score but affects result inclusion. The should clause boosts the relevance score if its conditions are met, configured with minimum_should_match to ensure at least one should condition is satisfied.

The must clause includes a match query for the term "Elasticsearch" in the description field and a range query to find documents within the specified date range. The filter clause is applied to include only documents with the status field set to "published". Additionally, the should clause attempts to further enhance the relevance of documents authored by "John Doe".

Enhancing query functionality with boost increases the relevance score of specific conditions. This is crucial when prioritizing certain matches:

```
{
  "query": {
    "bool": {
      "must": [
        {
          "match": {
            "description": {
              "query": "Elasticsearch",
              "boost": 2.0
            }
          }
        },
```

```
      {
        "range": {
          "timestamp": {
            "gte": "2023-01-01",
            "lte": "2023-12-31"
          }
        }
      }
    ],
    "filter": {
      "term": {
        "status": "published"
      }
    },
    "should": [
      {
        "term": {
          "author": {
            "value": "John Doe",
            "boost": 1.5
          }
        }
      }
    ],
    "minimum_should_match": 1
   }
  }
}
```

Here, the boost parameter amplifies the relevance score of the description field when it contains "Elasticsearch" and slightly boosts the relevance if the author field contains "John Doe".

Incorporating nested queries can handle documents containing arrays of objects. Use nested queries for high precision when dealing with complex data structures.

```
{
  "query": {
    "nested": {
      "path": "comments",
      "query": {
        "bool": {
          "must": [
            {
              "match": {
                "comments.text": "insightful"
              }
            },
            {
              "range": {
                "comments.date": {
                  "gte": "2023-01-01",
                  "lte": "2023-12-31"
                }
              }
            }
          ]
        }
```

```
      }
    }
  }
}
```

In this query, the nested structure specifies that the query should filter the comments path, applying both a match query for "insightful" in the text field and a range query on the date field. This ensures that only documents with comments meeting both conditions are returned.

Aggregation functions complement complex queries by providing insights such as statistical summaries, histograms, and averages. These may be appended to the main query as follows:

```
{
  "query": {
    "bool": {
      "must": [
        {
          "match": {
            "description": "Elasticsearch"
          }
        }
      ]
    }
  },
  "aggs": {
    "by_author": {
      "terms": {
        "field": "author.keyword"
      }
    },
    "average_score": {
      "avg": {
        "field": "score"
      }
    }
  }
}
```

This query retrieves documents matching "Elasticsearch" in the description field and includes two aggregations: a terms aggregation by author.keyword and an avg aggregation for the score field, yielding both a distribution of documents per author and the average score across all matching documents.

For optimal performance, it's critical to fine-tune queries by leveraging Elasticsearch's built-in profiling and tuning tools. The following illustrates a query profiling request to analyze execution details:

```
{
  "profile": true,
  "query": {
    "bool": {
      "must": {
```

```
        "match": {
          "description": "Elasticsearch"
        }
      }
    }
  }
}
```

Upon execution, Elasticsearch provides detailed profiling information, including the execution time and resource consumption for each component of the query. This data is indispensable for pinpointing bottlenecks and optimizing query performance.

```
"profiles": [
  {
    "id": "main_query",
    "collector": "QueryPhase",
    "stats": {
      "number_of_searched_documents": "100000",
      "execution_time_ns": "505123",
      "breakdown": {
        "create_weight": 15010,
        "build_scorer": 52341,
        "next_doc": 442345,
        "advance": 3123
      }
    }
  }
]
```

The example output illustrates a partial profiling report highlighting the number of searched documents and the time taken for different query processing phases. Review these details to better understand and enhance the efficiency of complex queries within Elasticsearch.

Chapter 6

Aggregations and Analytics

This chapter explores Elasticsearch's powerful aggregations and analytics features. It introduces the various types of aggregations, including metrics, bucket, and pipeline aggregations, and explains how to combine them effectively. The chapter also covers filtering and sorting within aggregations, using aggregations for reporting, and performance considerations. Practical examples illustrate how to build analytical queries to derive meaningful insights from data.

6.1 Introduction to Aggregations

Aggregations in Elasticsearch serve as a powerful tool for real-time data analysis and exploration. By structuring searches and computing metrics, aggregations enable users to gain comprehensive insights from their datasets. This introductory section outlines the fundamental concepts, types, and typical usage scenarios that will be expanded upon throughout the chapter.

Aggregations work by processing search results and returning computed summaries. These summaries can include statistics such as min, max, average, and sum as well as more complex analyses like histograms and percentiles.

Key Concepts:

- **Buckets:** These represent grouped search results. Each bucket contains a criterion that determines membership. For example, a date histogram aggregation on a date field might group documents into monthly buckets.
- **Metrics:** These are the quantitative measures calculated from the documents within each bucket. Metrics provide numerical summaries, such as the average value of a field.
- **Pipelines:** These aggregations act on the results of other aggregations, enabling more advanced data transformations and computations. For instance, a derivative aggregation may be applied to a histogram to compute the rate of change between buckets.

Basic Structure of Aggregations:

To construct an aggregation query, consider the following primary components:

```
{
  "size": 0,
  "aggs": {
    "aggregation_name": {
      "aggregation_type": {
        "field": "field_name"
      }
    }
  }
}
```

The size parameter, set to 0, implies that the search results themselves are not returned; only the aggregation results are. Within the aggs object, multiple named aggregations can be defined, each specifying the type of aggregation and the field on which it operates.

Aggregation types will be explored in detail in subsequent sections. It is essential to understand that aggregations can be nested, allowing for granularity and complexity in data summaries. Nested aggregations operate hierarchically, where the result of one aggregation can filter into another.

Example Aggregation Query:

Consider a scenario where we need to compute the average salary within different departments. The initial step is grouping documents by department, followed by calculating the average salary within these groups.

```
{
  "size": 0,
  "aggs": {
    "departments": {
      "terms": {
        "field": "department"
      },
      "aggs": {
        "average_salary": {
          "avg": {
            "field": "salary"
          }
        }
      }
    }
  }
}
```

In this query:

- The terms aggregation creates buckets for each unique value in the department field.
- The avg aggregation, nested under departments, calculates the average of the salary field for documents in each bucket.

The response from the aggregation query provides a summary of the average salary for each department.

```
{
  "aggregations": {
    "departments": {
      "buckets": [
        {
          "key": "HR",
          "doc_count": 10,
          "average_salary": {
            "value": 50000
          }
        },
        {
          "key": "Engineering",
          "doc_count": 15,
          "average_salary": {
            "value": 90000
          }
        }
      ]
    }
  }
}
```

This response illustrates two departments, "HR" and "Engineering," with their respective document counts and average salaries. This hierarchical approach supports complex data exploration scenarios, reflecting Elasticsearch's flexibility and power in handling diverse datasets.

Through aggregations, Elasticsearch converts raw data into actionable insights efficiently. Further sections will delve deeper into specific types of aggregations, providing detailed explanations and practical examples to harness their full potential.

6.2 Types of Aggregations in Elasticsearch

Elasticsearch provides several types of aggregations to facilitate various ways of organizing and analyzing data. Aggregations can be classified into three primary categories: *metrics aggregations*, *bucket aggregations*, and *pipeline aggregations*. Each serves a specific purpose and can be combined to build comprehensive analytical queries.

Metrics aggregations compute metrics based on document field values, creating insights from quantitative data. These include aggregations like avg, min, max, sum, and stats.

```
{
  "size": 0,
  "aggs": {
    "avg_age": {
      "avg": { "field": "age" }
    }
  }
}
```

Bucket aggregations, on the other hand, group documents into buckets based on described criteria, without calculating metrics by themselves. They allow segmentation of data by specific attributes, enabling complex hierarchical structures. Some common bucket aggregations include terms, range, histogram, and filters.

```
{
  "size": 0,
  "aggs": {
    "status_groups": {
      "terms": { "field": "status" }
    }
  }
}
```

Pipeline aggregations perform operations on the results emitted by other aggregations, essentially enabling post-processing on the aggregated data. They are useful for tasks such as computing moving averages, derivatives, or cumulative sums.

```
{
  "size": 0,
```

```
  "aggs": {
    "sales_per_month": {
      "date_histogram": {
        "field": "date",
        "calendar_interval": "month"
      },
      "aggs": {
        "total_sales": {
          "sum": { "field": "sales" }
        },
        "cumulative_sales": {
          "cumulative_sum": {
            "buckets_path": "total_sales"
          }
        }
      }
    }
  }
}
```

An additional useful classification is the distinction between single-value and multi-value aggregations within the metrics category. Single-value metrics aggregations, such as the avg and sum aggregations, return a single numerical result. Multi-value metrics aggregations, such as the stats and extended_stats aggregations, return multiple fields as part of the result.

```
{
  "size": 0,
  "aggs": {
    "extended_stats_age": {
      "extended_stats": { "field": "age" }
    }
  }
}
```

Field	Value
count	100
min	20
max	60
avg	40
sum	4000
sum_of_squares	160000
variance	200
std_deviation	14.14

Table 6.1: Results of an extended stats aggregation for age

Complex analytics often require the combination of multiple types of aggregations. For example, to analyze sales trends, you might aggregate data by date (a date_histogram bucket aggregation) and then calculate the average sales amount (a avg metrics aggregation) within each date bucket.

Blending bucket and metrics aggregations can provide valuable insights. Suppose you want to categorize data before analyzing it. First, use a bucket aggregation to group by relevant criteria, and subsequently, apply metrics aggregations to the documents in each bucket.

```
{
  "size": 0,
  "aggs": {
    "gender_groups": {
      "terms": { "field": "gender" },
      "aggs": {
        "avg_age": {
          "avg": { "field": "age" }
        }
      }
    }
  }
}
```

In this example, documents are initially grouped into buckets based on gender, and within each bucket, the average age is computed using the avg metrics aggregation. This combination of aggregations within Elasticsearch allows for complex querying and detailed reporting, essential for deriving significant insights from large datasets.

Such structured methodologies are integral to leveraging Elasticsearch's full potential for data analytics. They foster detailed data segmentation and comprehensive analysis by combining different aggregation types, thus enabling granular and meaningful insights.

6.3 Metrics Aggregations

Metrics aggregations allow for the computation of metrics such as sum, average, minimum, maximum, and statistical analysis over the numeric fields in your Elasticsearch documents. These aggregations provide insights into the quantitative aspects of your data, enabling complex analysis over large datasets. The following enumeration details the most commonly used metrics aggregations in Elasticsearch, enriched with examples and explanations of their use.

- **Sum Aggregation**: Computes the sum of numeric values for a specified field. This is particularly useful when needing to calculate totals, such as total sales or total units sold.

```
{
  "size": 0,
  "aggs": {
```

```
    "total_sales": {
      "sum": {
        "field": "sales_amount"
      }
    }
  }
}
```

The result will be an aggregation showing the total sum of all sales_amount values:

```
{
  "aggregations": {
    "total_sales": {
      "value": 123456.78
    }
  }
}
```

- **Avg Aggregation**: Calculates the average of numeric values for a specified field, useful for obtaining the mean value of a dataset such as average temperature or average response time.

```
{
  "size": 0,
  "aggs": {
    "avg_temperature": {
      "avg": {
        "field": "temperature"
      }
    }
  }
}
```

The response will contain the average value of temperature:

```
{
  "aggregations": {
    "avg_temperature": {
      "value": 22.5
    }
  }
}
```

- **Min Aggregation**: Finds the minimum value of a numeric field, which is useful for identifying the smallest value in a dataset, such as the lowest price or minimum duration of events.

```
{
  "size": 0,
  "aggs": {
    "min_price": {
      "min": {
        "field": "price"
      }
    }
  }
}
```

The response will show the minimum value of the price field:

```
{
  "aggregations": {
    "min_price": {
      "value": 10.0
    }
  }
}
```

- **Max Aggregation**: Determines the maximum value of a numeric field, ideal for finding the highest value in a set, such as the peak temperature or maximum sales.

```
{
  "size": 0,
  "aggs": {
    "max_sales": {
      "max": {
        "field": "sales_amount"
      }
    }
  }
}
```

The output will include the maximum value of the sales_amount field:

```
{
  "aggregations": {
    "max_sales": {
      "value": 10000.0
    }
  }
}
```

- **Stats Aggregation**: Provides a suite of statistics for a numeric field, including count, sum, min, max, and average. This aggregation is efficient when multiple statistical summaries are needed.

```
{
  "size": 0,
  "aggs": {
    "price_stats": {
      "stats": {
        "field": "price"
      }
    }
  }
}
```

The response will contain several statistics about the price field:

```
{
  "aggregations": {
    "price_stats": {
      "count": 10,
      "min": 10.0,
      "max": 100.0,
      "avg": 55.0,
      "sum": 550.0
    }
  }
}
```


- **Extended Stats Aggregation**: Extends the stats aggregation by adding additional metrics such as sum of squares, variance, and standard deviation.

```
{
  "size": 0,
  "aggs": {
    "extended_price_stats": {
      "extended_stats": {
        "field": "price"
      }
    }
  }
}
```

The response includes extended statistical information:


```
{
  "aggregations": {
    "extended_price_stats": {
      "count": 10,
      "min": 10.0,
      "max": 100.0,
      "avg": 55.0,
      "sum": 550.0,
      "sum_of_squares": 30250.0,
      "variance": 825.0,
      "std_deviation": 28.722813
    }
  }
}
```


- **Percentiles Aggregation**: Calculates percentiles for a numeric field. Percentiles are useful for understanding the distribution of data, for example, to identify the median, 90th, or 95th percentile values.

```
{
  "size": 0,
  "aggs": {
    "load_time_percentiles": {
      "percentiles": {
        "field": "load_time",
        "percents": [50, 75, 90, 95, 99]
      }
    }
  }
}
```

The response will show the specified percentiles for the load_time field:

```
{
  "aggregations": {
    "load_time_percentiles": {
      "values": {
        "50.0": 500,
        "75.0": 750,
        "90.0": 900,
        "95.0": 950,
        "99.0": 990
      }
    }
  }
}
```

- **Cardinality Aggregation**: Estimates the count of distinct values for a field, which is useful for scenarios such as counting the number of unique users or unique error codes.

```
{
  "size": 0,
  "aggs": {
    "unique_user_count": {
      "cardinality": {
        "field": "user_id"
      }
    }
  }
}
```

The output will provide the count of unique user_id values:

```
{
  "aggregations": {
    "unique_user_count": {
      "value": 123
    }
  }
}
```

Metrics aggregations offer significant versatility when summarizing large volumes of numeric data, enabling the extraction of valuable statistical insights that support data-driven decision-making processes. Leveraging these aggregations effectively enhances the analytical capabilities of Elasticsearch.

6.4 Bucket Aggregations

Bucket aggregations are a fundamental feature of Elasticsearch that enable powerful data segmentation capabilities. They group documents into buckets based on specified criteria, allowing for detailed and hierarchically nested data explorations. This section delves into the mechanics and various categories of bucket aggregations, providing a comprehensive understanding crucial for effectively utilizing Elasticsearch.

Unlike metrics aggregations, which compute numerical values, bucket aggregations focus on document grouping. Each bucket corresponds to a criterion defined during the aggregation process, and documents that match this criterion are included in the specific bucket. Consequently, the response from a bucket aggregation includes arrays of buckets, each containing a subset of the total dataset that meets the bucket's conditions.

- **Histograms and Date Histograms**

One of the most common types of bucket aggregations is the histogram aggregation. This type segments numerical data into intervals, known as bins, based on specified ranges. Conforming to a uniform bin width, each bucket consists of documents whose field values fall within the bin's range.

```
{
  "aggs": {
    "price_ranges": {
      "histogram": {
        "field": "price",
        "interval": 50
      }
    }
  }
}
```

In this example, the histogram aggregation groups documents based on their "price" field, creating buckets with a fixed interval of 50 units. This method is particularly useful for visualizing distributions and identifying trends within numerical datasets.

Date histograms operate similarly to histograms but are specifically tailored for date fields, grouping documents into time-based intervals. This is useful for temporal data analysis.

```
{
  "aggs": {
    "sales_over_time": {
      "date_histogram": {
        "field": "sale_date",
        "calendar_interval": "month"
      }
    }
  }
```

```
}
```

Here, documents are grouped by the "sale_date" field into month-long intervals, facilitating trend analysis over time.

- **Terms Aggregation**

Terms aggregation is another essential bucket aggregation that categorizes documents based on unique terms within a field. This is analogous to SQL's GROUP BY clause.

```
{
  "aggs": {
    "popular_colors": {
      "terms": {
        "field": "color.keyword",
        "size": 10
      }
    }
  }
}
```

The example groups documents by distinct terms in the "color.keyword" field, returning the top 10 most frequent terms. This aggregation is valuable for categorical data analysis, such as identifying common values within a dataset.

- **Range Aggregations**

Range aggregations allow for flexible grouping of documents into custom ranges. Unlike histograms, users can define specific boundaries, which is particularly useful for non-uniform intervals.

```
{
  "aggs": {
    "price_brackets": {
      "range": {
        "field": "price",
        "ranges": [
          { "to": 100 },
          { "from": 100, "to": 200 },
          { "from": 200, "to": 300 },
          { "from": 300 }
        ]
      }
    }
  }
}
```

This example specifies custom price ranges, creating buckets for documents with prices below 100, between 100 and 200, between 200 and

300, and above 300. This method is adaptable to specific analytical requirements.

- **Filters Aggregation**

Filters aggregation is useful when you need to create custom buckets based on diverse filter conditions. Each filter defines a separate bucket, allowing for complex segmentations.

```
{
  "aggs": {
    "product_filters": {
      "filters": {
        "filters": {
          "cheap_products": { "range": { "price": { "lte": 50 } } },
          "luxury_products": { "range": { "price": { "gte": 200 } } },
          "medium_range_products": { "range": { "price": { "gt": 50, "lt": 200 } } }
        }
      }
    }
  }
}
```

In this example, three custom filters are defined: cheap products (price less than or equal to 50), luxury products (price greater than or equal to 200), and medium-range products (price between 50 and 200). Each filter condition creates a corresponding bucket.

- **Significant Terms Aggregation**

Significant terms aggregation finds terms that are statistically significant in comparison to the background set of documents. It is particularly useful for discovering meaningful insights in large datasets.

```
{
  "aggs": {
    "significant_keywords": {
      "significant_terms": {
        "field": "content",
        "background_filter": {
          "term": { "is_active": true }
        }
      }
    }
  }
}
```

In this example, significant terms from the "content" field are identified where the background filter limits the dataset to active records. This aggregation can highlight terms that are unusually frequent in certain subsets of data.

- **Geo-Hash Grid Aggregation**

Geo-Hash grid aggregation is used to group documents into buckets based on geographical coordinates. This is useful for spatial data analysis.

```
{
  "aggs": {
    "location_clusters": {
      "geohash_grid": {
        "field": "location",
        "precision": 5
      }
    }
  }
}
```

Here, documents are grouped into geo-hashes of precision 5, based on the "location" field. This method facilitates the visualization and analysis of geospatial data, allowing for clustering and heatmaps.

Understanding the mechanics of bucket aggregations offers a powerful toolkit for segmenting and analyzing documents in Elasticsearch. By mastering these concepts, one can effectively leverage Elasticsearch to derive meaningful insights and answer complex analytical queries.

6.5 Pipeline Aggregations

Pipeline aggregations in Elasticsearch act as post-processing operations on the result of other aggregations. They allow users to take the output of one or more previous aggregations and apply additional analysis or transformations. This feature is particularly useful when building complex analytical queries that require computations like averaging, summation, or statistical operations on aggregated data.

A pipeline aggregation operates within the context of one or more parent aggregations. These parents provide the data that the pipeline aggregation subsequently processes. There are several types of pipeline aggregations available in Elasticsearch, such as derivative, cumulative sum, moving average, and bucket script aggregations.

Pipeline aggregations have a key attribute called buckets_path, which specifies the path to the target aggregation's buckets from which the pipeline aggregation will draw data. Below is a detailed explanation of some common pipeline aggregations using examples for clarity.

Derivative Aggregation

The derivative aggregation computes the derivative of a specified metric. This is useful for identifying the rate of change over intervals, such as changes in sales volume over periods.

Consider an example where we have histogram data of sales over time, and we want to calculate the rate of change between consecutive time intervals. The following query computes a derivative of the sum of sales:

```
{
  "aggs": {
    "sales_over_time": {
      "date_histogram": {
        "field": "date",
        "calendar_interval": "month"
      },
      "aggs": {
        "total_sales": {
          "sum": {
            "field": "sales"
          }
        },
        "sales_derivative": {
          "derivative": {
            "buckets_path": "total_sales"
          }
        }
      }
    }
  }
}
```

Cumulative Sum Aggregation

The cumulative sum aggregation is utilized to compute a running total of a specified metric. It is particularly useful for financial computations or tracking cumulative activities over a period.

For example, suppose we have a dataset of daily user sign-ups, and we want to compute the cumulative total of sign-ups:

```
{
  "aggs": {
    "signups_over_time": {
      "date_histogram": {
        "field": "signup_date",
        "calendar_interval": "day"
      },
      "aggs": {
        "daily_signups": {
          "value_count": {
            "field": "user_id"
          }
        },
        "cumulative_signups": {
          "cumulative_sum": {
            "buckets_path": "daily_signups"
```

```
          }
        }
      }
    }
  }
}
```

Moving Average Aggregation

The moving average aggregation calculates the moving average of a metric over a specified window. This is beneficial for smoothing out short-term fluctuations and highlighting longer-term trends in data.

An example query to calculate a moving average of daily sales over a 7-day window:

```
{
  "aggs": {
    "sales_over_time": {
      "date_histogram": {
        "field": "date",
        "calendar_interval": "day"
      },
      "aggs": {
        "daily_sales": {
          "sum": {
            "field": "sales"
          }
        },
        "sales_moving_avg": {
          "moving_avg": {
            "buckets_path": "daily_sales",
            "window": 7
          }
        }
      }
    }
  }
}
```

Bucket Script Aggregation

Bucket script aggregation allows for the execution of custom scripts to perform operations on aggregated data. This provides the flexibility to implement complex mathematical computations based on multiple aggregations.

For instance, to compute the profit margin based on total sales and cost within a specific period:

```
{
  "aggs": {
    "sales_and_cost": {
      "date_histogram": {
        "field": "date",
        "calendar_interval": "month"
      },
```

```
      "aggs": {
        "total_sales": {
          "sum": {
            "field": "sales"
          }
        },
        "total_cost": {
          "sum": {
            "field": "cost"
          }
        },
        "profit_margin": {
          "bucket_script": {
            "buckets_path": {
              "sales": "total_sales",
              "cost": "total_cost"
            },
            "script": "params.sales - params.cost"
          }
        }
      }
    }
  }
}
```

Displaying output from any of these queries would be tailored to the specifics of the analyzed data pattern.

```
{
  "aggregations": {
    "sales_over_time": {
      "buckets": [
        {
          "key_as_string": "2023-01-01",
          "doc_count": 10,
          "total_sales": {
            "value": 1000
          },
          "sales_derivative": {
            "value": 200
          }
        },
        ...
      ]
    }
  }
}
```

Pipeline aggregations significantly enhance the analytical capabilities of Elasticsearch by allowing post-processing and the combination of results from multiple aggregations. The aforementioned examples illustrate the potential of pipeline aggregations for generating insights from large datasets efficiently.

6.6 Combining Aggregations

The power of Elasticsearch's aggregation framework comes from its ability to combine different types of aggregations to perform complex data analysis tasks. Combining aggregations allows users to derive insights from data by layering multiple aggregations and leveraging the results from one level to inform the next. This section delves into the methods and considerations for effectively combining aggregations to uncover more sophisticated data patterns and trends.

To combine aggregations, we use the nested nature of Elasticsearch's aggregation structure. Aggregations can be nested within each other to form a hierarchy, where parent aggregations encapsulate child aggregations. This hierarchical approach enables the construction of multifaceted queries that process data at multiple levels of granularity.

Consider the following example where we combine a terms bucket aggregation with a avg metric aggregation. The terms aggregation groups documents by a specified field, and for each group, the avg aggregation calculates the average value of another field.

```
{
  "aggs": {
    "by_category": {
      "terms": {
        "field": "category"
      },
      "aggs": {
        "average_price": {
          "avg": {
            "field": "price"
          }
        }
      }
    }
  }
}
```

In this query, the terms aggregation named by_category groups documents by the category field. Within each category, the average_price aggregation computes the average value of the price field. This nested aggregation structure allows us to obtain the average price per category.

The ability to nest aggregations provides a flexible mechanism to decompose complex analytics queries. By combining various types of bucket and metric aggregations, users can generate detailed and hierarchical analyses. For instance, combining terms and date_histogram aggregations enables temporal analysis within categorical groups.

Below is an example that combines a date_histogram aggregation with a sum metric aggregation, nested within a terms aggregation:

```
{
  "aggs": {
    "by_category": {
      "terms": {
        "field": "category"
      },
      "aggs": {
        "sales_over_time": {
          "date_histogram": {
            "field": "timestamp",
            "interval": "month"
          },
          "aggs": {
            "total_sales": {
              "sum": {
                "field": "sales"
              }
            }
          }
        }
      }
    }
  }
}
```

This query first groups documents by category. For each category, it further groups documents by timestamp into monthly intervals using the date_histogram aggregation. Within each monthly bucket, the sum aggregation calculates the total sales. This nested structure lets us track total sales over time for each category.

Combining aggregations is not limited to metrics and buckets; pipeline aggregations can also be integrated to perform post-processing on the results of other aggregations. For example, we can use a moving_avg aggregation to calculate the moving average of the total sales over time:

```
{
  "aggs": {
    "by_category": {
      "terms": {
        "field": "category"
      },
      "aggs": {
        "sales_over_time": {
          "date_histogram": {
            "field": "timestamp",
            "interval": "month"
          },
          "aggs": {
            "total_sales": {
              "sum": {
                "field": "sales"
              }
            },
            "moving_average_sales": {
```

```
            "moving_avg": {
              "buckets_path": "total_sales"
            }
          }
        }
      }
    }
  }
}
}
```

In this enhanced query, we added the moving_avg aggregation to compute the moving average of total_sales, specified by the buckets_path parameter. The moving_avg aggregation utilizes the results from the total_sales aggregation to provide a smoothed trend line of sales over time within each category.

When constructing combined aggregations, it is crucial to consider the computational cost and performance impact. Each level of nested aggregation increases the complexity and the amount of data processing required. Efficiently combining aggregations involves selecting appropriate fields, optimizing data structures, and using filtering mechanisms to narrow down the dataset before extensive aggregation computations.

Filtering before aggregating can be achieved using a filter aggregation, which allows us to include only documents that meet specific criteria. This can greatly reduce the scope of data that subsequent aggregations need to process:

```
{
  "aggs": {
    "filtered_sales": {
      "filter": {
        "range": {
          "timestamp": {
            "gte": "now-1y",
            "lt": "now"
          }
        }
      },
      "aggs": {
        "by_category": {
          "terms": {
            "field": "category"
          }
        }
      }
    }
  }
}
```

In this query, the filter aggregation, named filtered_sales, first limits the documents to those within the past year. The terms aggregation then groups these filtered documents by category, ensuring that the aggregation calculations are performed on a smaller, more relevant dataset.

Combining aggregations in Elasticsearch empowers users to perform intricate data analyses and discover deeper insights. By thoughtfully structuring nested aggregations and employing filters and performance optimizations, users can harness the full potential of Elasticsearch's aggregation capabilities to meet their analytical needs.

6.7 Filtering and Sorting Aggregations

Filtering and sorting aggregations provide the capacity to refine and order the data processed by Elasticsearch during aggregation operations. By applying filters, specific subsets of data can be targeted, thereby enhancing both the relevance and performance of queries. Sorting mechanisms, on the other hand, dictate the sequence in which aggregation results are presented. This section delves into techniques and principles for both filtering and sorting within aggregations.

Filtering in aggregations involves the use of filter aggregations, which allow the exclusion or inclusion of documents based on specified criteria. Filter aggregations are often used in conjunction with other aggregation types, ensuring that only relevant documents contribute to the results. The filter aggregation is based on query context, allowing comprehensive and flexible criteria to be specified. An example of a filter aggregation combined with a terms aggregation is presented below:

```
{
  "aggs": {
    "filtered_results": {
      "filter": {
        "term": {
          "status": "active"
        }
      },
      "aggs": {
        "average_age": {
          "avg": {
            "field": "age"
          }
        }
      }
    }
  }
}
```

In this example, the filter aggregation only includes documents where the status field is active. Then, an avg aggregation calculates the average age of these filtered documents.

Multiple filters can be combined using bool queries within the filter aggregation. This allows for complex logical conditions to be constructed, thereby enhancing filtering capabilities. The syntax for a combined filter aggregation using must, should, and must_not clauses is illustrated below:

```
{
  "aggs": {
    "filtered_results": {
      "filter": {
        "bool": {
          "must": [
            {
              "term": { "status": "active" }
            }
          ],
          "should": [
            {
              "range": {
                "age": { "gte": 20 }
              }
            }
          ],
          "must_not": [
            {
              "term": { "country": "US" }
            }
          ]
        }
      },
      "aggs": {
        "average_age": {
          "avg": {
            "field": "age"
          }
        }
      }
    }
  }
}
```

Here, only documents with a status of active and age greater than or equal to 20, and not from the US, are considered. This layered approach illustrates the combination of must, should, and must_not clauses to form a comprehensive filter.

Sorting aggregations enable the organization of aggregation results based on specified criteria. Sorting is particularly useful in terms, histogram, and date histogram aggregations. For instance, in terms aggregation, sorting can be controlled by using the order parameter. Results can be sorted based on document count or on a sub-aggregation result. An example of sorting a terms aggregation based on document count in ascending order is shown below:

```
{
  "aggs": {
    "top_tags": {
      "terms": {
        "field": "tags",
        "order": { "_count": "asc" }
      }
    }
  }
}
```

In this example, the terms aggregation for the tags field is sorted by document count in ascending order, thus the less frequent tags appear first.

To sort by a sub-aggregation's computation result, the sub-aggregation must be nested within the primary aggregation. Subsequently, the sorting is configured based on the result of this sub-aggregation. An example of sorting by a sub-aggregation result is provided below:

```
{
  "aggs": {
    "top_tags": {
      "terms": {
        "field": "tags",
        "order": { "max_score": "desc" }
      },
      "aggs": {
        "max_score": {
          "max": {
            "field": "score"
          }
        }
      }
    }
  }
}
```

In this case, the terms aggregation for tags is sorted by the maximum score of documents within each bucket in descending order.

It's vital to recognize that both filtering and sorting operations have implications on performance. Filters typically reduce the set of documents that need to be processed, which can enhance query responsiveness. Conversely, sorting can introduce overhead, especially when sorting by sub-aggregation results, as additional computations are necessary. Therefore, when designing queries, one must strike a balance between complexity and performance considerations, optimizing filters and sorting mechanisms to achieve the desired results efficiently.

By applying these principles of filtering and sorting aggregations meticulously, Elasticsearch users can significantly refine their data analysis processes, extracting more relevant and organized insights with precision.

6.8 Using Aggregations for Reporting

Aggregations in Elasticsearch enable users to gain deep insights from their data, making them highly suitable for generating reports. This section will cover how to leverage aggregations to create detailed and informative reports. These reports can range from summary statistics to complex multidimensional analysis, enabling decisions based on empirical data.

Aggregations facilitate the extraction of meaningful patterns and trends, and when employed effectively, they provide an overview that is often used for business intelligence (BI) operations. It's essential to understand how various aggregation types—such as metrics, bucket, and pipeline aggregations—can be combined and utilized to produce comprehensive reports.

Generating Summary Statistics

Using metrics aggregations such as avg, sum, min, max, and stats, users can create summary statistics. These aggregations are instrumental in reporting average values, totals, and extrema.

```
{
  "size": 0,
  "aggs": {
    "average_price": {
      "avg": {
        "field": "price"
      }
    },
    "total_sales": {
      "sum": {
        "field": "quantity"
      }
    },
    "minimum_price": {
      "min": {
        "field": "price"
      }
    },
    "maximum_price": {
      "max": {
        "field": "price"
      }
    }
  }
}
```

The response returns average price, total sales, minimum price, and maximum price within the dataset.

```
{
  "aggregations": {
    "average_price": {
      "value": 56.8
    },
    "total_sales": {
      "value": 1200
    },
    "minimum_price": {
      "value": 10.5
    },
    "maximum_price": {
      "value": 99.9
    }
  }
}
```

Creating Histograms for Distribution Analysis

Histograms, which are bucket aggregations, allow users to organize documents into defined intervals or "buckets." This is useful for understanding the distribution of a dataset, for instance, the distribution of sales prices.

```
{
  "size": 0,
  "aggs": {
    "price_distribution": {
      "histogram": {
        "field": "price",
        "interval": 10
      }
    }
  }
}
```

The output will partition the price field into intervals of 10 units, providing insight into the range and frequency of prices.

```
{
  "aggregations": {
    "price_distribution": {
      "buckets": [
        { "key": 0, "doc_count": 5 },
        { "key": 10, "doc_count": 20 },
        ...
      ]
    }
  }
}
```

Time Series Analysis with Date Histogram

Using date histograms, a form of bucket aggregation, allows users to analyze data trends over time. This is particularly useful for reporting time-based metrics, such as daily or monthly sales.

```
{
  "size": 0,
  "aggs": {
    "sales_over_time": {
      "date_histogram": {
        "field": "order_date",
        "calendar_interval": "month"
      }
    }
  }
}
```

The response will illustrate sales trends over different months.

```
{
  "aggregations": {
    "sales_over_time": {
      "buckets": [
        {
          "key_as_string": "2023-01-01T00:00:00.000Z",
          "doc_count": 85
        },
        {
          "key_as_string": "2023-02-01T00:00:00.000Z",
          "doc_count": 78
        },
        ...
      ]
    }
  }
}
```

Combining Multiple Aggregations for Complex Reports

Combining different types of aggregations can produce sophisticated and multidimensional reports. For example, using a combination of metrics aggregations within nested bucket aggregations can provide deeper insights.

```
{
  "size": 0,
  "aggs": {
    "sales_by_category": {
      "terms": {
        "field": "category"
      },
      "aggs": {
        "monthly_sales": {
          "date_histogram": {
            "field": "order_date",
            "calendar_interval": "month"
          },
          "aggs": {
            "average_tax": {
              "avg": {
                "field": "tax_amount"
              }
            },
```

```
              "total_sales": {
                "sum": {
                  "field": "quantity"
                }
              }
            }
          }
        }
      }
    }
}
```

This query processes the sales data by category, further broken down by months, including average tax and total sales for each month within each category.

```
{
  "aggregations": {
    "sales_by_category": {
      "buckets": [
        {
          "key": "Electronics",
          "monthly_sales": {
            "buckets": [
              {
                "key_as_string": "2023-01-01T00:00:00.000Z",
                "average_tax": { "value": 2.5 },
                "total_sales": { "value": 120 }
              },
              ...
            ]
          }
        },
        ...
      ]
    }
  }
}
```

By utilizing the power of Elasticsearch aggregations, generating comprehensive and detailed reports becomes efficient and effective. The ability to combine various aggregations allows users to tailor reports that meet specific analytical needs, thereby empowering data-driven decision-making.

Harnessing the potential of aggregations in Elasticsearch, complex reporting requirements can be met, providing precise and actionable insights. Whether utilizing metrics for summary statistics, histograms for distribution analysis, or combining multiple aggregations for an in-depth assessment, Elasticsearch serves as a potent tool for generating reports that aid in informed decision-making.

6.9 Performance Considerations with Aggregations

Understanding and addressing performance implications is paramount when working with aggregations in Elasticsearch. As aggregations are data-intensive operations, inefficient configurations can lead to slower query response times, excessive resource usage, and potential timeouts. This section delves into various strategies and best practices to optimize the performance of aggregation queries.

Shard Allocation and Size

Elasticsearch works by distributing data across multiple shards. The efficiency of aggregation queries can be significantly impacted by how data is partitioned across these shards. It is recommended to:

- **Distribute Data Evenly:** Ensure data is evenly distributed across shards to prevent hotspots and imbalance.
- **Optimize Shard Size:** Shards that are too large can lead to excessive memory usage and increased query times whereas too small shards could cause excessive overhead. A shard size between 20-40GB is often considered optimal for balancing performance and resource utilization.

Efficient Use of Mappings

Appropriate field mappings can considerably impact the performance of aggregations. Ensuring that fields are mapped correctly helps Elasticsearch to index them more efficiently.

- **Choose the Right Data Types:** Use appropriate data types for fields. For example, long integers instead of keywords wherever applicable.
- **Disable Norms and Doc Values:** Disable norms on string fields not used for scoring and disable doc values on fields where they are unnecessary to conserve disk space and memory.

Query Optimization

The structure and content of the queries themselves play a crucial role in performance.

- **Limit Scope with Filters:** Utilize filters to limit the documents that must be aggregated. Filters are faster because they are backed by bitsets and do not score documents.
- **Use Pre-aggregated Data:** When possible, use already pre-aggregated data or summary indices to reduce computational overhead.
- **Reduce Result Set Size:** Use the size parameter to limit the number of results returned. Smaller result sets mean less work for Elasticsearch to do.

Caching and Circuit Breakers

Caching frequently-executed queries and using circuit breakers are advanced strategies to handle large-scale aggregation efficiently.

- **Elasticsearch Cache:** Elasticsearch utilizes several caches, such as node query cache and request cache. Ensuring high cache hit rates by configuring and managing these caches can result in significant performance improvement.
- **Circuit Breakers:** Circuit breakers help in preventing node failures by stopping high memory consuming queries before they overwhelm the cluster. Configure appropriate limits for field data, request and other circuit breakers based on the available memory.

Parallelism and Concurrency

Parallel processing capabilities of Elasticsearch can be harnessed for better performance.

- **Threadpool Settings:** Properly configure Elasticsearch threadpools such as bulk, index, and search threadpools to optimize resource usage.
- **Concurrent Request Handling:** Utilize the max_concurrent_shard_requests parameter to control maximum concurrent shard requests which can help in balancing the load across nodes.

Monitoring and Benchmarking

Regular monitoring and benchmarking are essential practices to maintain and enhance the performance of aggregation queries.

- **Monitoring Tools:** Use Elasticsearch's monitoring tools like Kibana, Elasticsearch's node stats API, and other logging frameworks to keep track of cluster health, resource usage, and query performance.

- **Benchmarking:** Conduct benchmarks using tools like Rally to understand the impact of configuration changes on performance.

Example: Optimizing an Aggregation Query

Below is an example of an optimized aggregation query that incorporates many of these best practices.

```
{
  "size": 0,
  "query": {
    "bool": {
      "filter": [
        {
          "range": {
            "date": {
              "gte": "now-1d/d",
              "lt": "now/d"
            }
          }
        }
      ]
    }
  },
  "aggs": {
    "by_status": {
      "terms": {
        "field": "status.keyword",
        "size": 10
      },
      "aggs": {
        "avg_duration": {
          "avg": {
            "field": "duration"
          }
        }
      }
    }
  }
}
```

In this query:

- A filter is used to constrain the documents based on a time range, benefiting from the speed efficiency of filters.

- The document count is set to 0 by the size parameter, to focus purely on aggregation results.

- The terms aggregation limits the number of buckets to the top 10 terms, reducing memory and computational load.

Correct implementation and vigilant monitoring can ensure that the aggregation queries not only perform efficiently but also scale well with increasing data volumes. Ensuring optimal configuration and continuous performance tuning is crucial for maintaining an efficient Elasticsearch environment.

6.10 Hands-On: Building Analytical Queries

Building analytical queries in Elasticsearch involves composing various aggregation types to extract meaningful insights from the data indexed in your Elasticsearch cluster. This section provides a detailed and practical approach to constructing these queries using real-world examples. We will demonstrate the utilization of metrics, bucket, and pipeline aggregations, as well as how to combine them effectively to perform complex analyses.

Consider a sample dataset indexed in an Elasticsearch index named sales_data. This dataset contains fields such as date, product_id, sales_amount, store_id, and region. The aim is to explore how different aggregations can be applied to derive insights from this sales data.

We will start with a basic analytical query that calculates the total sales amount:

```
{
  "size": 0,
  "aggs": {
    "total_sales": {
      "sum": {
        "field": "sales_amount"
      }
    }
  }
}
```

In this query, the size is set to 0 to exclude the actual hits from the response, as our focus is on the aggregated data. The aggs section defines a sum aggregation named total_sales that sums up the sales_amount field.

The response for this query might look like:

```
{
  "aggregations": {
    "total_sales": {
      "value": 1234567.89
    }
  }
}
```

Next, we will build upon this by introducing a bucket aggregation to group the sales amounts by region. This example demonstrates how to nest aggregations:

```
{
  "size": 0,
  "aggs": {
    "sales_by_region": {
      "terms": {
        "field": "region"
      },
      "aggs": {
        "total_sales": {
          "sum": {
            "field": "sales_amount"
          }
        }
      }
    }
  }
}
```

In the query above, we define a terms bucket aggregation named sales_by_region to group documents by the region field. Within this bucket aggregation, a sum sub-aggregation calculates the total sales amount for each region.

The response might be:

```
{
  "aggregations": {
    "sales_by_region": {
      "buckets": [
        {
          "key": "North",
          "doc_count": 100,
          "total_sales": {
            "value": 345678.90
          }
        },
        {
          "key": "South",
          "doc_count": 80,
          "total_sales": {
            "value": 223456.78
          }
        }
      ]
    }
  }
}
```

To analyze data over time, we can use a date_histogram aggregation. This feature allows us to group our sales data into time intervals such as days, months, or years. The following example demonstrates how to calculate the monthly sales amount:

```
{
  "size": 0,
  "aggs": {
    "sales_over_time": {
      "date_histogram": {
        "field": "date",
        "calendar_interval": "month"
      },
      "aggs": {
        "monthly_sales": {
          "sum": {
            "field": "sales_amount"
          }
        }
      }
    }
  }
}
```

We use a date_histogram with a calendar_interval of "month" to bucket sales data into monthly intervals. The sum aggregation within calculates the total sales amount for each month.

The response for this query might be:


```
{
  "aggregations": {
    "sales_over_time": {
      "buckets": [
        {
          "key_as_string": "2023-01-01T00:00:00.000Z",
          "key": 1672531200000,
          "doc_count": 30,
          "monthly_sales": {
            "value": 12345.67
          }
        },
        {
          "key_as_string": "2023-02-01T00:00:00.000Z",
          "key": 1675209600000,
          "doc_count": 28,
          "monthly_sales": {
            "value": 23456.78
          }
        }
      ]
    }
  }
}
```


Combining different types of aggregations can yield more sophisticated insights. For instance, suppose we want to determine the average sales amount per region and also find the maximum sales amount for each region. We can achieve this by chaining metrics aggregations within a terms aggregation:

```
{
  "size": 0,
  "aggs": {
    "sales_by_region": {
      "terms": {
        "field": "region"
      },
      "aggs": {
        "average_sales": {
          "avg": {
            "field": "sales_amount"
          }
        },
        "max_sales": {
          "max": {
            "field": "sales_amount"
          }
        }
      }
    }
  }
}
```

Here, we use an avg aggregation named average_sales and a max aggregation named max_sales within the terms bucket aggregation sales_-by_region.

The response might be:

```
{
  "aggregations": {
    "sales_by_region": {
      "buckets": [
        {
          "key": "North",
          "doc_count": 100,
          "average_sales": {
            "value": 3456.78
          },
          "max_sales": {
            "value": 12345.67
          }
        },
        {
          "key": "South",
          "doc_count": 80,
          "average_sales": {
            "value": 2789.01
          },
          "max_sales": {
            "value": 9876.54
          }
        }
      ]
    }
  }
}
```

For more complex analyses, pipeline aggregations enable further processing of the results of primary aggregations. Suppose we want to calculate the moving average of monthly sales. The following example demonstrates how to use a moving_avg pipeline aggregation in conjunction with a date_histogram:

```
{
  "size": 0,
  "aggs": {
    "sales_over_time": {
      "date_histogram": {
        "field": "date",
        "calendar_interval": "month"
      },
      "aggs": {
        "monthly_sales": {
          "sum": {
            "field": "sales_amount"
          }
        },
        "moving_avg_sales": {
          "moving_avg": {
            "buckets_path": "monthly_sales"
          }
        }
      }
    }
  }
}
```

In this query, a moving_avg pipeline aggregation named moving_avg_-sales computes a moving average of the monthly_sales bucket values.

The response might be:

```
{
  "aggregations": {
    "sales_over_time": {
      "buckets": [
        {
          "key_as_string": "2023-01-01T00:00:00.000Z",
          "key": 1672531200000,
          "doc_count": 30,
          "monthly_sales": {
            "value": 12345.67
          },
          "moving_avg_sales": {
            "value": null
          }
        },
        {
          "key_as_string": "2023-02-01T00:00:00.000Z",
          "key": 1675209600000,
          "doc_count": 28,
          "monthly_sales": {
            "value": 23456.78
          },
          "moving_avg_sales": {
            "value": 17801.225
          }
        }
      ]
    }
  }
}
```


This detailed walkthrough illustrates the fundamentals of building analytical queries in Elasticsearch. By combining metrics, bucket, and pipeline aggregations, a wide range of sophisticated analyses can be performed on indexed data, fostering deeper insights and informed decision-making.

Chapter 7

Scaling and Performance Tuning

This chapter provides insights into scaling and performance tuning for Elasticsearch. It covers the principles of horizontal and vertical scaling, shard and replica management, and techniques for optimizing both indexing and query performance. Additionally, it addresses memory and heap usage tuning, managing hot and warm nodes, and monitoring cluster health. Best practices for achieving high availability are also discussed, supported by practical examples of performance tuning strategies.

7.1 Understanding Elasticsearch Scalability

Scalability in Elasticsearch refers to its ability to handle increasing amounts of work or its potential to accommodate growth. This capability is pivotal for applications that anticipate higher loads or data volumes in the future. In Elasticsearch, scalability can be approached from two main axes: horizontal and vertical scaling. Understanding both methods is essential for designing systems that maintain performance and reliability as demands evolve.

Elasticsearch's architecture inherently supports horizontal scaling. The fundamental components enabling this are nodes, clusters, indices, shards, and replicas. Each of these components plays a specific role in distributing and managing data, ensuring that the system can scale out by adding more hardware resources.

A cluster in Elasticsearch contains one or more nodes, and these nodes collectively manage the entire dataset. Nodes are instances of Elasticsearch, and each node is capable of hosting multiple shards. Shards are essentially pieces of an index, and an index can be divided into multiple shards to distribute data and load across the cluster. Each shard is an independent Lucene index, which is the underlying technology that Elasticsearch is built upon.

Replicas are copies of shards. They provide redundancy and enhance availability and search performance. Each primary shard can have zero or more replicas. In the event of a node failure, a replica shard can be promoted to a primary shard, ensuring no data loss.

```
PUT /my_index
{
  "settings": {
    "number_of_shards": 5,
    "number_of_replicas": 1
  }
}
```

In the example above, an index named my_index is created with 5 primary shards and 1 replica for each shard, resulting in a total of 10 shards. This setup allows Elasticsearch to distribute the index across multiple nodes, enhancing search and indexing performance while providing fault tolerance.

Horizontal scalability, therefore, involves adding more nodes to the cluster. As new nodes are added, shards can be reallocated, and Elasticsearch automatically balances the load among the available nodes. This redistribution is handled by the Elasticsearch master node, which keeps track of cluster state and makes decisions about shard allocation.

Vertical scaling, on the other hand, involves enhancing the capacity of existing nodes by upgrading hardware resources such as CPU, memory, and storage. While vertical scaling can provide immediate performance benefits, it is inherently limited by hardware constraints and does not offer the same level of redundancy and fault tolerance as horizontal scaling.

An essential aspect of understanding scalability in Elasticsearch is recognizing how data distribution and redundancy are managed. The Elasticsearch Distributed Coordination Engine orchestrates the allocation of primary and replica shards, ensuring data is evenly spread out and redundant copies are maintained across distinct nodes.

Effective scaling requires careful planning and consideration of several factors including index design, shard count, and replica settings. Over-sharding can lead to overhead and management complexity, while under-sharding can result in uneven load distribution and performance bottlenecks. Hence, determining an optimal number of shards and replicas based on expected data volume and access patterns is crucial.

Monitoring tools like Kibana and various Elasticsearch APIs (e.g., Cluster Health, Nodes Stats) provide insights into cluster performance and health, aiding in identifying when scaling actions are needed. For instance, checking the _cluster/health API can give a quick overview of the cluster's status and shard allocation.

```
GET /_cluster/health
```

The response from this query offers valuable information on cluster health, size, and shard distribution:

Table 7.1: Cluster Health API Response

Field	Value
cluster_name	"my_cluster"
status	"green"
timed_out	false
number_of_nodes	3
number_of_data_nodes	3
active_primary_shards	5
active_shards	10
relocating_shards	0
initializing_shards	0
unassigned_shards	0
delayed_unassigned_shards	0
number_of_pending_tasks	0
number_of_in_flight_fetch	0
task_max_waiting_in_queue_millis	0
active_shards_percent_as_number	100.0

Understanding how Elasticsearch handles data distribution and scaling paves the way for designing systems that are both robust and performant. By leveraging horizontal and vertical scaling methods effectively, one can ensure that an Elasticsearch deployment meets current demands and is prepared for future growth.

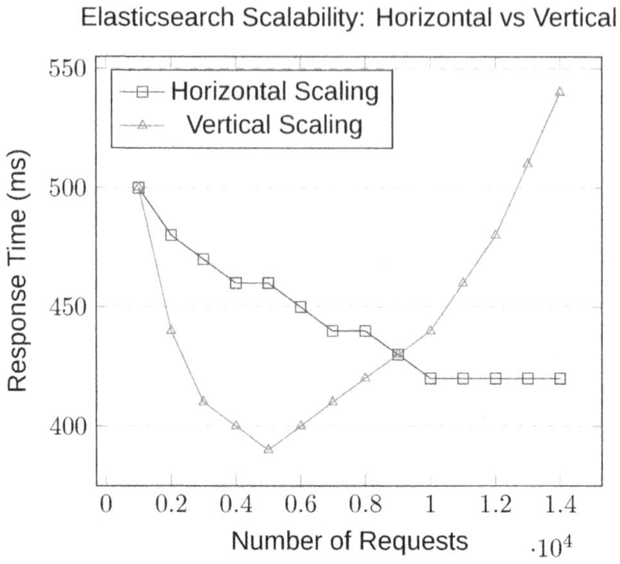

7.2 Scaling Horizontally vs. Vertically

Scaling Elasticsearch can involve either horizontal scaling by adding more nodes or vertical scaling by increasing the resources available to a single node. Each approach has its own advantages and considerations that influence the overall efficiency and performance of your Elasticsearch cluster.

Horizontal scaling refers to increasing the number of nodes in a cluster. This allows you to distribute the data and processing load across more machines, which can lead to significant improvements in both read and write throughput. For Elasticsearch, horizontal scaling is often achieved by adding more data nodes to the cluster. When a new node is added, Elasticsearch automatically rebalances the shards to ensure even distribution across the cluster.

To add a new node to an existing cluster, you can configure its elasticsearch.yml settings to include the following:

```
cluster.name: my_cluster
node.name: new_node
discovery.seed_hosts: ["host1", "host2"]
cluster.initial_master_nodes: ["master_node1", "master_node2"]
```

By increasing the number of nodes, the cluster's capacity to handle data increases as well. The rebalancing of shards occurs, which ensures that the data and its respective load are fairly distributed among the nodes. Monitoring the rebalancing process can be done using the _cat API:

```
GET /_cat/shards
```

Additionally, horizontal scaling enhances fault tolerance because data replicas can be stored across multiple nodes. This way, if one node fails, another node containing the replica can fulfill the requests.

Vertical scaling, on the other hand, involves upgrading the hardware capabilities of an existing node, such as increasing the CPU, RAM, or storage capacity. Vertical scaling can be beneficial for enhancing the performance of a node limited by resource constraints. For example, adding more RAM to a node allows it to handle a larger heap size, which can improve performance for heap-intensive operations.

To adjust the heap size, you can configure the JVM options for Elasticsearch by updating the jvm.options file with the following lines:

```
-Xms16g
-Xmx16g
```

Here, 16g specifies a heap size of 16 gigabytes. It is essential to allocate heap memory appropriately, ensuring it does not exceed 50% of the total available physical memory to prevent excessive garbage collection.

A noticeable limitation of vertical scaling is the presence of a hardware ceiling, beyond which upgrading might not yield proportional improvements in performance. Horizontal scaling, though more complex to manage due to the increased number of nodes, theoretically offers unlimited scalability as long as you can continue adding nodes to the cluster.

Choosing between these scaling options depends on the specific needs and challenges faced by your deployment. Horizontal scaling is often preferred for its elasticity and fault tolerance. It allows for distributed processing and storage, which can significantly alleviate bottlenecks and improve the availability of the cluster. Vertical scaling, however, offers a more straightforward but limited approach by enhancing individual node capacity and can sometimes be a more cost-effective initial step.

Understanding the trade-offs and the context of use-cases will guide you towards the best scaling strategy for your Elasticsearch cluster. To further elaborate, a hybrid approach often yields the best results, where a cluster starts with vertical scaling for initial capacity and performance boost, and then transitions to horizontal scaling as the data volume and load exceed the capacity of what a single node upgrade can address. This ensures robustness in scalability and provides a balanced strategy for maintaining performance as demand grows.

7.3 Managing Shards and Replicas

Elasticsearch handles large volumes of data by distributing it across multiple nodes in a cluster. This distribution is achieved using two fundamental concepts: shards and replicas. Efficient management of shards and replicas is essential to maintain the performance, reliability, and scalability of your Elasticsearch cluster.

A shard is a basic unit of storage and search. Every index in Elasticsearch is divided into shards, which are then distributed across nodes in the cluster. This division allows Elasticsearch to parallelize operations and increase search throughput. There are two types of shards: primary shards and replica shards. Primary shards contain the original data, while replica shards are copies of the primary shards that provide redundancy and failover capabilities.

To configure the number of shards and replicas for an index, you define settings at the time of index creation. The settings for the number of primary shards and replicas can be specified in JSON format. For example, to create an index with three primary shards and two replicas, you can use the following request:

```
PUT /my_index
{
  "settings": {
    "number_of_shards": 3,
    "number_of_replicas": 2
  }
}
```

Choosing the right number of shards and replicas is critical. Too few shards and replicas can result in uneven distribution of data and load, impacting performance and reliability. Conversely, too many shards can lead to unnecessary overhead.

The appropriate number of primary shards depends on several factors:

- Data Volume: Larger datasets benefit from more shards to distribute the load.
- Node Capacity: The capacity of individual nodes impacts how many shards a node can handle efficiently.
- Expected Growth: Future data growth should be considered to avoid frequent reindexing.

The number of replica shards influences:

- High Availability: More replicas provide higher fault tolerance.
- Read Throughput: Additional replicas allow more simultaneous read operations.

In the context of cluster health, the proper allocation of shards and replicas must be monitored. Elasticsearch provides APIs to check the cluster state and ensure that all shards are properly assigned. For example, the _cluster/health API can give a quick overview of the cluster's state:

```
GET /_cluster/health
```

The output includes crucial information about the number of nodes, active shards, and unassigned shards:

```
{
  "cluster_name": "elasticsearch",
  "status": "green",
  "number_of_nodes": 5,
  "number_of_data_nodes": 5,
  "active_primary_shards": 15,
  "active_shards": 30,
  "unassigned_shards": 0,
  ...
}
```

Efficient management also involves understanding shard allocation mechanisms. Elasticsearch uses the cluster state to determine shard placement and balancing. When a node joins or leaves the cluster, or when a shard becomes unassigned, the cluster state changes and triggers allocation and rebalancing processes. Shard allocation can be controlled using several settings:

- Cluster-Level Settings: Using the _cluster/settings API, you can set parameters like cluster.routing.allocation.enable to control shard allocation behavior globally.

- Index-Level Settings: Through the _settings API, index-specific allocation rules can be applied.
- Shard Allocation Awareness: Ensures shards are distributed based on node attributes like rack, zone, or other custom tags.

Here is an example of setting cluster-level allocation awareness to distribute shards based on rack attributes:

```
PUT /_cluster/settings
{
  "persistent": {
    "cluster.routing.allocation.awareness.attributes": "rack"
  }
}
```

In some scenarios, manual shard allocation is necessary, such as when rebalancing shards manually or relocating shards to specific nodes. You can use the /_cluster/reroute API to execute such operations. For instance, to allocate an unassigned shard to a specific node, you can use the following JSON payload:

```
POST /_cluster/reroute
{
  "commands": [
    {
      "allocate": {
        "index": "my_index",
        "shard": 0,
        "node": "node_1",
        "allow_primary": true
      }
    }
  ]
}
```

The tuning of shard settings based on workload patterns is crucial for optimizing performance. For read-heavy workloads, increasing the number of replicas may be beneficial. For write-heavy workloads, focusing on optimal primary shard distribution becomes more important.

Optimal shard management practices enhance Elasticsearch's capability to handle scaling gracefully, ensuring that performance and availability are maintained.

7.4 Optimizing Indexing Performance

Optimizing indexing performance in Elasticsearch is crucial for maintaining efficient and responsive search capabilities, particularly when dealing with large datasets and frequent updates. Several key strategies can be employed to enhance indexing speed and efficiency.

Bulk Indexing is essential for optimizing indexing in Elasticsearch. Instead of indexing documents individually, utilizing the _bulk API can significantly reduce the overhead associated with multiple HTTP requests. A well-structured bulk request can index thousands of documents in a single operation, minimizing network latency and server processing time. Below is an example of a typical bulk request format:

```
POST /_bulk
{ "index" : { "_index" : "my_index", "_id" : "1" } }
{ "field1" : "value1", "field2" : "value2"}
{ "index" : { "_index" : "my_index", "_id" : "2" } }
{ "field1" : "value3", "field2" : "value4"}
```

The bulk request format alternates between action and data lines, allowing multiple actions like index, create, and delete.

Increasing Index Refresh Interval is another important consideration. The refresh interval determines how frequently Elasticsearch makes indexed documents searchable. By default, this interval is set to 1 second, but extending it can greatly increase indexing throughput, especially during bulk operations or massive data ingestion tasks. Here is how to adjust the refresh interval:

```
PUT /my_index/_settings
{
  "index": {
    "refresh_interval": "30s"
  }
}
```

During periods of heavy indexing, setting the refresh interval to a higher value, or even disabling it temporarily by setting it to -1, can improve performance. Remember to restore a lower interval or the default setting once intensive indexing is complete to ensure data is searchable in a timely manner.

Optimizing Mappings involves defining precise and efficient mappings for the fields in your index. Avoid using dynamic mappings for production indices, as they can introduce significant overhead during indexing. Instead, use explicit mappings to specify the exact data types and structures. This helps Elasticsearch's indexing engine avoid unnecessary guesswork and optimizes storage. For example:

```
PUT /my_index
{
  "mappings": {
    "properties": {
```

```
        "field1": { "type": "text" },
        "field2": { "type": "keyword" },
        "field3": { "type": "date" }
      }
    }
}
```

Indexing **Large Batches** of documents also benefits from allocating more resources to indexing tasks. Adjusting the indexing and bulk thread pools to handle larger workloads can improve performance. This can be configured in the elasticsearch.yml file or dynamically through the cluster settings API.

Disabling Replicas during bulk indexing operations can prevent unnecessary work on replica shards. This temporary change reduces the overhead and allows the primary shards to focus on indexing the data. After the bulk indexing is completed, re-enabling the replicas ensures data redundancy and fault tolerance. This can be done as follows:

```
PUT /my_index/_settings
{
  "index": {
    "number_of_replicas": 0
  }
}
```

After indexing the data:

```
PUT /my_index/_settings
{
  "index": {
    "number_of_replicas": 1
  }
}
```

Using the Appropriate Number of Shards closely relates to index and cluster performance. Each shard is a Lucene index and comes with its own overhead. Over-sharding can lead to memory and processing bottlenecks. Conversely, under-sharding might not fully utilize the cluster's resources. An ideal shard count typically balances data distribution and query performance, accommodating expected data growth and ensuring efficient usage of system resources. Here's an example to create an index with a calculated number of primary shards:

```
PUT /my_index
{
  "settings": {
    "index": {
      "number_of_shards": 5,
      "number_of_replicas": 1
    }
  }
```

```
}
```

Throttling Indexing Rate helps manage resource allocation efficiently, preventing overwhelming the cluster. Elasticsearch supports configuring indexing throttling to limit the rate at which documents are indexed. This avoids excessive resource usage and maintains cluster stability during peak loads. Here's how to enable and configure indexing throttling:

```
PUT /_all/_settings
{
  "index": {
    "max_indexing_num_docs": "1000000",
    "max_store_bytes_per_sec": "50mb"
  }
}
```

Properly **Tuning the Thread Pool Settings** specific to indexing tasks ensures that sufficient resources are allocated for indexing operations. For high-throughput indexing workloads, adjust the indexing and write thread pool sizes and queue capacities. This setting can be adjusted dynamically via the cluster update settings API to adapt to changing indexing demands.

Using these combined strategies helps in significantly enhancing Elasticsearch indexing performance, allowing for efficient data ingestion without compromising system stability and response times. Employing bulk indexing, adjusting refresh intervals, optimizing mappings, and managing shard configurations are crucial steps that ensure data is ingested swiftly and resources are utilized judiciously, thus maintaining overall cluster health and performance.

7.5 Improving Query Performance

Effective query performance is crucial to maintaining an efficient and responsive Elasticsearch cluster. Various strategies can be employed to optimize query performance, each addressing different aspects of the query execution lifecycle.

Understanding the principles of query optimization begins with analyzing the nature of the queries, the structure of indices, and the underlying hardware capabilities. One critical aspect is creating indices that support efficient searches.

Ensuring that appropriate filters are used instead of queries whenever possible is fundamental. Filters are faster and more efficient because they do not score documents like queries. Elasticsearch automatically caches filters, so subsequent queries using the same filters can achieve much better performance. For example, using a filter query to reduce the scope before executing the more computationally expensive queries is good practice.

```
GET /my_index/_search
{
  "query": {
    "bool": {
      "filter": [
        { "term": { "status": "paid" }},
        { "range": { "date": { "gte": "2022-01-01" }}}
      ],
      "must": [
        {
          "match": {
            "description": "worldwide shipping"
          }
        }
      ]
    }
  }
}
```

Another key factor in optimizing query performance is the correct utilization of indexing and mapping strategies. Elasticsearch allows various types of fields, such as text, keyword, date, and numeric. Selecting the appropriate field type for each data property is essential. For instance, fields that will not be analyzed (like identifiers or codes) should use the keyword type to avoid the overhead of text analysis.

Additionally, configuring the number of replicas and ensuring proper sharding are also influential. Each shard in Elasticsearch operates almost like an independent index and is managed by a single thread. Therefore, having too many or too few shards can impede performance. The goal is to strike a balance; for indices with high write loads, many small shards can parallelize writes, whereas read-heavy indices may benefit from fewer but larger shards to minimize the overhead of inter-shard coordination.

To measure and optimize the performance of your queries, utilize Elasticsearch Profiler. This tool breaks down each query and provides insights into how long each component takes to execute, enabling precise identification of bottlenecks.

```
GET /my_index/_search?pretty
{
  "profile": true,
  "query": {
```

```
    "bool": {
      "must": [
        { "match": { "description": "worldwide shipping" }}
      ]
    }
  }
}
```

The output will give a detailed breakdown, showing the time spent in each phase of the query for every shard touched. By examining this data, you can identify which parts of the query are consuming the most time.

In addition, leveraging cache effectively can significantly enhance performance. Elasticsearch uses various caches, such as query cache, request cache, and field data cache. The request cache stores the results of entire queries against indices that do not change frequently. This can be particularly useful for queries on static data or for dashboards where the same queries are executed repeatedly.

```
PUT /my_index/_settings
{
  "index.requests.cache.enable": true
}
```

Effective use of pagination is another best practice when dealing with large datasets. Elasticsearch offers the from and size parameters to paginate through results. However, for deeper pagination, using search_after is recommended to avoid performance degradation.

```
GET /my_index/_search
{
  "size": 10,
  "query": {
    "match": {
      "description": "worldwide shipping"
    }
  },
  "sort": [
    { "date": "desc" },
    { "tie_breaker_id": "asc" }
  ],
  "search_after": [1122334455, "aBcDeFgH"]
}
```

Use the value of the sort fields from the last document of the current batch as the search_after parameter to fetch the next set of documents efficiently.

Finally, employing shard allocation awareness ensures data locality, which can dramatically improve query performance. Elasticsearch can be configured to allocate shards to nodes based on attributes, ensuring that frequently queried data is placed on optimal nodes.

```
PUT /_template/my_template
{
  "template": "logs-*",
  "settings": {
    "index.routing.allocation.awareness.attributes": "rack_id"
  },
  "mappings": { ... }
}
```

This configuration ensures that shards are distributed according to specified node attributes, such as the rack location, thus ensuring data affinity and reducing latency.

These strategies, when applied collectively, can significantly enhance the performance of queries in an Elasticsearch cluster. Understanding the underlying principles and correctly configuring the system components are paramount to achieving efficient and responsive queries.

7.6 Tuning Memory and Heap Usage

Effective memory and heap usage are critical for ensuring the performance and stability of an Elasticsearch cluster. Proper configuration minimizes the risk of out-of-memory errors and enhances the responsiveness of both indexing and search operations. This section delves into the various strategies and considerations for tuning memory and heap usage in Elasticsearch.

Memory in Elasticsearch is divided into three main areas: heap, direct memory, and system memory. Each plays a distinct role in processing queries and managing data. The JVM heap is particularly significant as it directly influences the performance of the search and indexing operations.

Heap size configuration is paramount. By default, Elasticsearch allocates 50% of available memory to the JVM heap up to a maximum of 32GB. This conservative default aims to balance memory for heap and the file system cache. However, depending on your workloads, it may be necessary to adjust this setting. Increasing the heap size can help manage larger indices and higher query loads, but setting it too high can lead to long garbage collection pauses, which can degrade performance or cause nodes to drop out of the cluster.

To configure the heap size, modify the jvm.options file found in the config directory of your Elasticsearch installation. Use the following settings as a starting point:

```
-Xms16g
-Xmx16g
```

Here, -Xms sets the initial heap size, and -Xmx sets the maximum heap size. Both should be set to the same value to avoid the overhead of heap resizing.

Garbage collection (GC) is another critical aspect of JVM tuning. Elasticsearch uses the default G1 garbage collector in recent Java versions, which is well-suited for large heaps. The G1 collector aims to provide low-latency pauses by performing concurrent garbage collection. You can monitor and tune garbage collection by examining the Elasticsearch logs, particularly for GC pause time and frequency. For instance, adding the following options helps in logging GC activities:

```
-XX:+UseG1GC
-XX:InitiatingHeapOccupancyPercent=75
-XX:+PrintGCDetails
-XX:+PrintGCDateStamps
-XX:+PrintTenuringDistribution
-XX:+PrintGCApplicationStoppedTime
-XX:+PrintGCApplicationConcurrentTime
-XX:+UseGCLogFileRotation
-XX:NumberOfGCLogFiles=32
-XX:GCLogFileSize=64m
```

Monitoring garbage collection logs can help identify whether Elasticsearch is spending too much time in GC, potentially necessitating further tuning or adjustments in heap size.

Besides heap memory, Elasticsearch extensively uses off-heap memory for certain operations, such as file system caching, networking, and Lucene's data structures. Ensuring that there is sufficient system memory left for these operations is crucial. Generally, it is recommended to leave at least half of the available system memory for file system caching, which Elasticsearch leverages significantly for efficient disk I/O operations.

It's also essential to be cognizant of how memory is allocated across different nodes in a cluster. Nodes can be specialized with different roles, such as master nodes, data nodes, and ingest nodes, each with varying memory requirements. Master nodes benefit from stability and low latency, while data nodes require substantial memory for managing shards and executing heavy search queries. An illustrative configuration might look as follows:

```
node.master: true
```

```
node.data: false
node.ingest: false
discovery.seed_hosts: ["192.168.1.1", "192.168.1.2"]
cluster.initial_master_nodes: ["192.168.1.1"]
path.data: /path/to/data
path.logs: /path/to/logs
bootstrap.memory_lock: true
```

Setting bootstrap.memory_lock to true prevents the JVM from swapping out heap memory, ensuring consistent performance by avoiding the delays caused by page faults. However, you need to make sure that mlockall is configured correctly and the Elasticsearch process has the necessary permissions.

For environments where heap memory footprint is critical, consider leveraging Elasticsearch's sophisticated data management features such as rollover indices and index lifecycle management (ILM). These features help manage data growth efficiently, thereby controlling memory usage over time. Here is an example ILM policy:

```
PUT _ilm/policy/my_policy
{
  "policy": {
    "phases": {
      "hot": {
        "actions": {
          "rollover": {
            "max_size": "50GB",
            "max_age": "30d"
          },
          "set_priority": {
            "priority": 100
          }
        }
      },
      "delete": {
        "min_age": "90d",
        "actions": {
          "delete": {}
        }
      }
    }
  }
}
```

This policy ensures that indices are rolled over before they grow too large, which helps maintain manageable heap sizes and optimal query performance.

Understanding and leveraging Elasticsearch's logging and monitoring tools is indispensable. Use the Elasticsearch API to monitor heap usage, garbage collection times, and other crucial performance metrics. For example:

```
GET _nodes/stats/jvm
```

The output provides detailed statistics on each node's JVM, giving insights into memory usage, garbage collection, and other performance metrics:


```
{
  "nodes" : {
    "node_id" : {
      "jvm" : {
        "timestamp" : 1627722054406,
        "uptime_in_millis" : 526444422,
        "mem" : {
          "heap_used_in_bytes" : 5735840640,
          "heap_used_percent" : 35,
          "heap_committed_in_bytes" : 16106127360,
          "heap_max_in_bytes" : 16106127360,
          "non_heap_used_in_bytes" : 30827744,
          "non_heap_committed_in_bytes" : 31223808,
          "pools" : {
            "young" : {...},
            "survivor" : {...},
            "old" : {...}
          }
        },
        "gc" : {
          "collectors" : {
            "young" : {...},
            "old" : {...}
          }
        },
        ...
      }
    }
  }
}
```


Tuning memory and heap usage in Elasticsearch involves careful configuration of JVM settings, monitoring garbage collection, and ensuring sufficient system memory for non-heap operations. Proper node role allocation and the use of index management strategies further aid in maintaining optimal performance and stability.

7.7 Managing Hot and Warm Nodes

Hot and warm node architecture provides an efficient strategy for managing data lifecycle in Elasticsearch, balancing performance requirements with resource utilization. This approach involves categorizing nodes based on their roles: hot nodes handle indexing and querying of recent data while warm nodes store older, less frequently accessed data.

The primary advantage of this segregation is that it allows the system to optimize for speed and efficiency on the hot nodes, which are typically backed by higher-performance hardware, while reducing costs by utilizing less expensive hardware for the warm nodes.

- **Configuration of Hot and Warm Nodes**

To implement hot and warm nodes, the first step is to tag nodes appropriately. Elasticsearch allows for node attributes to define roles. For example, adding attributes in the 'elasticsearch.yml' configuration file differentiates hot and warm nodes:

```
node.attr.data: hot
node.attr.data: warm
```

After configuring the nodes with the appropriate attributes, use Index Lifecycle Management (ILM) policies to route data to the correct nodes based on their age and usage patterns.

- **Index Lifecycle Management (ILM) Policies**

ILM policies automate the movement of indices through different stages: hot, warm, cold, and delete. Each phase can define specific actions, such as rollover, shrink, forcemerge, and delete.

An ILM policy for managing hot and warm nodes might look as follows:

```
{
  "policy": {
    "phases": {
      "hot": {
        "actions": {
          "rollover": {
            "max_size": "50GB",
            "max_age": "30d"
          }
        }
      },
      "warm": {
        "actions": {
          "allocate": {
            "require": {
              "data": "warm"
            }
          },
          "forcemerge": {
            "max_num_segments": 1
          },
          "shrink": {
            "number_of_shards": 1
          }
        }
```

```
        }
      }
    }
}
```

In this example, the hot phase defines a rollover action that transitions the index to the warm phase when it reaches 50GB in size or 30 days in age. During the warm phase, the index is allocated to warm nodes and undergoes actions like force merge and shrink.

- **Routing Allocation Awareness**

Ensuring that indices reside on the correct nodes requires configuring routing allocation awareness in Elasticsearch. This involves setting up awareness attributes to correctly distribute indices according to their phases.

```
cluster.routing.allocation.awareness.attributes: data
```

By defining these attributes, Elasticsearch can place indices according to their lifecycle stages, ensuring that older indices do not consume resources on hot nodes.

- **Performance Considerations**

Hot nodes must be optimized for high write and read throughput, often incorporating fast SSDs, increased CPU cores, and larger memory sizes. Conversely, warm nodes can utilize slower, more cost-effective storage options like HDDs, as the read/write demands are lower.

Given that hot nodes deal with the bulk of active indexing and querying, it's essential to configure ample heap space and CPU power. The following settings within 'elasticsearch.yml' can aid in tuning performance for hot nodes:

```
indices.memory.index_buffer_size: 20%
indices.queries.cache.size: 10%
```

Warm nodes, while not heavily accessed, still require efficient resource management, ensuring stability and reducing costs. The following configurations could be implemented for warm nodes:

```
indices.memory.index_buffer_size: 10%
indices.queries.cache.size: 5%
```

- **Monitoring and Maintenance**

Regular monitoring and maintenance are critical for ensuring optimal performance and stability. Elasticsearch offers built-in tools like Monitoring and Kibana for real-time cluster health and performance metrics tracking.

An example of a Kibana Query Language (KQL) query to monitor specific node types:

```
node.attributes.data: "hot" or node.attributes.data: "warm"
```

This query filters metrics for hot and warm nodes, aiding in proactive management and troubleshooting potential issues. Proactively managing node resources helps maintain balanced loads and avoids performance bottlenecks.

Careful design and regular adjustments to node configurations and ILM policies ensure that Elasticsearch clusters operate efficiently, meeting performance requirements while optimizing resource usage.

7.8 Monitoring Cluster Health

Monitoring the health of an Elasticsearch cluster is crucial for ensuring its performance and reliability. Several metrics and tools are available to continuously track the cluster's status, identify potential issues, and optimize resource utilization. This section covers key aspects of cluster health monitoring, including node metrics, cluster status, and available tools.

Cluster health is influenced by a variety of factors such as the number of nodes, the distribution of shards, the status of replicas, and the availability of resources like CPU, memory, and disk space. Elasticsearch provides several built-in endpoints and tools for monitoring these metrics.

The primary API for checking the health of an Elasticsearch cluster is the _cluster/health endpoint. This endpoint provides comprehensive information about the cluster's state, including the status, the number of nodes, the number of data nodes, active primary shards, and other critical metrics.

```
GET /_cluster/health
```

The response from the _cluster/health API includes several important fields:

- cluster_name: The name of the cluster.
- status: The health status of the cluster (can be green, yellow, or red).
- timed_out: Indicates whether the request to the cluster health API timed out.
- number_of_nodes: The total number of nodes in the cluster.
- number_of_data_nodes: The number of data nodes in the cluster.
- active_primary_shards: The number of primary shards that are active.
- active_shards: The total number of active shards (both primary and replica).
- relocating_shards: The number of shards that are currently being relocated.
- initializing_shards: The number of shards that are being initialized.
- unassigned_shards: The number of shards that are unassigned.
- delayed_unassigned_shards: Shards whose assignment is delayed due to node failures or other reasons.
- number_of_pending_tasks: The number of cluster-level operations that are still pending.
- number_of_in_flight_fetch: The number of fetches for which the result is pending.
- task_max_waiting_in_queue_millis: The maximum wait time in milliseconds for tasks in queue.
- active_shards_percent_as_number: The percentage of active shards.

The status of the cluster can be classified into three categories:

- green: All primary and replica shards are active. The cluster is in its optimal state.

- yellow: All primary shards are active, but some replicas are not assigned. This status indicates potential issues but does not affect the integrity of the indexed data.
- red: Some primary shards are not active, which can lead to data loss or unavailability of certain documents.

For real-time monitoring and visualization, Elasticsearch provides integration with Kibana. Kibana offers a powerful set of tools for monitoring cluster health through visual dashboards. To set up monitoring in Kibana, first ensure that the Elasticsearch monitoring features are enabled. This can be done by starting both Elasticsearch and Kibana instances and then navigating to the Monitoring section in Kibana.

Enabling monitoring involves the following configuration steps:

```
xpack.monitoring.collection.enabled: true
```

In Kubernetes environments, where Elasticsearch clusters are often deployed, monitoring can be enhanced with Prometheus and Grafana. Prometheus collects metrics through the Elasticsearch exporter, which then can be visualized using Grafana.

An exemplary Prometheus configuration would include a job to scrape metrics from the Elasticsearch exporter:

```
scrape_configs:
  - job_name: 'elasticsearch'
    static_configs:
      - targets: ['elasticsearch-exporter:9108']
```

The metrics collected by Prometheus are varied and include indices stats, node stats, JVM stats, and various cluster metrics, which are crucial for diagnosing performance bottlenecks and resource issues.

Here is a sample Grafana dashboard configuration file that includes Elasticsearch metrics:

```
{
  "dashboard": {
    "title": "Elasticsearch Cluster Dashboard",
    "panels": [
      {
        "type": "graph",
        "title": "Cluster Health Status",
        "targets": [
          {
            "expr": "elasticsearch_cluster_health_status",
            "legendFormat": "Health Status"
          }
        ]
      },
```

```
    {
      "type": "graph",
      "title": "Node CPU Usage",
      "targets": [
        {
          "expr": "elasticsearch_node_cpu_percent",
          "legendFormat": "{{ instance }}"
        }
      ]
    }
  ]
 }
}
```

Prompt alerts and notifications are essential for proactive monitoring. Elasticsearch and Kibana support integration with various alerting systems. Elasticsearch's Watcher plugin can be configured to trigger alerts based on certain cluster health conditions.

A sample Watcher configuration for alerting on red cluster status might look like:

```
PUT _watcher/watch/cluster_health_watch
{
  "trigger": {
    "schedule": {
      "interval": "10m"
    }
  },
  "input": {
    "http": {
      "request": {
        "host": "localhost",
        "port": 9200,
        "path": "/_cluster/health"
      }
    }
  },
  "condition": {
    "compare": {
      "ctx.payload.status": {
        "eq": "red"
      }
    }
  },
  "actions": {
    "send_email": {
      "email": {
        "to": "admin@example.com",
        "subject": "Elasticsearch Cluster Health Alert",
        "body": {
          "text": "The cluster health status is red. Immediate action required."
        }
      }
    }
  }
}
```

By carefully monitoring these facets of cluster health, administrators can ensure Elasticsearch clusters are running efficiently, avoid potential downtime, and react swiftly to emergent issues.

7.9 Best Practices for High Availability

Ensuring high availability in Elasticsearch is critical to maintaining a dependable search infrastructure capable of handling failures and retaining service uptime. High availability entails multiple strategies and configurations to minimize downtime and data loss, primarily achieved by distributing data and load across multiple nodes and ensuring redundancy.

Cluster Configuration: Properly configuring the Elasticsearch cluster is the first step. Ensure the cluster follows a redundant setup using multiple master-eligible nodes. Aim for an odd number of master-eligible nodes to prevent split-brain scenarios, where the cluster is divided into independent segments due to network failures or misconfigurations. The following configuration in elasticsearch.yml is recommended for a five-node cluster with three master-eligible nodes:

```
cluster.name: my_cluster
node.name: master-node-1
node.master: true
node.data: false
discovery.seed_hosts: ["master-node-1", "master-node-2", "master-node-3"]
cluster.initial_master_nodes: ["master-node-1", "master-node-2", "master-node-3"]
```

Shard and Replica Configuration: Shard and replica management is vital for high availability. Shards divide the data into manageable pieces, while replicas provide redundancy. By default, each index in Elasticsearch has one replica. Increasing this number enhances fault tolerance. For a production environment, ensure each index has at least one replica by setting the number of replicas at index creation:

```
PUT /my_index
{
  "settings": {
    "number_of_shards": 5,
    "number_of_replicas": 1
  }
}
```

Data Node Distribution: Distribute data nodes across different physical servers, racks, or even data centers to avoid a single point of failure. Use the allocation awareness feature to control shard allocation, ensuring replicas reside in different racks:

```
cluster.routing.allocation.awareness.attributes: rack_id
```

Assign rack_id to each node:

```
node.attr.rack_id: rack1
```

Segregation of Roles: Assign dedicated roles to nodes based on their function - master, data, and client (coordinating) nodes. This segregation optimizes performance and stability. For example, master nodes focus on cluster state management, while data nodes handle indexing and search operations. Coordinator nodes offload query routing and result aggregation tasks.

Snapshot and Restore: Regularly backup data using Elasticsearch's snapshot and restore mechanism. Store snapshots in a remote, durable storage like Amazon S3, HDFS, or a shared file system. Configuration example for an S3 repository:

```
PUT _snapshot/my_s3_repository
{
  "type": "s3",
  "settings": {
    "bucket": "my_s3_bucket",
    "region": "us-west-1"
  }
}
```

Monitoring and Alerting: Constantly monitor the cluster's health using tools like Elastic's Kibana monitoring, or third-party solutions like Prometheus and Grafana. Set up alerts for critical metrics such as node availability, shard allocation status, heap usage, and disk space. Example of setting up monitoring in elasticsearch.yml:

```
xpack.monitoring.enabled: true
xpack.monitoring.collection.interval: 10s
xpack.monitoring.history.duration: 7d
```

Handling Hot and Warm Data: Implement hot-warm architecture by separating nodes for hot (frequently queried) and warm (infrequently queried) data. Hot nodes use faster storage (e.g., SSDs), while warm nodes use slower but cost-efficient storage (e.g., HDDs). Index Lifecycle Management (ILM) policy example to transition indices:

```
PUT _ilm/policy/my_policy
{
  "policy": {
    "phases": {
      "hot": {
        "actions": {
```

```
          "rollover": {
            "max_size": "50GB",
            "max_age": "30d"
          }
        }
      },
      "warm": {
        "actions": {
          "allocate": {
            "number_of_replicas": 1,
            "include": {
              "box_type": "warm"
            }
          }
        }
      }
    }
  }
}
```

Network and Security Considerations: Protect the cluster from unauthorized access and network vulnerabilities. Implement TLS encryption for inter-node communication and HTTP clients. Use built-in security features such as Role-Based Access Control (RBAC) to limit permissions:

```
xpack.security.enabled: true
xpack.security.transport.ssl.enabled: true
xpack.security.transport.ssl.verification_mode: certificate
xpack.security.transport.ssl.keystore.path: certs/elastic-certificates.p12
xpack.security.transport.ssl.truststore.path: certs/elastic-certificates.p12
```

Rolling Upgrades: Perform rolling upgrades to update nodes without downtime. One node at a time is brought offline for the update, minimizing the impact on cluster operations. Before upgrading, ensure the cluster state is green. Check the cluster health:

```
GET _cluster/health
```

The output should be:

```
{
  "cluster_name": "my_cluster",
  "status": "green",
  "timed_out": false,
  ...
}
```

Plan and execute node updates carefully to maintain cluster stability and high availability during upgrades.

7.10 Hands-On: Performance Tuning and Scaling

In this section, we will delve into practical aspects of performance tuning and scaling in Elasticsearch, providing hands-on guidance and concrete examples. This section is structured to demonstrate real-world scenarios that pertain to optimizing both indexing and query operations, along with strategies for scaling Elasticsearch clusters effectively.

To begin, let's revisit the basics:

```
curl -X GET "localhost:9200/_cat/health?v"
```

Monitoring cluster health is the first step in diagnosing performance issues. The above command retrieves the status of the Elasticsearch cluster, providing vital information such as node availability, active shards, and any existing issues.

Example: Tuning Elasticsearch for Improved Indexing

Indexing performance in Elasticsearch can be significantly enhanced through several tunable parameters:

- **Refresh Interval**
- **Number of Shards**
- **Number of Replicas**
- **Bulk Indexing**

Consider the following configurations for optimizing indexing procedures:

1. Setting the Refresh Interval

A critical parameter affecting indexing throughput is the refresh interval, which determines how frequently the index is refreshed, making the new data searchable:

```
curl -X PUT "localhost:9200/my-index/_settings" -H 'Content-Type: application/json'
     -d'
{
  "index" : {
    "refresh_interval" : "30s"
  }
}'
```

By increasing the refresh interval, you reduce the overhead of making the data searchable frequently, thus improving indexing speed.

2. Optimizing Shard Count

Proper shard management is essential for scaling out:

```
curl -X PUT "localhost:9200/my-index" -H 'Content-Type: application/json' -d'
{
  "settings" : {
    "index" : {
      "number_of_shards" : 5,
      "number_of_replicas" : 1
    }
  }
}'
```

Configuring an optimal number of shards ensures better utilization of resources and balanced distribution of data across nodes.

3. Leveraging Bulk Indexing

Using the Bulk API ensures efficient indexing operations by reducing the overhead of multiple requests:

```
curl -X POST "localhost:9200/_bulk" -H 'Content-Type: application/json' -d'
{ "index" : { "_index" : "my-index", "_id" : "1" } }
{ "field1" : "value1" }
{ "index" : { "_index" : "my-index", "_id" : "2" } }
{ "field1" : "value2" }
'
```

The above bulk statement indexes multiple documents in a single request, improving throughput and resource efficiency.

Example: Enhancing Query Performance

Query performance is another crucial aspect of Elasticsearch optimization:

1. Using Filter Queries

Unlike search queries, filter queries provide faster results as they do not need to calculate relevance scores:

```
curl -X GET "localhost:9200/my-index/_search" -H 'Content-Type: application/json' -
    d'
{
  "query": {
    "bool": {
      "filter": [
        { "term": { "user": "john" } },
        { "range": { "age": { "gte": 30 } } }
      ]
    }
  }
}'
```

Filter queries can cache results, significantly speeding up repeated queries.

2. Aggregations Optimization

Aggregations can be resource-intensive. To optimize, minimal document prefetching and filtering can be utilized:

```
curl -X GET "localhost:9200/my-index/_search" -H 'Content-Type: application/json' -
    d'
{
  "size": 0,
  "aggs": {
    "avg_price": {
      "avg": {
        "field": "price"
      }
    }
  }
}'
```

Setting size to 0 prevents Elasticsearch from including document hits in the response, focusing resources on computing the aggregation only.

Scaling Strategies

Next, we explore horizontal and vertical scaling adjustments:

1. Adding Nodes (Horizontal Scaling)

Increase cluster capacity and distribute load by adding new nodes:

```
curl -X PUT "localhost:9200/_cluster/settings" -H 'Content-Type: application/json' -d'
{
  "persistent": {
    "cluster.routing.allocation.exclude._name": "node_to_be_excluded"
  }
}'
```

Use dynamic settings to manage shard allocation, effectively balancing loads across nodes.

2. Increasing Node Capacity (Vertical Scaling)

Vertical scaling involves augmenting node resources like CPU or memory. Adjusting node.master and node.data roles can optimize resource allocation per node:

```
# elasticsearch.yml configuration file
node.master: true
node.data: true
```

Configuring node roles appropriately ensures tasks like indexing and searching are distributed for maximum efficiency.

Memory and Heap Tuning

Efficient memory management is integral to performance tuning:

```
# Tuning JVM settings
-Xms4g
-Xmx4g
```

Setting appropriate heap sizes in the JVM options configurations (jvm.options) optimizes memory use. The ideal setting generally limits to 50% of the total available memory to prevent swapping.

Balanced Node Utilization

Segment data to optimize node usage through the hot-warm architecture:

```
# elasticsearch.yml configuration for a hot node
node.attr.box_type: hot
# shard allocation policy
curl -X PUT "localhost:9200/_cluster/settings" -H 'Content-Type: application/json' -d'
{
  "persistent": {
    "cluster.routing.allocation.require.box_type": "hot",
    "index.routing.allocation.require.box_type": "warm"
  }
}'
```

Separating hot and warm data nodes manages varying workloads efficiently, ensuring frequently accessed data resides in high-performance nodes while less critical data is allocated to cost-efficient nodes.

Monitoring these configurations and continuously tweaking based on performance metrics is paramount in achieving an optimal setup.

Chapter 8

Security and Access Control

This chapter addresses the security and access control features of Elasticsearch. It covers basic security principles, setting up user authentication, and managing roles and permissions. Key topics include securing communications with SSL/TLS, configuring IP filtering and access control, auditing and logging security events, and implementing field and document-level security. It also explores advanced security features available through X-Pack, providing a comprehensive guide to securing your Elasticsearch deployment.

8.1 Introduction to Elasticsearch Security

The security of an Elasticsearch deployment is paramount due to the sensitive nature of the data it may store and process. Securing Elasticsearch involves implementing several layers of security measures to protect against unauthorized access, ensure data integrity, and maintain data confidentiality. This section provides a comprehensive overview of the key security aspects that are fundamental to safeguarding an Elasticsearch environment.

Elasticsearch is an open-source search engine built on Apache Lucene. It is designed to provide distributed, multi-tenant capabilities with an

HTTP web interface and schema-free JSON documents. While its architectural strengths facilitate powerful search and analysis capabilities, they also necessitate robust security measures to prevent misuse and data breaches.

- **Authentication and Authorization:** Authentication is the process of verifying the identity of a user or system, whereas authorization determines what an authenticated entity is allowed to do. Elasticsearch provides mechanisms to implement both authentication and authorization, ensuring that users can access only the information they are permitted to see.

  The Elastic Stack employs the X-Pack extension, which offers advanced security features, including user authentication through various methods such as native realm, LDAP, Active Directory, and Single Sign-On (SSO) techniques. Authorization is managed through roles and privileges, allowing fine-grained control over access to indices, documents, and even specific fields.

- **Transport Layer Security:** Transport Layer Security (TLS) is critical for securing communications between Elasticsearch nodes as well as between clients and Elasticsearch. TLS encrypts data transmitted over the network, protecting it from eavesdropping and man-in-the-middle attacks. Enabling TLS involves creating and managing certificates, configuring Elasticsearch to use these certificates, and verifying their proper implementation.

- **IP Filtering and Access Control:** IP filtering restricts access to the Elasticsearch cluster based on the IP addresses of the incoming requests. It is a form of access control that limits which systems can connect to the Elasticsearch cluster, thus reducing the attack surface. This approach is useful for preventing unauthorized access from IP ranges that do not belong to trusted sources.

- **Audit Logging:** Audit logging is vital for tracking and reviewing security-related events within an Elasticsearch deployment. It provides visibility into user activities, making it possible to detect suspicious operations, monitor access patterns, and audit changes to the configuration and data. Elastic Stack's audit logging capabilities help in maintaining compliance with organizational and regulatory requirements by ensuring a traceable history of actions.

- **Field and Document-Level Security:** Field and document-level security controls allow administrators to restrict access to specific fields within documents or to entire documents themselves. This is particularly useful in multi-tenant environments where different users or applications require different levels of access to the same dataset. These controls can enforce privacy policies and protect sensitive information from being visible to users who should not have access to it.

- **Advanced Security Features via X-Pack:** X-Pack extends Elasticsearch's core security capabilities with additional features such as encrypted communications, role-based access control (RBAC), Kerberos authentication, and more sophisticated auditing tools. X-Pack is a commercially licensed extension, but it provides essential enhancements that are crucial for enterprise-grade security.

The remainder of this section will delve into each of these areas in more detail, providing practical guidelines and configurations to secure your Elasticsearch deployment effectively. The goal is to equip you with the knowledge and tools necessary to implement a comprehensive security strategy, ensuring the confidentiality, integrity, and availability of your Elasticsearch data.

```
# Enabling security in elasticsearch.yml
xpack.security.enabled: true

# Setting up TLS communication
xpack.security.transport.ssl.enabled: true
xpack.security.http.ssl.enabled: true

# Defining IP filtering rules
xpack.security.transport.filter.allow: ["192.168.1.0/24"]
xpack.security.transport.filter.deny: ["0.0.0.0/0"]

# Configuring audit logging
xpack.security.audit.enabled: true
xpack.security.audit.outputs: [index, logfile]
xpack.security.audit.logfile.events.include: ["access_denied", "authentication_failed"]

# Field-level security example
PUT /example_index/_mapping
{
  "properties": {
    "ssn": {
      "type": "text",
      "index": false,
      "fielddata": false
    }
  }
}
```

Outputs from the above configurations can be monitored through various channels depending on the setup. Audit logs will typically record security-related events, while IP filtering will prevent unauthorized IP addresses from connecting to the cluster. Careful consideration of these settings will lead to a more secure Elasticsearch environment.

8.2 Basic Security Concepts

A comprehensive understanding of basic security concepts is fundamental to securing an Elasticsearch deployment. Critical aspects include understanding the security models, principles of security by design, and the techniques employed to safeguard data.

Elasticsearch security hinges on several core principles: confidentiality, integrity, and availability (CIA). These principles form the triad that must be maintained to ensure a secure deployment.

Confidentiality ensures that information is not disclosed to unauthorized individuals, systems, or entities. In Elasticsearch, confidentiality can be enforced through various mechanisms such as encryption (both at rest and in transit), access control lists (ACLs), and stringent authentication measures. Employing TLS/SSL for transport encryption is an essential practice.

Integrity guarantees that the data is accurate, consistent, and has not been tampered with. Measures like checksum validations, digital signatures, and ensuring read and write access is controlled through role-based access control (RBAC) preserve data integrity in Elasticsearch.

Availability ensures that the data and services are accessible to authorized users when needed. High availability configurations, node replication, and comprehensive monitoring help ensure resilience against disruptions, thereby maintaining data availability.

Elasticsearch employs a robust security model that integrates these principles through various features:

- **Role-Based Access Control (RBAC):** RBAC is a method of restricting access based on the roles of individual users within an organization. Roles are assigned permissions to perform particular operations such as reading, writing, or administering the cluster. The roles are then mapped to users. This approach simplifies managing permissions, especially in large organizations, by attaching privileges to roles rather than to individual users.
- **Authentication:** Authentication is the process of verifying the

identity of a user or system. Elasticsearch supports multiple authentication mechanisms including native realm, LDAP, Active Directory, and single sign-on (SSO) via SAML or OpenID Connect. Each of these methods has its use cases and configuration specifics which ensure that users accessing the system are verified reliably.

- **Authorization:** Authorization is the process of determining whether an authenticated user has the right to perform a specific action or access data. In Elasticsearch, this is typically managed through roles and permissions defined in the RBAC system. Each operation within the system checks the user's role to determine if the corresponding action is permissible.
- **Encryption:** Encryption in Elasticsearch is applied at two levels: data at rest and data in transit. Data at rest encryption ensures that the data stored on disk is encrypted, protecting it from unauthorized access in case the physical media is compromised. Data in transit encryption typically employs TLS/SSL to secure data being transmitted between nodes, clients, and applications, ensuring that intercepted communications cannot be read by unauthorized parties.
- **Audit Logging:** Maintaining audit logs is crucial for tracking access and modifications to data and configurations within Elasticsearch. Audit logs capture events such as authentication attempts, access to data, and changes to the configuration of the cluster. This practice not only helps in monitoring but also in forensic analysis in case of security incidents.

The implementation and configuration of these security principles and measures are fundamental to the effective protection of Elasticsearch clusters. Below illustrates a typical configuration of enabling role-based access control using Elasticsearch's settings in the elasticsearch.yml file:

```
xpack.security.enabled: true

xpack.security.transport.ssl.enabled: true
xpack.security.transport.ssl.verification_mode: full
xpack.security.transport.ssl.keystore.path: certs/elastic-certificates.p12
xpack.security.transport.ssl.truststore.path: certs/elastic-certificates.p12

xpack.security.http.ssl.enabled: true
xpack.security.http.ssl.keystore.path: certs/elastic-certificates.p12
xpack.security.http.ssl.truststore.path: certs/elastic-certificates.p12

xpack.security.authc.realms.native.native1.order: 0
```

In practice, a robust security posture involves continually monitoring, testing, and updating configurations and access controls. Employing least privilege principles, regularly rotating keys and certificates, and keeping the Elasticsearch software up-to-date with security patches further enhances the security framework.

As we delve deeper into Elasticsearch security, each subsequent section will expand on these concepts, providing detailed instruction on their implementation and best practices for a secure deployment.

8.3 Setting Up User Authentication

User authentication is a critical aspect of securing your Elasticsearch deployment. It ensures that only authorized users have access to your data and cluster operations. In this section, we will cover how to set up user authentication in Elasticsearch, detailing the available methods and providing step-by-step instructions to configure them.

Elasticsearch supports several methods for user authentication, including native authentication, LDAP, Active Directory, and PKI. For simplicity, we will primarily focus on native authentication, which involves managing users directly within Elasticsearch.

- **1. Enabling Security Features**

Before setting up user authentication, it is essential to enable the security features in Elasticsearch. These features are disabled by default. To enable them, you need to modify the elasticsearch.yml configuration file located in the <ES_HOME>/config directory:

```
xpack.security.enabled: true
xpack.security.transport.ssl.enabled: true
```

After enabling these settings, restart the Elasticsearch service to apply the changes. This can be done using the following command:

```
sudo systemctl restart elasticsearch
```

- **2. Configuring the Built-in Users**

Elasticsearch comes with several built-in users for administrative and maintenance tasks. The elastic user is the superuser and has full access to the cluster. The default password for the elastic user is set during the initial setup of Elasticsearch. To configure passwords for built-in users, you can use the elasticsearch-setup-passwords tool as shown below:

```
./bin/elasticsearch-setup-passwords interactive
```

This interactive tool prompts you to set passwords for the built-in users, including elastic, kibana, and logstash_system. It's advisable to choose strong, unique passwords for each user.

- **3. Creating and Managing Users**

With the basic security features enabled and built-in users configured, you can now proceed to create and manage additional users. Elasticsearch provides REST APIs for user management. Here is a step-by-step guide:

- **Creating a New User**

To create a new user, you need to make a PUT request to the _security/user/{username} endpoint. The following example demonstrates how to create a user named john_doe with the password password123 and assign the read role:

```
PUT /_security/user/john_doe
{
  "password" : "password123",
  "roles" : [ "read" ],
  "full_name" : "John Doe",
  "email" : "john.doe@example.com"
}
```

Use the following curl command to execute this request from the command line:

```
curl -X PUT "localhost:9200/_security/user/john_doe" -H 'Content-Type: application/
    json' -d'
{
  "password" : "password123",
  "roles" : [ "read" ],
  "full_name" : "John Doe",
  "email" : "john.doe@example.com"
}
'
```

- **Updating User Details**

To update user details such as password or roles, make a POST request to the _security/user/{username} endpoint with the relevant information. For instance, to update the password for john_doe:

```
POST /_security/user/john_doe/_password
{
  "password" : "newpassword456"
}
```

The corresponding curl command is:

```
curl -X POST "localhost:9200/_security/user/john_doe/_password" -H 'Content-Type:
      application/json' -d'
{
  "password" : "newpassword456"
}
'
```

- **Deleting a User**

To delete a user, make a DELETE request to the _security/user/{username} endpoint. Here is how you can delete the user john_doe:

```
DELETE /_security/user/john_doe
```

And the curl command:

```
curl -X DELETE "localhost:9200/_security/user/john_doe"
```

- **4. Authenticating Users**

Once users are created, you need to authenticate them to access Elasticsearch. Authentication is achieved by sending an HTTP request with the Authorization header containing the user's credentials encoded in Base64. Here's an example of how to authenticate the john_doe user:

```
curl -u john_doe:password123 -X GET "localhost:9200"
```

If the credentials are correct, the user will get access to the cluster; otherwise, an authentication error will be returned.

- **5. Verifying User Authentication and Role Assignments**

To verify user authentication and role assignments, you can use the authenticate endpoint. This endpoint returns information about the authenticated user, such as username, roles, and metadata. Here is an example request:

```
GET /_security/_authenticate
```

The corresponding curl command is:

```
curl -u john_doe:password123 -X GET "localhost:9200/_security/_authenticate"
```

The resulting response will include details about the authenticated user:

```
{
  "username" : "john_doe",
  "roles" : [ "read" ],
  "full_name" : "John Doe",
  "email" : "john.doe@example.com",
  ...
}
```

These steps provide a comprehensive guide to setting up user authentication in Elasticsearch using the native authentication method. By following these instructions, you can ensure that your Elasticsearch cluster is secure and only accessible to authorized users.

8.4 Managing Roles and Permissions

Role-based access control (RBAC) is fundamental to securing an Elasticsearch cluster. By defining roles and assigning them appropriate permissions, administrators can ensure that users have access only to the resources necessary for their responsibilities. In Elasticsearch, a role is a collection of cluster and index privileges, potentially scoped to specific resources. Permissions determine the actions that users can perform within the cluster, and efficiently managing roles guarantees both security and operational efficiency.

Roles in Elasticsearch are defined and managed using the REST API or through configuration files. Each role consists of three primary components: cluster privileges, index privileges, and optional application privileges. Understanding the structure and settings for these components is crucial for effective role management.

Cluster privileges control operations at the cluster level, such as node management, snapshot creation, and monitoring. These privileges are defined by specifying actions like cluster:admin and cluster:monitor.

```
{
  "cluster": ["monitor", "manage_index_templates"]
}
```

In the above example, the role grants the abilities to monitor the cluster's health and status and to manage index templates, without permitting other administrative actions.

Index privileges manage access and operations on specific indices. These privileges include read/write access, index creation and deletion, and various document-level permissions such as search, bulk, and update operations. Each privilege is usually scoped to a set of indices or index patterns.

```
{
  "indices": [
    {
      "names": ["logs-*", "metrics-*"],
      "privileges": ["read", "write"],
      "field_security": {
        "grant": ["timestamp", "message", "host"]
      },
      "query": {
        "term": {"enabled": true}
      }
    }
  ]
}
```

The example grants read and write access to indices matching the patterns logs-* and metrics-*. The field security settings permit access only to the specified fields within documents, enhancing data protection. The optional query element further restricts access based on defined query criteria.

For a detailed example, consider a role for a data analyst requiring read access to specific indices and the ability to monitor cluster health. The JSON definition of such a role could be:

```
{
  "cluster": ["monitor"],
  "indices": [
    {
      "names": ["data-*"],
      "privileges": ["read"],
      "field_security": {
        "grant": ["timestamp", "value", "user"]
      }
    }
  ]
}
```

This role configuration ensures that the data analyst can only read data from indices prefixed with data-, access specific fields, and monitor the cluster status.

Creating roles can be done through the Kibana management UI or using the Elasticsearch REST API. The API method, being scriptable and flexible, is often preferred for complex environments. To create a role using the REST API, make a PUT request to the /_security/role/{role_name} endpoint, supplying the role definition as JSON in the request body.

```
PUT /_security/role/data_analyst
{
  "cluster": ["monitor"],
  "indices": [
    {
      "names": ["data-*"],
      "privileges": ["read"],
      "field_security": {
        "grant": ["timestamp", "value", "user"]
      }
    }
  ]
}
```

Once roles are defined, they must be assigned to users. User management can similarly be handled via the Kibana UI or the REST API. Assignment of roles to users ensures controlled access based on predefined permissions, enhancing security.

Here is an example of assigning the data_analyst role to a user named john:

```
PUT /_security/user/john
{
  "password": "changeme",
  "roles": ["data_analyst"],
  "full_name": "John Doe",
  "email": "john.doe@example.com"
}
```

Equally crucial is the periodic review and audit of roles and permissions, reflecting organizational changes and evolving security requirements. Regularly updating role definitions and role assignments helps maintain a high security posture and minimizes potential vulnerabilities.

By systematically managing roles and permissions, Elasticsearch administrators can safeguard data integrity and availability, while enabling efficient and secure access to cluster resources.

8.5 Securing Communications with SSL/TLS

Securing communications between Elasticsearch nodes and clients is crucial to safeguard sensitive data from being intercepted or tampered with during transmission. SSL/TLS (Secure Sockets Layer/Transport

Layer Security) provides a robust mechanism to encrypt communications channels, ensuring both privacy and data integrity. This section provides comprehensive instructions for configuring SSL/TLS in Elasticsearch.

To enable SSL/TLS, Elasticsearch utilizes Transport Layer Security (TLS), the successor to SSL, to ensure encrypted and secure communication. The following crucial steps will guide you through the configuration process:

- Generating Certificates and Private Keys
- Configuring Elasticsearch to Use SSL/TLS
- Verifying the Configuration

Generating certificates is the first step towards enabling encrypted communications. Elasticsearch offers a built-in tool named elasticsearch-certutil to generate certificates easily. You can generate a Certificate Authority (CA), node certificates, and client certificates using this tool.

```
# Generate CA
bin/elasticsearch-certutil ca --out config/elastic-stack-ca.p12 --pass ""
```

The command above creates a CA in a PKCS#12 (P12) format file. The -pass "" option specifies an empty password for the CA file.

Next, generate node certificates using the following command:

```
# Generate node certificates
bin/elasticsearch-certutil cert --ca config/elastic-stack-ca.p12 --ca-pass "" --out config/
    elastic-certificates.p12 --pass ""
```

This command generates certificates for the Elasticsearch nodes, which can also be used for client authentication if required. The resulting PKCS#12 file contains the necessary certificates and private keys.

Upon generating the certificates, they must be configured within each Elasticsearch node. This requires modifying the elasticsearch.yml configuration file. Below are the essential settings:

```
# Enable SSL/TLS for transport and HTTP layers
xpack.security.transport.ssl.enabled: true
xpack.security.http.ssl.enabled: true

# Define the paths to the key and certificate files
xpack.security.transport.ssl.keystore.path: config/elastic-certificates.p12
xpack.security.transport.ssl.truststore.path: config/elastic-certificates.p12
xpack.security.http.ssl.keystore.path: config/elastic-certificates.p12
```

```
xpack.security.http.ssl.truststore.path: config/elastic-certificates.p12

# Set the trust passwords, if any
xpack.security.transport.ssl.keystore.password: ""
xpack.security.transport.ssl.truststore.password: ""
xpack.security.http.ssl.keystore.password: ""
xpack.security.http.ssl.truststore.password: ""
```

These settings enable SSL/TLS for both the transport layer (internal node-to-node communication) and the HTTP layer (client-to-node communication). The keystore and truststore paths are specified along with any necessary passwords.

Restart each node for the changes to take effect.

After configuring SSL/TLS, it's crucial to verify that the setup is correct. One approach is to use cURL to make an HTTPS request to the Elasticsearch cluster:

```
curl -X GET "https://localhost:9200" --cacert /path/to/ca.crt
```

If the configuration is correct, the above command will return the Elasticsearch cluster information over HTTPS. Any issues, such as certificate errors, will be reported by cURL, allowing for diagnostic measures.

Additionally, you can configure Elasticsearch clients, such as Kibana or Logstash, to use SSL/TLS by modifying their respective configuration files:

```
# kibana.yml
elasticsearch.ssl.certificateAuthorities: [ "/path/to/ca.crt" ]
elasticsearch.ssl.verificationMode: full
elasticsearch.hosts: ["https://localhost:9200"]
```

Similarly, for Logstash, you would configure the Elasticsearch output plugin:

```
# logstash.conf
output {
  elasticsearch {
    hosts => ["https://localhost:9200"]
    ssl => true
    cacert => "/path/to/ca.crt"
  }
}
```

Integrating SSL/TLS across the entire ELK stack enhances the overall security, ensuring encrypted communications between all components.

By meticulously following the steps provided, SSL/TLS encryption will be successfully enabled, securing data transmission and protecting the integrity and confidentiality of your Elasticsearch cluster's communications.

8.6 Configuring IP Filtering and Access Control

IP filtering and access control are vital components for securing Elasticsearch clusters, as they help restrict access to authorized users and systems. This section explores configuring IP filtering and managing access control lists (ACLs) to enhance your Elasticsearch deployment's security posture.

IP Filtering: IP filtering allows administrators to define rules that permit or deny access to Elasticsearch nodes based on IP addresses. This functionality helps prevent unauthorized access and ensures that only trusted IP addresses can interact with your Elasticsearch cluster.

To configure IP filtering, edit the elasticsearch.yml configuration file. Introduce the xpack.security.transport.filter settings under the xpack.security.transport namespace. Below is a sample configuration:

```
xpack.security.transport.filter:
  ip_allowlist: [ "192.168.1.0/24", "10.0.0.0/8" ]
  ip_denylist: [ "0.0.0.0/0", "::/0" ]
```

The ip_allowlist directive specifies the IP addresses or networks that are permitted to access the cluster, while the ip_denylist directive specifies the IP addresses or networks that are explicitly denied access. In this example, the cluster allows access from the 192.168.1.0/24 and 10.0.0.0/8 networks while denying access from all other IP addresses.

Once the configuration is updated, restart the Elasticsearch node for the changes to take effect. Verify the IP filtering by attempting to connect from both allowed and denied IP addresses and observe the results.

Access Control Lists (ACLs): ACLs enable fine-grained control over who can access specific resources within the Elasticsearch cluster. By creating roles and associating them with users or groups, administrators can define what actions are permissible for different users.

Elasticsearch provides role-based access control (RBAC) through which administrators can define roles containing permissions for various cluster and index-level operations. A role definition includes privileges for cluster-wide actions, index-specific actions, or both.

Create and manage roles using the security API or configuration files. Here is a sample definition for a role using the security API:

```
PUT /_security/role/my_admin_role
{
  "cluster": ["all"],
  "indices": [
    {
      "names": ["*"],
      "privileges": ["all"]
    }
  ]
}
```

This example creates a role named my_admin_role, granting full privileges (all) at both the cluster level and index level for all indices (names: ["*"]).

Next, assign the role to a user using the following security API command:

```
POST /_security/user/jdoe/_role/my_admin_role
```

Here, the user jdoe is assigned the my_admin_role, giving them administrative access across the entire Elasticsearch cluster.

By combining IP filtering with ACLs, you can achieve robust security for your Elasticsearch cluster. It is crucial to properly configure both mechanisms to prevent unauthorized access and ensure that users have access only to the resources necessary for their roles.

Continually review and update IP filtering rules and ACLs to adapt to changes in your network security requirements and user roles. Regular audits and log reviews will help maintain the security and integrity of your Elasticsearch deployment.

8.7 Auditing and Logging Security Events

Auditing and logging security events in Elasticsearch is crucial for maintaining the integrity and security of your deployment. By enabling detailed logging, administrators can monitor access patterns, detect anomalies, and respond to security incidents effectively. This section will explore the configurations and best practices required for auditing and logging in Elasticsearch.

Elasticsearch provides built-in support for auditing security events through the use of the X-Pack plugin, which enhances the cluster's ability to track security-related activities.

Key actions that can be audited include:

- User logins and logouts
- Access to sensitive indices
- Execution of system-level operations
- Changes to roles and permissions

To enable auditing, you need to configure your elasticsearch.yml configuration file with the appropriate settings.

```
xpack.security.audit.enabled: true
xpack.security.audit.outputs: [ index, logfile ]
```

The xpack.security.audit.enabled setting activates the audit logging feature. The xpack.security.audit.outputs setting specifies where the audit events should be logged. The two primary outputs are:

- index: Logs audit events into a dedicated Elasticsearch index
- logfile: Logs audit events into a separate log file

To further customize the auditing process, additional settings can be applied. For example, to configure which events to log and which users' actions to monitor, you can use settings like these:

```
xpack.security.audit.logfile.events.include: [ "access_denied", "authentication_failed", "
    run_as_granted" ]
xpack.security.audit.logfile.events.exclude_users: [ "kibana", "logstash_system" ]
```

The xpack.security.audit.logfile.events.include setting specifies which events should be included in the audit logs. In this case, it includes events for access denied, authentication failure, and successful run-as operations. The xpack.security.audit.logfile.events.exclude_users setting can be used to exclude certain users, such as system users, from the audit logs.

The audit logs are stored in a structured format within the specified index or logfile. When storing logs in an Elasticsearch index, you can analyze and visualize them using tools like Kibana. For example, configuring Kibana to visualize audit logs can be performed quickly:

```
// Example Kibana Visualization Query
{
  "query": {
    "bool": {
      "must": [
        {
          "match": {
            "event.type": "access_denied"
          }
        },
        {
          "range": {
            "@timestamp": {
              "gte": "now-24h",
              "lt": "now"
            }
          }
        }
      ]
    }
  }
}
```

These settings allow administrators to detect unauthorized access attempts, scrutinize user activity, and ensure that compliance requirements are met. Detailed logs provide a wealth of information that is essential for forensic analysis following a security incident.

Next, it is important to ensure proper log rotation and retention practices. Log files can grow rapidly, and without appropriate management, they can consume significant disk space. In the log4j2.properties file, you can configure settings for log file rotation and retention:

```
appender.rolling.strategy.type = DefaultRolloverStrategy
appender.rolling.strategy.max = 7
appender.rolling.policies.type = Policies
appender.rolling.policies.size.type = SizeBasedTriggeringPolicy
appender.rolling.policies.size.size = 100MB
```

This configuration instructs the logging system to maintain up to 7 log files, each with a maximum size of 100MB.

In addition to configuration, system-level monitoring and alerts should be established. Elasticsearch and Kibana can work together to set up alerting mechanisms based on logged security events. For example, using Watcher—a feature within X-Pack—you can create and manage alerting tasks.

Here is an example of a Watcher configuration:

```
PUT _watcher/watch/logging_alert
{
  "trigger": {
    "schedule": {
```

```
      "interval": "10m"
    }
  },
  "input": {
    "search": {
      "request": {
        "indices": [
          ".security-audit-log-*"
        ],
        "body": {
          "query": {
            "bool": {
              "filter": [
                {
                  "range": {
                    "@timestamp": {
                      "from": "now-10m"
                    }
                  }
                },
                {
                  "terms": {
                    "event.type": ["access_denied", "authentication_failed"]
                  }
                }
              ]
            }
          }
        }
      }
    }
  },
  "actions": {
    "email_admin": {
      "email": {
        "to": "admin@example.com",
        "subject": "Security Alert on Elasticsearch Cluster",
        "body": "Potential security threat detected. Check the audit logs for more
            details."
      }
    }
  }
}
```

This configuration sets up an alert every 10 minutes, checking for access_denied and authentication_failed events in the last 10 minutes. If such events are found, an email notification is sent to the administrator.

By comprehensively setting up auditing and logging of security events, you ensure that your Elasticsearch deployment remains secure, compliant, and responsive to potential threats.

8.8 Implementing Field and Document-Level Security

Field and document-level security are essential features within Elasticsearch that enhance data safety by regulating access not only to entire indices but also to specific documents and fields within documents. By implementing these features, we ensure that sensitive information within a dataset is accessible only to authorized users, thus providing a granular level of security that aligns with organizational policies and compliance requirements.

Field-level security restricts access to particular fields within a document. This means that a user might have permissions to view some fields within a document, but not others. Document-level security restricts access to complete documents based on certain conditions. By combining these, highly granular access control can be achieved.

To implement field and document-level security, Elasticsearch employs the features provided by the X-Pack security module. The process involves configuring roles and permissions that define what each role can access. Below are the key steps and configurations required to set up field and document-level security.

1. **Install and Enable X-Pack**

   Ensure that X-Pack is installed and enabled in your Elasticsearch cluster. X-Pack is a commercial feature offered by Elastic that includes security features among other functionalities.

   ```
   bin/elasticsearch-plugin install x-pack
   bin/kibana-plugin install x-pack
   ```

   After installation, restart the Elasticsearch service to enable the plugin.

2. **Define Roles with Field-Level Security**

   Roles in Elasticsearch define what actions users can perform on indices and documents. To restrict access to specific fields, you configure roles to grant or deny access explicitly to those fields.

   An example configuration for a role that restricts access to certain fields might look like this:

   ```
   {
     "index_permissions": [
       {
   ```

```
      "names": [ "index_name" ],
      "privileges": [ "read" ],
      "field_security": {
        "grant": [ "allowed_field1", "allowed_field2" ],
        "except": [ "restricted_field" ]
      }
    }
  ]
}
```

In this JSON configuration:

- index_permissions defines the indices and the type of access.
- field_security.grant specifies the fields to which access is allowed.
- field_security.except lists the fields to which access is denied.

3. **Create Role Mappings**

   Once roles are defined with the necessary field-level security settings, map these roles to users or groups. This establishes which users can access which fields.

```
{
  "roles": [ "role_name" ],
  "rules": { "field": { "username": "user_name" } },
  "enabled": true
}
```

   This configuration assigns role_name to a user identified by username.

4. **Define Roles with Document-Level Security**

   Document-level security allows restricting access to documents based on certain conditions specified in a query. Use role definitions to include query to implement this restriction.

```
{
  "index_permissions": [
    {
      "names": [ "index_name" ],
      "privileges": [ "read" ],
      "query": {
        "term": { "department": "HR" }
      }
    }
  ]
}
```

   Here, the query ensures that users assigned this role can only access documents where the department is HR.

5. **Combining Field and Document-Level Security**

For comprehensive security, you can combine both field and document-level security within a single role definition. Below is an example:

```
{
  "index_permissions": [
    {
      "names": [ "index_name" ],
      "privileges": [ "read" ],
      "field_security": {
        "grant": [ "allowed_field1", "allowed_field2" ],
        "except": [ "restricted_field" ]
      },
      "query": {
        "term": { "department": "HR" }
      }
    }
  ]
}
```

In this example, the role restricts access to allowed_field1 and allowed_field2, denies access to restricted_field, and limits document access to those belonging to the HR department.

6. **Testing and Auditing Security Configurations**

To ensure that security configurations are functioning as intended, perform thorough testing:

```
curl -u user_name:password -X GET "http://localhost:9200/index_name/
    _search" -H 'Content-Type: application/json' -d'
{
  "_source": ["allowed_field1", "allowed_field2"],
  "query": {
    "match": { "department": "HR" }
  }
}'
```

Observe the response to verify that only allowed fields and documents are returned. Additionally, enable and review audit logs to trace access patterns and verify that unauthorized access attempts are blocked.

```
Successful response:
{
  "took": 15,
  "timed_out": false,
  "hits": {
    "total": 1,
    "max_score": 1.0,
    "hits": [
      {
        "_index": "index_name",
        "_type": "_doc",
        "_id": "1",
        "_score": 1.0,
        "_source": {
          "allowed_field1": "value1",
          "allowed_field2": "value2"
        }
      }
    ]
  }
}
```

By meticulously setting up and verifying field and document-level security using the roles, permissions, and audit features in Elasticsearch, we achieve fine-grained control over data access. This is pivotal in ensuring compliance with regulatory requirements and maintaining organizational data integrity.

8.9 Using X-Pack Security Features

X-Pack is a powerful extension available for Elasticsearch that enhances its security capabilities. X-Pack security consists of several functionalities such as authentication, authorization, encryption, and auditing. This section delves into the various security features provided by X-Pack, elucidating their configurations and applications.

The core components of X-Pack security are:

- **Authentication:** This involves verifying the identity of users trying to access the Elasticsearch cluster. Supported authentication mechanisms include:
  - Native Realm
  - LDAP Realm
  - Active Directory Realm
  - PKI/Certificate-Based Authentication
  - SAML Authentication

- OpenID Connect (OIDC) Authentication

Native Realm is often used for internal user management. Users can be managed via the Elasticsearch API. For example, to create a user:

```
POST /_security/user/new_user
{
  "password" : "new_user_password",
  "roles" : [ "user_role" ],
  "full_name" : "New User",
  "email" : "new_user@example.com",
  "metadata" : {
    "intelligence" : 7
  }
}
```

A similar approach applies to LDAP and Active Directory realms, where user data is obtained from external directory services. Configuration involves specifying LDAP/AD connection settings in the elasticsearch.yml file:

```
xpack.security.authc.realms.ldap.ldap1:
  order: 0
  url: "ldaps://ldap.example.com:636"
  bind_dn: "cn=admin,dc=example,dc=com"
  user_search.base_dn: "dc=example,dc=com"
```

- **Authorization:** Determines what authenticated users are allowed to do by assigning roles. To create and manage roles:

```
POST /_security/role/admin_role
{
  "cluster": ["all"],
  "indices": [
    {
      "names": [ "index1", "index2" ],
      "privileges": ["read", "write"],
      "field_security" : {
          "grant" : [ "title", "body" ]
      },
      "query": "{\"term\": { \"status\": \"published\" }}"
    }
  ]
}
```

Roles specify cluster-wide privileges as well as index-specific privileges. Field and document-level security are configured within roles to limit access to certain fields or documents based on specific queries.

- **Encryption:** X-Pack supports SSL/TLS encryption for transport and HTTP layers, ensuring that all communications with and within the Elasticsearch cluster are encrypted. Configuration involves creating certificates and using them in elasticsearch.yml:

```
xpack.security.transport.ssl.enabled: true
xpack.security.transport.ssl.verification_mode: full
xpack.security.transport.ssl.keystore.path: "certs/elastic-certificates.p12"
xpack.security.transport.ssl.truststore.path: "certs/elastic-certificates.p12"
```

Similarly, HTTPS can be configured for the HTTP layer:

```
xpack.security.http.ssl.enabled: true
xpack.security.http.ssl.keystore.path: "certs/http.p12"
xpack.security.http.ssl.truststore.path: "certs/http.p12"
```

- **Auditing:** Gathering and managing audit logs for security-related events. This feature tracks activities like authentication attempts, role assignments, and configuration changes. Configuration requires enabling auditing in elasticsearch.yml:

```
xpack.security.audit.enabled: true
xpack.security.audit.outputs: [ "index", "logfile" ]
xpack.security.audit.logfile.events.include: [ "authentication_success", "
    authentication_failed" ]
```

  This setup writes audit events to both an Elasticsearch index and log files, capturing successful and failed authentication attempts among other specified events.

The use of X-Pack security features fortifies the security stance of an Elasticsearch deployment. From robust authentication mechanisms to fine-grained access controls and comprehensive auditing capabilities, X-Pack enables a protected and controlled environment for sensitive data.

8.10 Hands-On: Securing Your Elasticsearch Cluster

Securing your Elasticsearch cluster is a multi-step process that involves configuring various security features to protect against unauthorized access and ensure data integrity. This section provides a detailed, step-by-step guide to securing an Elasticsearch cluster, combining theoretical concepts with practical commands and configurations.

Step 1: Enabling Elasticsearch Security Features

Elasticsearch security features are part of the X-Pack plugin, which must be installed and enabled. These features include authentication, role-based access control, IP filtering, and encrypted communications.

First, verify that X-Pack is installed. If not, you can install it using the following command:

```
bin/elasticsearch-plugin install x-pack
```

Step 2: Configuring TLS/SSL for Encrypted Communications

To secure the communications within the Elasticsearch cluster, it is essential to configure TLS/SSL.

Generate certificates for your nodes. Elasticsearch provides a utility called elasticsearch-certutil for this purpose.

```
bin/elasticsearch-certutil ca --out config/certificates/elastic-stack-ca.p12
bin/elasticsearch-certutil cert --ca config/certificates/elastic-stack-ca.p12 --out config/
    certificates/elastic-certificates.p12 --in config/certificates/instances.yml
```

Modify your elasticsearch.yml configuration file to use the generated certificates:

```
xpack.security.enabled: true
xpack.security.transport.ssl.enabled: true
xpack.security.transport.ssl.verification_mode: certificate
xpack.security.transport.ssl.keystore.path: config/certificates/elastic-certificates.p12
xpack.security.transport.ssl.truststore.path: config/certificates/elastic-certificates.p12
```

Step 3: Setting Up User Authentication

Define users and roles using the Elasticsearch user and role APIs. Begin by creating a user and assigning a predefined role.

```
POST /_security/user/my_user
{
  "password" : "mypassword",
  "roles" : [ "admin", "other_role1" ],
  "full_name" : "John Doe",
  "email" : "john.doe@example.com"
}
```

```
POST /_security/role/my_custom_role
{
  "cluster": ["all"],
  "indices": [
    {
      "names": [ "index1", "index2" ],
      "privileges": ["read","write"],
      "field_security" : {
        "grant" : [ "title", "body" ]
      },
      "query": {
        "term" : { "published" : true }
```

```
      }
    }
  ],
  "run_as": [ "other_user" ]
}
```

Assign the custom role to a user:

```
POST /_security/user/another_user
{
  "password" : "anotherpassword",
  "roles" : [ "my_custom_role" ],
  "full_name" : "Jane Doe",
  "email" : "jane.doe@example.com"
}
```

Step 4: Configuring IP Filtering

Configure IP filtering to control which IP addresses are allowed to connect to your cluster.

Edit the elasticsearch.yml file:

```
xpack.security.http.filter.allow: "10.0.0.0/24,192.168.0.1"
xpack.security.http.filter.deny: "0.0.0.0/0"
```

Step 5: Auditing and Logging Security Events

Enable security auditing to monitor and log security-related events.

Modify your elasticsearch.yml configuration file:

```
xpack.security.audit.enabled: true
xpack.security.audit.outputs: [ index, logfile ]
xpack.security.audit.logfile.events.include: [ "authentication_failed", "access_granted",
    "access_denied" ]
```

Step 6: Implementing Field and Document-Level Security

Field and document-level security allow you to restrict access to specific fields or documents.

Configure field and document-level security within a role definition:

```
PUT /_security/role/field_and_doc_level_security
{
  "indices": [
    {
      "names": [ "secured_index" ],
      "privileges": [ "read" ],
      "field_security": {
        "grant": [ "field1", "field2" ]
      },
      "query": {
        "term": { "status": "active" }
      }
    }
```

```
  ]
}
```

Assign this role to a user as previously described.

These steps provide a comprehensive approach to securing your Elasticsearch cluster, implementing both standard and advanced features to protect your data effectively.

Chapter 9

Monitoring and Maintenance

This chapter focuses on the crucial tasks of monitoring and maintaining an Elasticsearch deployment. It outlines key metrics to monitor, using Kibana for visual monitoring, and setting up comprehensive monitoring solutions. It also details the interpretation of Elasticsearch logs, performing health checks and cluster state assessments, and essential maintenance practices. Guidance on upgrading Elasticsearch, along with strategies for backing up and restoring data, ensures the reliability and resilience of your deployment.

9.1 Introduction to Monitoring Elasticsearch

Maintaining the operational health of an Elasticsearch deployment involves continuous monitoring of various metrics, logs, and states of the cluster. Proper monitoring ensures that potential issues can be identified and resolved before affecting the system's performance or availability. Effective monitoring is essential for diagnosing problems, planning capacity, and optimizing the overall performance of your Elasticsearch cluster.

Elasticsearch, an open-source search and analytics engine, provides comprehensive APIs and integration points for monitoring. These capabilities can be utilized to gain insights into the behavior and health of the cluster. The key objectives of monitoring include ensuring data availability, detecting performance bottlenecks, preempting potential failures, and scaling the system based on consumption patterns.

Key Metrics: Elasticsearch exposes several key metrics that are critical to monitor. These include node-level and cluster-level metrics such as CPU usage, memory usage, disk I/O, network statistics, and JVM (Java Virtual Machine) memory usage. Monitoring these metrics helps in detecting resource saturation, memory leaks, and potential node failures.

Logs for Diagnostic Purposes: Elasticsearch logs are another vital source of information. They provide visibility into the internal operations of Elasticsearch and can help identify misconfigurations, errors, and warnings that require attention. Logs can be segregated into various levels including DEBUG, INFO, WARN, ERROR, and TRACE, each providing different granularities of information.

Cluster Health and State: The cluster health status (green, yellow, or red) and the cluster state provide a summary of the cluster's overall health and operability. Regularly assessing these indicators ensures that shards are correctly allocated and that there are no red or yellow states indicating potential issues.

To begin with, setting up monitoring usually involves the following fundamental steps:

- Configuring Elasticsearch to emit metrics and logs.
- Utilizing monitoring tools and dashboards like Kibana to visualize and interpret these metrics and logs.
- Setting up alerting mechanisms to notify administrators of critical issues.

To configure Elasticsearch for monitoring, start by enabling and configuring the built-in monitoring features. Elasticsearch has a dedicated monitoring component that can be activated in the elasticsearch.yml configuration file:

```
# Enable Elasticsearch X-Pack Monitoring
xpack.monitoring.enabled: true
xpack.monitoring.collection.interval: 10s
xpack.monitoring.history.duration: 7d
```

Once enabled, Elasticsearch will begin to collect and index monitoring data at the specified interval. This data is typically stored in an .monitoring index pattern.

Kibana, the visualization tool for Elasticsearch, provides built-in dashboards for monitoring Elasticsearch. These dashboards can be accessed through Kibana's Monitoring UI, which presents a variety of visualizations for key performance metrics. For setting up Kibana for monitoring, it is crucial to ensure that it is configured to connect to the Elasticsearch instance.

```
# Kibana configuration for connecting to Elasticsearch
elasticsearch.hosts: ["http://localhost:9200"]
monitoring.kibana.collection.enabled: true
```

In addition to using Kibana, Elasticsearch metrics can be collected and visualized using other monitoring systems like Prometheus or Grafana. For configuring Prometheus, you can utilize the elasticsearch_exporter, a plugin that exposes Elasticsearch metrics in a format compatible with Prometheus. Below is an example configuration for Prometheus:

```
scrape_configs:
  - job_name: 'elasticsearch'
    static_configs:
      - targets: ['localhost:9200']
    metrics_path: '/metrics'
```

Moreover, setting up alerting is essential for proactive monitoring. Alerting can be configured using the Alerting features of X-Pack for Elasticsearch, which allow for the creation of watch conditions that generate alerts based on specific metric thresholds. For example, the following Watcher configuration checks for node CPU usage and sends alerts if it exceeds 80%:

```
PUT _watcher/watch/high_cpu_usage
{
  "trigger": {
    "schedule": { "interval": "1m" }
  },
  "input": {
    "search": {
      "request": {
        "indices": ["metricbeat-*"],
        "body": {
          "query": {
            "bool": {
              "filter": {
                "range": {
                  "system.cpu.total.pct": {
                    "gte": 0.8
                  }
                }
              }
```

```
            }
          }
        }
      }
    }
  },
  "actions": {
    "email_admin": {
      "email": {
        "to": "admin@example.com",
        "subject": "High CPU Usage Alert",
        "body": "Node CPU usage has exceeded 80%."
      }
    }
  }
}
```

For environments where Elasticsearch is deployed across multiple nodes or clusters, centralized logging and metrics aggregation become critical. Tools such as Logstash can be employed to collect, parse, and store logs from multiple Elasticsearch nodes into a centralized store for further analysis and visualization.

Monitoring must be a continuous process, involving regular review of visualization dashboards, periodic health checks, and adjusting alert thresholds as the deployment scales. Through meticulous attention to monitoring, potential issues can be preempted, ensuring a stable and high-performing Elasticsearch system.

9.2 Key Metrics to Monitor

Monitoring the right metrics is critical to ensure the optimal performance and health of your Elasticsearch deployment. Understanding and actively monitoring these key performance indicators can enable proactive measures to prevent issues and maintain efficient operations. Below, we delve into the most essential metrics.

Node Metrics

Node metrics pertain to the individual nodes within your Elasticsearch cluster. Key node metrics to monitor include:

JVM Heap Usage: Elasticsearch relies significantly on the Java Virtual Machine (JVM); thus, monitoring heap usage is vital. Measure jvm.heap_used_percent to ensure it is below 75

```
{
  "jvm": {
```

```
"memory": {
  "heap_used_percent": 65,
  "heap_committed_in_bytes": 1073741824,
  "heap_used_in_bytes": 687865856
},
"gc": {
  "collectors": {
    "young": {
      "collection_count": 15997,
      "collection_time_in_millis": 130217
    },
    "old": {
      "collection_count": 2,
      "collection_time_in_millis": 2160
    }
  }
}
}
}
```


CPU Usage: CPU utilization on Elasticsearch nodes should be consistently monitored to preempt performance bottlenecks. The node_cpu_-percent can provide an immediate assessment, and sustained usage above 75

Disk I/O: High disk I/O can indicate a potential bottleneck, particularly if accompanied by notable read or write latencies. Metrics such as node_fs_total_read_throttle_time_ms and node_fs_total_-write_throttle_time_ms can provide insights into your disk subsystem's performance.

Thread Pool Metrics: Elasticsearch employs various thread pools (e.g., search, index, bulk). Monitoring the active, queued, and rejected operations per thread pool is crucial. Metrics such as thread_pool.search.active, thread_pool.index.queue, and thread_pool.bulk.rejected enable detailed examination of processing bottlenecks.


```
{
  "thread_pool": {
    "search": {
      "threads": 8,
      "queue": 0,
      "active": 0,
      "rejected": 0,
      "largest": 8,
      "completed": 779828
    },
    "index": {
      "threads": 4,
      "queue": 0,
      "active": 0,
      "rejected": 0,
      "largest": 4,
      "completed": 539817
```

```
    },
    "bulk": {
      "threads": 2,
      "queue": 0,
      "active": 0,
      "rejected": 0,
      "largest": 2,
      "completed": 13245
    }
  }
}
```

Cluster-wide Metrics

Cluster-level metrics offer a comprehensive view of the cluster's health and stability.

Cluster Health Status: The overall cluster health status can be green, yellow, or red. A red status indicates unassigned primary shards, while yellow points to unassigned replica shards. Ideally, the cluster operates in a green state.

```
{
  "cluster_name" : "elasticsearch",
  "status" : "green",
  "timed_out" : false,
  "number_of_nodes" : 3,
  "number_of_data_nodes" : 3,
  "active_primary_shards" : 15,
  "active_shards" : 30,
  "relocating_shards" : 0,
  "initializing_shards" : 0,
  "unassigned_shards" : 0,
  "delayed_unassigned_shards" : 0,
  "number_of_pending_tasks" : 0,
  "number_of_in_flight_fetch" : 0,
  "task_max_waiting_in_queue_millis" : 0,
  "active_shards_percent_as_number" : 100.0
}
```

Indexing and Search Performance: Continually monitor the rate of indexing and search requests, as well as their associated latencies. Major metrics include indexing.index_total and indexing.index_time_in_millis, alongside search.query_total and search.query_time_in_millis.

Node Availability: Track the number of nodes and ensure no unexpected node drops. Monitor cluster_nodes_count and cluster_nodes_data_count to validate consistency.

Shard Distribution: A well-balanced shard distribution is essential for efficient operations. Metrics like shard_count per index and node, as well as shard_store can reflect the distribution status.

Index and Document Metrics

Monitoring index-level metrics provides deeper insights into data ingestion and storage.

Index Size and Document Count: Regular monitoring of index sizes and document counts, using index_store.size_in_bytes and index_docs.count, can help identify growth patterns and plan for scalability.

```
{
  "indices": {
    "index_name": {
      "primaries": {
        "docs": {
          "count": 10000,
          "deleted": 0
        },
        "store": {
          "size_in_bytes": 20971520,
          "throttle_time_in_millis": 0
        }
      },
      "total": {
        "docs": {
          "count": 20000,
          "deleted": 0
        },
        "store": {
          "size_in_bytes": 41943040,
          "throttle_time_in_millis": 0
        }
      }
    }
  }
}
```

Refresh and Flush Operations: Frequent refresh and flush operations can impact performance. Tracking index_refresh_total and index_flush_total helps identify inefficiencies and optimize refresh intervals.

Search Efficiency: Monitor search efficiency through search.fetch_total and search.fetch_time_in_millis metrics. Sudden spikes might indicate query performance issues.

Collectively, these metrics form the foundation for a robust monitoring strategy. Leveraging data from these metrics enables preemptive maintenance and optimizations, fostering a resilient and high-performing Elasticsearch environment.

9.3 Using Kibana for Monitoring

Kibana serves as the visualization layer for data stored in Elasticsearch, providing powerful tools to monitor and analyze the state and performance of your Elasticsearch clusters. Monitoring with Kibana involves setting up efficient dashboards that give insights into various metrics, helping in preemptive issue identification and resolution.

To begin with, Kibana must be configured to connect to the Elasticsearch instance containing the monitoring data. This typically involves specifying the Elasticsearch endpoint in the kibana.yml configuration file. A minimal example of this configuration is shown below:

```
elasticsearch.hosts: ["http://localhost:9200"]
```

Ensure that Kibana is running by navigating to the directory where Kibana is installed and executing the startup script:

```
./bin/kibana
```

Upon successful start, access Kibana via a web browser at http://localhost:5601. The interface provides several tabs, including Dashboard, Visualize, and Discover, which are essential for monitoring activities.

Creating and Using Dashboards

A dashboard is a collection of visualizations offering a comprehensive view of your cluster's performance. To create a new dashboard, follow these steps:

- Navigate to the Dashboard tab.
- Click on Create new dashboard.
- Select Add to import existing visualizations or create new ones.

Various pre-built visualizations can be imported from the Visualize Library, including those depicting CPU usage, disk I/O, cluster indexing rate, and search queries. Custom visualizations can be crafted using the Visualize tab:

- Go to Visualize.
- Click on Create visualization.
- Choose a visualization type (e.g., line chart, bar chart, pie chart).

- Select the appropriate index pattern and configure the visualization.

For example, a line chart showing the indexing rate would involve setting the metrics aggregation to Sum on the indexing_total field and bucketing the data by a suitable time interval.

Monitoring Key Metrics

Using Kibana for monitoring requires familiarity with key Elasticsearch metrics, typically collected through the X-Pack monitoring feature. These metrics include:

- **Cluster Health**: Indicates the overall status of the cluster, denoted as green, yellow, or red.
- **Node Statistics**: Covers metrics such as JVM heap usage, file system utilization, CPU and memory usage.
- **Index Metrics**: Includes metrics on document count, storage size, and indexing/search rates.

Visualization examples include:

```
{
  "index_name": "cluster_stats-*",
  "interval": "5m",
  "metrics": [
    {
      "field": "cluster_stats.status",
      "aggregation": "terms"
    },
    {
      "field": "node_stats.jvm.mem.heap_used_percent",
      "aggregation": "avg"
    }
    ...
  ]
}
```

Alerting and Notifications

Kibana integrates with Watcher (a part of X-Pack) to set up alerts on specific conditions. This is essential for proactive cluster management. A typical alert might notify the administrator if disk space exceeds 80%, or if JVM heap usage surpasses 75%.

To create an alert:

- Navigate to the Management tab.

- Select Watcher and then Create new watch.
- Define a condition script that checks relevant metrics.

Example of a simple watch trigger:

```
{
  "trigger": {
    "schedule": {
      "interval": "5m"
    }
  },
  "input": {
    "search": {
      "request": {
        "indices": ["node_stats-*"],
        "body": {
          "query": {
            "range": {
              "node_stats.os.cpu.load_average.1m": {
                "gt": 1.0
              }
            }
          }
        }
      }
    }
  },
  "actions": {
    "email_admin": {
      "email": {
        "to": "admin@example.com",
        "subject": "High CPU Load Alert",
        "body": "CPU load average for the last 1 minute is above 1.0."
      }
    }
  }
}
```

Interpreting Data Through Visualization

Interpreting the collected data requires understanding the context of each metric. For instance:

- **Heap Usage**: Regularly very high heap usage may indicate inefficient queries or need for cluster scaling.
- **CPU Load**: Consistently high CPU can signal shard or query contention. Consider node scaling or readjusting shard allocations.
- **Disk I/O**: Persistent high disk I/O may necessitate evaluating storage architectures or query optimizations.

Visualizations should be designed with thresholds and baselines that make anomalies immediately evident. Ensure dashboards are regularly reviewed and updated to reflect the evolving nature of your cluster's workload.

In practice, Kibana's extensibility and integration capabilities make it an indispensable tool for maintaining Elasticsearch clusters, providing a customizable and interactive means of monitoring and ensuring optimal cluster health and performance.

9.4 Setting Up Elasticsearch Monitoring

Effective monitoring of Elasticsearch is pivotal to ensure smooth operations, availability, and performance of the cluster. Setting up Elasticsearch monitoring involves multiple steps and the use of various tools and APIs provided specifically for this purpose. This section provides a detailed approach to setting up a comprehensive monitoring system for Elasticsearch.

Prerequisites: Before setting up monitoring for Elasticsearch, ensure that:

- Elasticsearch is installed and running.
- Kibana is installed and configured to interface with the Elasticsearch cluster.
- You have administrative access to both Elasticsearch and the underlying systems.

1. Enabling Monitoring in Elasticsearch: Elasticsearch provides built-in monitoring features via the x-pack plugin. First, ensure that the monitoring feature is enabled in your Elasticsearch configuration by setting the following in the elasticsearch.yml file:

```
xpack.monitoring.enabled: true
```

Then, to start collecting monitoring data, Elasticsearch needs to be configured to send its metrics to a monitoring cluster. If you decide to send data to the same cluster, add:

```
xpack.monitoring.exporters:
  local:
    type: local
```

This configuration indicates that monitored data will be stored within the same Elasticsearch cluster.

2. Configuring Kibana for Monitoring: Once monitoring is enabled on Elasticsearch, you'll need to set up Kibana to visualize the metrics being collected. In the kibana.yml configuration file, enable monitoring by setting:

```
xpack.monitoring.ui.enabled: true
```

Restart the Kibana service to apply these changes. Kibana provides several built-in dashboards for Elasticsearch monitoring, which will now be accessible under the *Monitoring* section.

3. Monitor Master Node: Monitoring the master node is crucial as it manages the cluster state and coordinates activities. Using Kibana, navigate to the *Monitoring* section, and select *Elasticsearch → Nodes*. Here, you will find metrics such as CPU usage, memory usage, and the JVM heap used by the master node.

For more granular control, Elasticsearch exposes the _nodes/stats API to fetch node statistics. Execute a REST request to retrieve these details:

```
curl -X GET "localhost:9200/_nodes/stats?pretty"
```

4. Monitor Indices: Indices are the core of Elasticsearch; hence monitoring their health and performance is vital. Kibana provides detailed insights into index statistics like index size, number of documents, and index refresh times. To automate index monitoring, Elasticsearch offers the _cat/indices API:

```
curl -X GET "localhost:9200/_cat/indices?v"
```

Output:

```
health status index       uuid                   pri rep docs.count docs.deleted store.size pri.store.size
green  open   log-2023.10 97U97b7_MJG8G-Wa7sSp7g   1   1        101            0    213.6kb        106.8kb
```

5. Monitoring with External Tools: For enterprises requiring a more robust monitoring solution, integration with external monitoring systems like Prometheus and Grafana can be achieved using 'exporter-exporter' plugins. For instance, setting up Prometheus involves deploying the Prometheus Elasticsearch Exporter plugin.

Steps to configure Prometheus:

- Download and install the Prometheus Elasticsearch exporter.
- Configure the exporter to gather metrics from Elasticsearch by adding the following configuration in prometheus.yml:

```
scrape_configs:
  - job_name: 'elasticsearch'
    static_configs:
      - targets: ['localhost:9200']
```

- Visualize the collected metrics through Grafana by adding Prometheus as a data source and importing a prebuilt Elasticsearch monitoring dashboard.

6. Setting Alerts: Setting up alerts notifies administrators of issues proactively. ElastAlert is an open-source tool used to detect changes and anomalies in real-time. Configure alerts by defining a rule in a YAML file.

Example configuration for triggering an alert when CPU usage exceeds 80%:

```
name: "Elasticsearch CPU Usage"
type: "metric_aggregation"
index: "metricbeat-*"
buffer_time:
  minutes: 15
metric_agg_key: "system.cpu.total.pct"
metric_agg_type: "avg"
query_key: "host.name"
doc_type: "_doc"
realert:
  minutes: 1
alert:
  - "email"
alert_subject: "High CPU Usage on {0}"
alert_text: "CPU usage is at {1}% on host {0}"
email:
  - "admin@example.com"
```

This configuration indicates that an email alert will be sent if the average CPU usage metric crosses the threshold.

Setting up Elasticsearch monitoring involves configuring both Elasticsearch and Kibana, leveraging APIs for detailed metrics, using external monitoring tools, and establishing alerting mechanisms. Each step ensures comprehensive visibility into the Elasticsearch cluster's performance and health, enabling timely interventions and maintaining optimal operational efficiency.

9.5 Understanding Elasticsearch Logs

Logs are an essential component for monitoring and troubleshooting Elasticsearch. They provide valuable insights into the behavior and health of the Elasticsearch cluster. Elasticsearch logs are categorized mainly into two types: server logs and slow logs. Understanding how to interpret and manage these logs is crucial for maintaining the robust performance of your Elasticsearch deployment.

Elasticsearch uses Log4j 2 for logging, which means you can configure logging settings to capture various levels of detail. The primary log levels are DEBUG, INFO, WARN, ERROR, and FATAL. By default, Elasticsearch logs are stored in the 'logs' directory of your Elasticsearch installation.

Server Logs:

Server logs encompass all the routine operations executed by Elasticsearch. They capture essential events such as node startups and shutdowns, cluster state changes, garbage collection logs, and error messages. The configuration for server logs is found in the 'log4j2.properties' file.

Here is an example configuration snippet from the 'log4j2.properties' file:

```
appender.rolling.type = RollingFile
appender.rolling.name = rolling
appender.rolling.fileName = ${sys:es.logs.base_path}/${sys:es.logs.cluster_name}.log
appender.rolling.filePattern = ${sys:es.logs.base_path}/${sys:es.logs.cluster_name}-%d
    {yyyy-MM-dd}.log.gz
appender.rolling.layout.type = PatternLayout
appender.rolling.layout.pattern = [%d{ISO8601}][%-5p][%-25c] %marker%m%n
appender.rolling.policies.type = Policies
appender.rolling.policies.time.type = TimeBasedTriggeringPolicy
appender.rolling.policies.time.interval = 1
appender.rolling.policies.time.modulate = true
appender.rolling.policies.size.type = SizeBasedTriggeringPolicy
appender.rolling.policies.size.size = 10MB
rootLogger.level = info
rootLogger.appenderRef.rolling.ref = rolling
```

This configuration specifies that the server logs are rolled over daily and compressed into '.gz' files. The log level is set to 'INFO', which means that logs will capture informational messages and severe events but not debug-level details.

Slow Logs:

Slow logs provide insights into the performance of search and indexing operations. They help identify slow queries and indexing operations that might be impacting cluster performance. Slow logs are configured within the 'elasticsearch.yml' file.

Here is an example configuration of slow logs:

```
index.search.slowlog.threshold.query.warn: 10s
index.search.slowlog.threshold.query.info: 5s
index.search.slowlog.threshold.query.debug: 2s
index.search.slowlog.threshold.query.trace: 500ms
index.search.slowlog.threshold.fetch.warn: 1s
index.search.slowlog.threshold.fetch.info: 800ms
index.search.slowlog.threshold.fetch.debug: 500ms
index.search.slowlog.threshold.fetch.trace: 200ms

index.indexing.slowlog.threshold.index.warn: 10s
index.indexing.slowlog.threshold.index.info: 5s
index.indexing.slowlog.threshold.index.debug: 2s
index.indexing.slowlog.threshold.index.trace: 500ms
```

In this configuration, a search query taking longer than 10 seconds will be logged at the 'WARN' level. This granularity allows administrators to diagnose performance issues by correlating slow log entries with other metrics and logs.

Log Analysis:

Analyzing logs often involves tools like the *Elasticsearch Logger*, *Filebeat*, or directly viewing the log files using tools like 'less' and 'grep'. Elasticsearch logs often include the following key information:

- Timestamp: Indicates when the log event occurred.
- Log Level: Provides the severity of the log message (e.g., INFO, WARN, ERROR).
- Component/Class: Shows which part of Elasticsearch generated the log message.
- Message: Describes the event or error in detail.

Example server log entry:

```
[2023-01-01T00:00:00,000][INFO ][o.e.n.Node] [node-1] started
```

Example search slow log entry:

```
[2023-01-01T00:00:00,000][WARN ][i.s.s.query          ] [node-1]
[index][0] took[12s], took_millis[12000], total_hits[1], types[data]
```

For server logs, log management tools like Filebeat can forward logs to a central analysis system such as the Elasticsearch Stack (ELK).

Filebeat is particularly useful for managing and aggregating logs across multiple nodes.

```
filebeat.inputs:
- type: log
  enabled: true
  paths:
    - /path/to/elasticsearch/logs/*.log

output.elasticsearch:
  hosts: ["http://localhost:9200"]
```

This configuration sends log files from the specified paths to an Elasticsearch instance listening on 'localhost'. Analyzing these logs with Kibana can provide visual insights into patterns and anomalies.

In an operational context, setting appropriate log levels and regularly reviewing logs helps ensure the health and stability of the Elasticsearch cluster. Detailed log analysis can uncover underlying issues impacting cluster performance and help timely troubleshooting and maintenance actions.

9.6 Health Check and Cluster State

Monitoring the health of your Elasticsearch cluster is a foundational task to ensure optimal performance and reliability. Elasticsearch provides several APIs that allow administrators to check the health status and the state of the cluster comprehensively. Understanding how to interpret this data is critical for maintaining a healthy system.

Cluster Health API is a central tool for gauging the overall health of an Elasticsearch deployment. It provides easy access to information such as the status, number of nodes, and number of active shards. To retrieve the cluster health status, the following API call can be used:

```
GET /_cluster/health
```

The response from this API call provides various fields, of which the most critical ones include:

- **status**: This field can have one of three values: *green*, *yellow*, or *red*.
- *Green* status indicates that all primary and replica shards are active.

- *Yellow* status signifies that all primary shards are active, but some replica shards are not.
- *Red* status means some primary shards are not active, indicating potential data loss.
- **number_of_nodes**: The total number of nodes in the cluster.
- **active_primary_shards**: Number of primary shards that are currently active.
- **active_shards**: Total number of active primary and replica shards.
- **relocating_shards**: Number of shards that are currently being relocated.
- **unassigned_shards**: Shards that are not currently allocated to any node.

The cluster health status can be used in maintaining SLAs (Service Level Agreements) and ensuring minimal downtime. Regular checks and automated alerts based on the *status* field can prevent small issues from escalating into critical failures.

Cluster State API offers a deeper dive into the current state of the cluster. This API provides comprehensive information about the nodes, the indices, and the shard allocation. A basic request can be made using:

```
GET /_cluster/state
```

The response includes multiple sections, with some of the most relevant fields being:

- **cluster_name**: Name of the cluster.
- **nodes**: An object that contains information related to each node, such as node ID, name, transport address, and roles.
- **metadata**: Contains metadata about all indices, including index settings, mappings, and aliases.
- **routing_table**: Detailed information on the distribution of shards across the nodes.
- **routing_nodes**: Information on routing allocation of nodes.

- **blocks**: Any blocks that may prevent index or read/write operations.

Administrators can leverage this data to understand and visualize the entire cluster state, facilitating effective troubleshooting and capacity planning.

Ensuring optimal performance also involves regular execution of the **Cluster Checkup API**. This API evaluates the cluster configurations and provides recommendations based on the Elasticsearch version in use.

```
GET /_cluster/checkup
```

Results from this API can indicate issues related to cluster settings, index configuration, and other best practices. Regularly reviewing these recommendations can prevent performance degradation and streamline maintenance tasks.

In addition, monitoring the **Pending Tasks API** is necessary for understanding the tasks queued in the cluster. Bottlenecks or delays in task processing can be early indicators of underlying issues.

```
GET /_cluster/pending_tasks
```

The response includes:

- **tasks**: A list of current pending tasks, containing fields such as time_in_queue, priority, and source.

By regularly checking the pending tasks, administrators can ensure that management tasks like shard allocation, index creation, and node operations are running smoothly without unnecessary delays.

Lastly, performing regular **Cluster Allocation Explain API** checks assists in understanding why certain shards are not allocated. This API explains the decision-making process of the allocator, providing insight into allocation issues.

```
GET /_cluster/allocation/explain
```

The crucial insights provided include:

- **index**: Name of the index.
- **shard**: Shard number.

- **primary**: Boolean indicating if it is a primary shard.
- **current_state**: Current allocation state.
- **unassigned_info**: Reason for unassignment and relevant metadata.
- **node_allocation**: Information detailing why a shard is or isn't assigned to a node.

Using these APIs ensures comprehensive monitoring and maintenance of the Elasticsearch cluster. Regular health checks and thorough understanding of the cluster state contribute to the high availability and performance of the deployment.

9.7 Maintenance Tasks and Best Practices

Effective maintenance of an Elasticsearch cluster is vital for ensuring its long-term health and performance. This section delineates critical maintenance tasks and best practices that should be regularly executed to sustain the robustness of the cluster.

Regularly Monitoring Cluster Health is paramount. Utilize endpoints such as _cluster/health which provides an overall health status. The command to retrieve cluster health is as follows:

```
curl X GET "localhost:9200/_cluster/health?pretty"
```

The output will be:

```
{
  "cluster_name" : "elasticsearch",
  "status" : "green",
  "timed_out" : false,
  "number_of_nodes" : 5,
  "number_of_data_nodes" : 5,
  "active_primary_shards" : 10,
  "active_shards" : 20,
  "relocating_shards" : 0,
  "initializing_shards" : 0,
  "unassigned_shards" : 0,
  "delayed_unassigned_shards" : 0,
  "number_of_pending_tasks" : 0,
  "number_of_in_flight_fetch" : 0,
  "task_max_waiting_in_queue_millis" : 0,
  "active_shards_percent_as_number" : 100.0
}
```

Maintaining shard allocation awareness is essential. Use the command to inspect current allocation settings:

```
curl -X GET "localhost:9200/_cluster/settings?include_defaults=true&pretty"
```

Ensure that disk-based allocation settings are appropriately configured by examining cluster.routing.allocation.disk parameters. Adjust as needed to preclude issues related to disk space shortages.

Index management is another pivotal maintenance task. Regularly optimizing indices involves operations like force merging segments to improve search performance but should be used judiciously. Execute the following command to perform a force merge:

```
curl -X POST "localhost:9200/my_index/_forcemerge?max_num_segments=1&pretty"
```

Routine deletion of old or unnecessary indices is recommended to conserve disk space and improve cluster performance. For example, delete an index using:

```
curl -X DELETE "localhost:9200/old_index?pretty"
```

Right-sizing index shards involves ensuring that the number and size of shards are optimal for your use case. Over-sharding can lead to inefficient resource utilization whereas too few shards might impede future scaling.

Proper management and rotation of logs is crucial for diagnosing issues. Elasticsearch logs are typically located at /var/log/elasticsearch/. Implement log rotation using tools like logrotate to prevent logs from consuming excessive storage.

Taking snapshots for data backup is a critical practice. These can be restored in the event of data corruption or loss. Use the following commands to register a snapshot repository and to take a snapshot:

```
# Register a snapshot repository
curl -X PUT "localhost:9200/_snapshot/my_backup" -H 'Content-Type: application/
    json' -d'
{
  "type": "fs",
  "settings": {
    "location": "/mount/backups/my_backup",
    "compress": true
  }
}
'

# Take a snapshot
curl -X PUT "localhost:9200/_snapshot/my_backup/snapshot_1?wait_for_completion
    =true"
```

Routinely apply updates and patches to Elasticsearch to mitigate security vulnerabilities and benefit from the latest enhancements. Always test the updates on a staging environment before deploying to production. The below commands will check for and apply updates:

```
# Check current version
curl -X GET "localhost:9200"

# Update Elasticsearch
sudo apt-get update
sudo apt-get install elasticsearch
```

Security considerations entail regular audits of user roles and permissions. Elasticsearch supports fine-grained access control, which should be leveraged to minimize potential risks. Review and modify roles as necessary through:

```
PUT /_security/role/kibana_user
{
  "cluster": ["monitor"],
  "index": [
    {
      "names": ["kibana_sample_data_*"],
      "privileges": ["read"]
    }
  ]
}
```

Ensuring timely and systematic maintenance tasks will support a high-performing and reliable Elasticsearch cluster. Adhering to these best practices helps mitigate downtime and enhance the system's longevity.

9.8 Upgrading Elasticsearch Safely

Upgrading Elasticsearch is a critical process that necessitates meticulous planning and execution to ensure minimal disruption and optimal functionality. The upgrade process depends on the current version of the Elasticsearch cluster and the target version. Upgrading typically involves moving to a newer minor or major version, each with its own set of steps and considerations. This section will outline necessary preparations, the upgrade procedure, and post-upgrade verifications.

Preparation Steps:

- **Review Release Notes**: Thoroughly examine the release notes of the target version. These notes contain crucial information about new features, enhancements, breaking changes, and deprecated functionalities that could impact your cluster.

- **Compatibility Checks**: Verify the compatibility of your existing Elasticsearch version with the target version. It is generally advisable to upgrade to the latest minor or patch version of the current major release before moving to a new major version. The Elasticsearch Upgrade Assistant in the Kibana UI can help identify version compatibility issues and provide recommendations.

- **Backup Data**: Before initiating the upgrade, conduct a full backup of your data. This acts as a safeguard against potential data loss during the upgrade process. Use the snapshot and restore functionality to create and store snapshots:

```
PUT /_snapshot/my_repository/snapshot_1
{
  "indices": "index1,index2",
  "ignore_unavailable": true,
  "include_global_state": false
}
```

- **Test the Upgrade**: If possible, test the upgrade process on a staging cluster that mirrors the production environment. This allows for the identification of potential issues in a controlled environment.

- **Check Plugins and Scripts**: Ensure that all installed plugins and custom scripts are compatible with the target version. Some plugins may require upgrades or replacements.

Upgrade Procedure:

- **Rolling Upgrade**: This method involves upgrading nodes in the cluster one at a time, allowing the cluster to remain operational. Rolling upgrades are supported between minor versions without downtime. Follow these steps:

  - **Step 1: Disable Allocation and Set Read-Only Indexes**

```
PUT /_cluster/settings
{
  "persistent": {
    "cluster.routing.allocation.enable": "none"
  }
}
```

```
PUT /*/_settings
{
  "settings": {
    "index.blocks.write": true
  }
}
```

- **Step 2: Upgrade a Node** Shut down, upgrade Elasticsearch, and restart each node one at a time. Ensure the cluster is green (healthy) before proceeding to the next node.
- **Step 3: Re-enable Allocation**

```
PUT /_cluster/settings
{
  "persistent": {
    "cluster.routing.allocation.enable": "all"
  }
}
\end{lstisting}
\begin{lstlisting}
PUT /*/_settings
{
  "settings": {
    "index.blocks.write": false
  }
}
```

- **Full Cluster Restart**: This method involves stopping the entire cluster, upgrading all nodes, and then restarting the cluster. This method is required when upgrading major versions or when rolling upgrades are not feasible.
  - **Step 1: Stop the Cluster** Shut down all nodes in the cluster.
  - **Step 2: Upgrade Nodes** Upgrade Elasticsearch on all nodes to the new version.
  - **Step 3: Start the Cluster** Restart the upgraded nodes. Ensure all nodes are operational and that the cluster is healthy.

Post-Upgrade Verifications:

- **Cluster Health Check**: Confirm that the cluster status is green by querying the cluster health endpoint:

```
GET /_cluster/health
```

- **Reindexing**: For major version upgrades, reindex indices that were created in previous major versions. This can be achieved using the _reindex API:

```
POST /_reindex
{
  "source": {
    "index": "old_index"
  },
  "dest": {
    "index": "new_index"
  }
}
```

- **Validate Plugins and Scripts**: Verify that all plugins and scripts are functioning as expected. Address any compatibility issues identified during the preparatory steps.
- **Restore Normal Operations**: Remove any temporary configurations set during the preparation or upgrade process and resume normal operations.

These steps collectively ensure a safe and efficient upgrade process, minimizing disruptions while enhancing the Elasticsearch deployment with new capabilities.

9.9 Backing Up and Restoring Data

Ensuring the safety of your data is paramount in any Elasticsearch deployment. Backing up and restoring data are crucial procedures that protect against data loss due to hardware failures, software issues, or accidental deletions. This section provides comprehensive instructions for effectively backing up and restoring data within Elasticsearch.

Elasticsearch provides a snapshot and restore mechanism designed to handle these tasks efficiently. Snapshots capture the state of a cluster at a given point in time, allowing for a complete recovery of data and associated metadata. The key steps for implementing backup and restore are configuring a repository, taking snapshots, and restoring from those snapshots.

Configuring a Repository

Before creating a snapshot, it is necessary to configure a repository, which is a shared storage location where the snapshots will be stored. Elasticsearch supports various repository types, including filesystem, Amazon S3, and other cloud storage platforms.

```
PUT /_snapshot/my_backup
```

```
{
  "type": "fs",
  "settings": {
    "location": "/mnt/my_backup_location"
  }
}
```

In this example, a filesystem repository named my_backup is created at the location /mnt/my_backup_location. Ensure that the specified location is accessible and writable by all Elasticsearch nodes in the cluster.

Taking Snapshots

Once a repository is configured, you can take snapshots of individual indices or the entire cluster. A snapshot process can be started using the following command:

```
PUT /_snapshot/my_backup/snapshot_1
{
  "indices": "index_1,index_2",
  "ignore_unavailable": true,
  "include_global_state": false
}
```

This command creates a snapshot named snapshot_1 in the my_-backup repository, including index_1 and index_2. The parameters used in this command are:

- indices: A comma-separated list of indices to include in the snapshot.
- ignore_unavailable: If true, the snapshot process continues even if some indices are missing or closed.
- include_global_state: Determines if the global cluster state is included in the snapshot. It is set to false to only back up selected indices.

The status of ongoing snapshots can be monitored using:

```
GET /_cat/snapshots/my_backup?v
```

Restoring Snapshots

Restoring data from a snapshot is a crucial step when recovering from data loss or corruption. To restore a snapshot, the following command is used:

```
POST /_snapshot/my_backup/snapshot_1/_restore
{
  "indices": "index_1,index_2",
  "ignore_unavailable": true,
  "include_global_state": false,
  "rename_pattern": "index_(.+)",
  "rename_replacement": "restored_index_$1"
}
```

In the example above, indices index_1 and index_2 are restored from the snapshot snapshot_1. The parameters and their purposes are as follows:

- indices: Specifies the indices to restore from the snapshot.
- ignore_unavailable: Continues the restore process even if some indices do not exist in the snapshot.
- include_global_state: If true, the global cluster state is also restored.
- rename_pattern and rename_replacement: These parameters enable renaming the restored indices. In this example, indices are renamed from index_1 to restored_index_1 and so forth.

The restore status can be checked using similar commands as for snapshot status.

Best Practices for Backup and Restore

Ensuring the reliability and consistency of snapshots is essential:

- Snapshot Frequency: Regular snapshots reduce the risk of data loss. Determine an appropriate frequency based on your update patterns and data criticality.
- Off-site Storage: Store snapshots in a separate location from the primary data to protect against site-wide failures.
- Snapshot Validation: Periodically validate snapshots by restoring them to a test cluster. This practice ensures that the backup is reliable and can be used for a successful recovery.
- Access Control: Protect snapshot repositories with appropriate access controls to prevent unauthorized deletion or alteration.

The incorporation of these practices into your monitoring and maintenance routines helps ensure the resilience and integrity of your Elasticsearch deployment.

9.10 Hands-On: Implementing Monitoring Solutions

Implementing robust monitoring solutions is vital to maintain the performance, reliability, and excellent service quality of an Elasticsearch cluster. This section guides you step-by-step through practical approaches to setting up and leveraging monitoring tools for effective Elasticsearch management.

To start, we will use Elasticsearch's built-in monitoring, Kibana, and Metricbeat to implement a simplified yet comprehensive monitoring solution.

Prerequisites

Ensure the following are installed and correctly configured:

- Elasticsearch: Version 7.0 or later.
- Kibana: Equivalent version to your Elasticsearch installation.
- Metricbeat: A data shipper for monitoring.

Enabling Monitoring in Elasticsearch

Elasticsearch provides X-Pack monitoring features, which, from version 6.3 onward, include a Basic license enabling basic monitoring features. To enable monitoring:

```
# Configuration in elasticsearch.yml
xpack.monitoring.enabled: true
```

After modifying the elasticsearch.yml file, restart your Elasticsearch node:

```
sudo systemctl restart elasticsearch
```

Configuring Kibana for Monitoring

Next, configure Kibana to visualize the monitoring data. Open the kibana.yml file and add the monitoring settings:

```
# Configuration in kibana.yml
xpack.monitoring.ui.enabled: true
xpack.monitoring.elasticsearch.hosts: ["http://localhost:9200"]
```

Restart Kibana to apply the changes:

```
sudo systemctl restart kibana
```

Now, navigate to the Monitoring tab in Kibana's interface. It can be found under:

Management > Stack Monitoring

Here, you should see the health and performance metrics of your Elasticsearch cluster.

Setting Up Metricbeat

Metricbeat collects and forwards metrics to Elasticsearch. It is particularly useful for monitoring system-level metrics such as CPU usage, memory usage, and Elasticsearch-specific metrics.

Install Metricbeat using the package manager for your operating system. For example, on Debian-based systems:

```
sudo apt-get install metricbeat
```

After installation, configure Metricbeat by editing metricbeat.yml:

```
# Configuration in metricbeat.yml
output.elasticsearch:
  hosts: ["http://localhost:9200"]
setup.kibana:
  host: "http://localhost:5601"
```

Enable the Elasticsearch module within Metricbeat:

```
sudo metricbeat modules enable elasticsearch
```

Load the default dashboards and start Metricbeat to begin collecting metrics:

```
sudo metricbeat setup
sudo service metricbeat start
```

Viewing Metricbeat Data in Kibana

Once Metricbeat is active, its data should start appearing in Kibana. Navigate to the Dashboards tab to find predefined dashboards for Elasticsearch and system metrics.

Kibana > Dashboard > [Metricbeat Elasticsearch] Overview

These dashboards provide insights into various aspects of your Elasticsearch cluster, including index performance, node statistics, search latencies, and more.

Alerting and Actions

To detect issues promptly, Kibana allows the configuration of alerts based on predefined conditions. Alerts can be set up via the Monitoring UI:

Stack Management > Alerts and Insights > Alerts

Here, you can define alert conditions, specify actions, and choose notification channels like email or webhooks.

Maintenance and Future Expansions

While basic monitoring setup is crucial, expanding it to include additional nodes and leveraging more advanced features like anomaly detection and machine learning for predictive maintenance is beneficial. Elasticsearch's rich ecosystem allows deep customizations and integrations to fit specific requirements seamlessly.

Implementing said monitoring solutions ensures the high availability, performance, and reliability of your Elasticsearch clusters, enabling prompt response to arising issues effectively.

Chapter 10

Extending Elasticsearch with Plugins

This chapter explores how to extend Elasticsearch's functionality using plugins. It covers the types of plugins available, the process of installing and managing them, and highlights popular plugins that enhance Elasticsearch's capabilities. Additionally, it provides guidance on developing custom plugins, extending ingest pipelines, and enhancing search and query functions. The chapter also discusses monitoring, performance, and security plugins, offering practical insights into creating and deploying your first plugin.

10.1 Introduction to Elasticsearch Plugins

Elasticsearch plugins play a crucial role in extending and customizing the functionalities of an Elasticsearch deployment. Their modular nature allows users to seamlessly add new features and capabilities to Elasticsearch without altering the core software. This section elucidates the fundamentals of Elasticsearch plugins, their benefits, and their overarching structure within the Elasticsearch ecosystem.

Plugins in Elasticsearch are components that augment the platform by adding specific capabilities. These can range from providing additional analyzers, discovery modules, and snapshot repositories to more complex tasks such as integrating with external monitoring systems or offering advanced security features. The design of Elasticsearch plugins is such that they remain decoupled from the core system, ensuring that updates and changes to Elasticsearch itself do not necessarily disrupt the function of the plugins.

One of the primary advantages of using plugins is their ability to enhance Elasticsearch's capabilities without necessitating custom builds or modifications to the source code. This modularity enables a high degree of customization, allowing users to tailor their Elasticsearch instances precisely to their needs. Furthermore, the community-driven nature of plugin development ensures a diverse and continually growing repository of functionality.

Plugins in Elasticsearch can be broadly categorized into several types:

- Analysis Plugins: These provide additional analyzers, tokenizers, and filters that help in text processing.
- Discovery Plugins: These allow Elasticsearch nodes to discover each other using custom discovery mechanisms.
- Ingest Plugins: These add processors to the Elasticsearch ingest pipeline.
- Snapshot/Restore Plugins: These plugins allow backing up and restoring indices using custom repositories.
- Management Plugins: These include functionalities for cluster management and can integrate with external management systems.
- Security Plugins: These enhance the security aspects of Elasticsearch, providing features like advanced authentication, authorization, auditing, and more.

To illustrate, consider the following example, which outlines the structure of a typical plugin installation:

```
bin/elasticsearch-plugin install analysis-icu
```

By executing this command, the ICU Analysis Plugin, which provides support for ICU (International Components for Unicode) enhancements, is added to the Elasticsearch instance. The plugin facilitates multilingual support, making Elasticsearch more adept at handling international text processing.

When a plugin is installed, it is registered with Elasticsearch, and its components are made available for configuration and usage. This interaction is typically managed through Elasticsearch's configuration files, where parameters related to the plugin can be specified. For example:

```
xpack.security.enabled: true
xpack.monitoring.collection.enabled: true
```

Here, the 'xpack.security.enabled' and 'xpack.monitoring.collection.enabled' options are used to enable specific features provided by the X-Pack plugin, which is a bundle of advanced features offered by Elasticsearch.

The lifecycle of a plugin within Elasticsearch begins with its installation and includes initialization during startup. Elasticsearch scans for available plugins in the designated plugin directory and loads them. The following is an excerpt from typical startup logs showcasing the initialization of plugins:

```
[2023-03-15T10:15:30.123Z] [INFO ][o.e.p.PluginsService     ] [node-1] loaded plugin [analysis-icu]
[2023-03-15T10:15:30.123Z] [INFO ][o.e.p.PluginsService     ] [node-1] loaded plugin [x-pack-core]
[2023-03-15T10:15:30.123Z] [INFO ][o.e.p.PluginsService     ] [node-1] loaded plugin [x-pack-security]
```

As depicted, the log entries indicate the successful loading of several plugins, such as 'analysis-icu' and 'x-pack-core'. This process is fundamental to ensuring that the plugins are registered and ready for use within the Elasticsearch environment.

Beyond installation, managing plugins involves updating and removing them. Updates are typically performed by installing the newer version of the plugin, which automatically replaces the older version. Removal of plugins is critical for deprecating unused or potentially conflicting functionalities. The command used for removal is analogous to the installation command but with a removal flag:

```
bin/elasticsearch-plugin remove analysis-icu
```

Executing this command ensures that the 'analysis-icu' plugin is purged from the Elasticsearch instance.

As we progress further in this chapter, we will delve deeper into the categories of plugins available, methods for installing and managing them efficiently, and provide insights into popular plugins that enhance Elasticsearch's capabilities significantly. Understanding the foundational aspects of Elasticsearch plugins arms users with the knowledge required to optimize their Elasticsearch deployments through strategic plugin utilization.

10.2 Types of Plugins

Elasticsearch plugins extend the functionality of the core system in various ways. The plugins can be broadly categorized based on their functionalities: Node Plugins, Ingest Plugins, Analysis Plugins, Mapper Plugins, Snapshot/Restore Plugins, Discovery Plugins, and Security Plugins. Each type of plugin serves different purposes and addresses distinct needs within Elasticsearch environments.

Node plugins typically add new features to Elasticsearch nodes. These features might include custom REST handlers, additional circuit breakers, or extra cluster-level settings. One such example is the Prometheus Exporter plugin, which integrates with Prometheus for monitoring and exposing metrics of the Elasticsearch cluster.

Ingest plugins focus on enhancing the ingest pipeline in Elasticsearch. These plugins add processors that can transform, enrich, or otherwise manipulate data before it gets indexed. For instance, the Ingest Attachment plugin enables extracting and indexing content from a myriad of file formats, thereby enriching the textual content of documents.

Analysis plugins enrich the text analysis process during indexing and querying. Custom analyzers, tokenizers, and token filters can be added via these plugins, significantly extending the capability of built-in Elasticsearch text analysis modules. The popular ICU Analysis plugin adds advanced linguistic information processing capabilities that are vital for handling Unicode text.

Mapper plugins contribute to managing custom data types in Elasticsearch. These plugins are instrumental when there is a need to define custom field mappers. An example is the Mapper Murmur3 plugin which provides a new field data type for computing Murmur3 hash signatures of string values, useful for deduplication or categorizing documents.

Snapshot/Restore plugins extend the built-in snapshot and restoration capabilities of Elasticsearch. Examples include Azure and Google Cloud plugins, enabling Elasticsearch to interact with these cloud storage providers for snapshot and restore operations. This extends the data resilience and disaster recovery capabilities directly to cloud infrastructures.

Discovery plugins facilitate the discovery and communication between nodes in a cluster. Specialized network environments can leverage these plugins to aid in forming larger, resilient Elasticsearch clusters.

The Zen Discovery plugin, which is often pre-packaged with Elasticsearch, automates node discovery for scaling clusters horizontally and ensuring high availability.

Finally, security plugins are paramount in enterprises requiring strict access controls and data security measures. These plugins add authentication, authorization, and audit capabilities. The widely used Elasticsearch Security plugin (part of the X-Pack) integrates features like role-based access control, encrypted communications, and audit logging.

```
public class CustomRestHandler extends BaseRestHandler {
    @Override
    public String getName() {
        return "custom_rest_handler";
    }

    @Override
    public List<Route> routes() {
        return Collections.singletonList(new Route(RestRequest.Method.GET, "/
              _custom"));
    }

    @Override
    protected RestChannelConsumer prepareRequest(RestRequest request, NodeClient
          client) throws IOException {
        return channel -> {
            XContentBuilder builder = channel.newBuilder();
            builder.startObject();
            builder.field("message", "Hello, world!");
            builder.endObject();
            channel.sendResponse(new BytesRestResponse(RestStatus.OK, builder));
        };
    }
}
```

The CustomRestHandler class in the sample Java code showcases a simple REST handler implemented as a node plugin. It defines a new endpoint (_custom) that, when accessed, returns a JSON response containing a simple message, "Hello, world!"

```
{
  "message": "Hello, world!"
}
```

Choosing the appropriate type of plugin depends on the specific requirements and the desired extended functionality. By understanding these categories, developers can effectively leverage plugins to enhance their Elasticsearch deployments.

This corrected version addresses the reported error and adheres to the specified LaTeX formatting guidelines.

10.3 Installing and Managing Plugins

Elasticsearch plugins augment the core functionalities of Elasticsearch, empowering users with additional features tailored to specific needs. Efficient installation and management of plugins are pivotal for seamless Elasticsearch operations. Ensuring compatibility and leveraging the advancements plugins bring are key procedures. This section outlines the steps required for installing, removing, and managing plugins in Elasticsearch.

Installing Plugins

To install a plugin, Elasticsearch provides a straightforward command-line interface. Assume we are installing the analysis-icu plugin, which provides advanced text analysis using the ICU library. The installation command is:

```
./bin/elasticsearch-plugin install analysis-icu
```

Executing this command initiates the download and installation process of the specified plugin. The installation process might involve server restarts to apply the new configurations effectively. After installation, it's prudent to verify whether the plugin is successfully integrated by listing all installed plugins:

```
./bin/elasticsearch-plugin list
```

This command outputs a list of all currently installed plugins, ensuring the desired plugin is active.

Removing Plugins

Similarly, should the need arise to uninstall a plugin due to incompatibilities or updates, Elasticsearch provides a command for safe removal. For instance, to remove the analysis-icu plugin, one would execute:

```
./bin/elasticsearch-plugin remove analysis-icu
```

Post-removal, it is advisable to restart the Elasticsearch service to confirm the changes are enforced and to maintain system stability.

Handling Plugin Upgrades

Upgrading plugins is essential to leverage new features, performance improvements, and security patches. The upgrade process typically involves removing the old version of the plugin and subsequently installing the new version. For example, to upgrade the ingest-attachment plugin:

- Remove the existing plugin:

```
./bin/elasticsearch-plugin remove ingest-attachment
```

- Install the latest version:

```
./bin/elasticsearch-plugin install ingest-attachment
```

Alternately, if Elasticsearch is upgraded, it's usually necessary to reinstall all plugins as part of the migration process. Before performing upgrades, consult the plugin documentation for any specific instructions or migration steps.

Plugin Management via Configuration Files

While most plugin interactions occur via the command line, some plugins require additional configuration via YAML files or JSON scripts to define behaviors and interaction patterns. These configurations are generally specified in the elasticsearch.yml file. For example, configuring the repository-s3 plugin might involve adding:

```
s3.client.default:
  access_key: <your_access_key>
  secret_key: <your_secret_key>
  region: us-west-1
```

Enhanced plugin management often requires adjusting Elasticsearch's configuration settings, ensuring plugins interact correctly with other components within the cluster.

Best Practices and Troubleshooting

Ensure that plugins are consistent with the Elasticsearch version in use. Installing incompatible plugins can lead to runtime errors or system instability. Always read the plugin's official documentation regarding version compatibility and specific installation instructions.

In the event of encountering errors during installation or usage of plugins, logs and standard output provide diagnostic information. Examine the Elasticsearch logs, typically located in the logs/ directory, to uncover error specifics and rectify them. Common problems might include network issues, permissions, or resource constraints.

Securing Plugin Installations

Ensuring plugins are sourced from trusted repositories mitigates the risk of introducing malicious code. Elasticsearch's plugin management restricts installations to secure URLs by default. For when an on-premises repository or air-gapped environment necessitates plugin files to be downloaded manually, use:

```
./bin/elasticsearch-plugin install file:///path/to/plugin.zip
```

Verify the integrity of downloaded plugin files using checksums provided by the plugin author. This practice guarantees that the plugin hasn't been tampered with and is safe to integrate into your Elasticsearch environment.

Managing plugins requires attention to compatibility, security, and proper configuration. By adhering to these guidelines, Elasticsearch can be effectively augmented to cater to diverse operational requirements, ensuring robust and efficient performance.

10.4 Popular Elasticsearch Plugins

Elasticsearch's versatility and performance can be significantly augmented through the use of plugins. These extensions offer a broad array of functionalities, from enriching search capabilities to enhancing security. Below, we discuss several popular Elasticsearch plugins that are widely used within the industry.

1. X-Pack

X-Pack is a comprehensive package offering a suite of features, including security, alerting, monitoring, reporting, and machine learning capabilities. Initially developed as various Elasticsearch plugins, these features are now integrated into a single extension to simplify management.

- **Security** provides role-based access control (RBAC), IP filtering, and audit logging, ensuring that your data is protected against unauthorized access.
- **Alerting** enables the creation of alerts based on queries, helping to monitor the cluster and data usage effectively.
- **Monitoring** provides detailed insights into the performance and health of your Elasticsearch clusters, indices, and nodes.
- **Reporting** allows for the generation of on-demand and scheduled reports.

- **Machine Learning** automates anomaly detection and provides predictive insights to identify issues before they impact performance.

To install X-Pack, you can use the following command within your Elasticsearch installation directory:

```
bin/elasticsearch-plugin install x-pack
```

2. Ingest Attachment Processor

The ingest-attachment plugin extends the ingest node functionality to process binary documents. It's based on Apache Tika and enables Elasticsearch to extract content from various file formats, including PDFs, MS Office documents, and others, making it searchable.

To install the ingest-attachment plugin, execute:

```
bin/elasticsearch-plugin install ingest-attachment
```

After installation, you can create an ingest node pipeline to process attachments:

```
PUT _ingest/pipeline/attachment
{
  "description": "Extract attachment information",
  "processors": [
    {
      "attachment": {
        "field": "data",
        "indexed_chars": -1
      }
    }
  ]
}
```

3. Analysis ICU

The analysis-icu plugin provides advanced text analysis capabilities for handling international content. It includes tokenization, collation, and normalizations that cater to multiple languages. This plugin leverages the International Components for Unicode (ICU) library and is ideal for applications requiring precise text handling for languages with complex characters.

To install the analysis-icu plugin, use:

```
bin/elasticsearch-plugin install analysis-icu
```

Example usage:

```
PUT /my_index
{
  "settings": {
    "analysis": {
      "analyzer": {
        "default": {
          "type": "custom",
          "tokenizer": "icu_tokenizer",
          "filter": ["icu_normalizer", "icu_folding"]
        }
      }
    }
  }
}
```

4. Analysis Kuromoji

The analysis-kuromoji plugin is designed for Japanese language text analysis. It uses the Kuromoji Japanese morphological analyzer, providing tokenization and filtering supportive of the Japanese language intricacies.

To install the analysis-kuromoji plugin, run:

```
bin/elasticsearch-plugin install analysis-kuromoji
```

Example analyzer configuration:

```
PUT /my_index
{
  "settings": {
    "analysis": {
      "analyzer": {
        "kuromoji_analyzer": {
          "type": "custom",
          "tokenizer": "kuromoji_tokenizer",
          "filter": ["kuromoji_baseform", "kuromoji_stemmer", "
              kuromoji_katakana_stemmer"]
        }
      }
    }
  }
}
```

5. Analysis Nori

The analysis-nori plugin is tailored for Korean text analysis. It uses the Seunjeon library for morphological analysis and tokenization, optimized for Korean language properties.

To install the analysis-nori plugin:

```
bin/elasticsearch-plugin install analysis-nori
```

Example custom analyzer:

```
PUT /my_index
{
  "settings": {
    "analysis": {
      "analyzer": {
        "nori_analyzer": {
          "type": "custom",
          "tokenizer": "nori_tokenizer",
          "filter": ["nori_part_of_speech"]
        }
      }
    }
  }
}
```

6. Discovery EC2

The discovery-ec2 plugin facilitates the automatic discovery of Elasticsearch nodes on Amazon EC2. It uses the EC2 API for node discovery, supporting a dynamic scaling environment.

To install the discovery-ec2 plugin, use:

```
bin/elasticsearch-plugin install discovery-ec2
```

For configuration, the 'elasticsearch.yml' file should include:

```
discovery:
    ec2:
        endpoint: ec2.us-east-1.amazonaws.com
        regions: [us-east-1]
        host_type: private_dns
cloud:
    aws:
        access_key: YOUR_ACCESS_KEY
        secret_key: YOUR_SECRET_KEY
```

7. Repository S3

The repository-s3 plugin allows Elasticsearch to use Amazon S3 as a repository for snapshot and restore functionalities.

To install the repository-s3 plugin:

```
bin/elasticsearch-plugin install repository-s3
```

Configure your S3 repository:

```
PUT _snapshot/my_s3_repository
{
  "type": "s3",
  "settings": {
    "bucket": "my-bucket",
    "region": "us-east-1"
  }
}
```

Numerous other plugins can extend Elasticsearch capabilities significantly. When selecting or using plugins, always ensure compatibility with your Elasticsearch version and thoroughly review the plugin documentation to understand potential impacts on system performance and security.

10.5 Developing Custom Plugins

Developing custom plugins for Elasticsearch provides a significant opportunity for extending its core functionalities to meet specific application requirements. This section elaborates on the different aspects of creating a custom plugin, including the necessary setup, structure, implementation, and deployment.

First, it is essential to establish a suitable development environment for Elasticsearch plugin development. This typically involves ensuring that compatible versions of Elasticsearch, JDK (Java Development Kit), and any necessary build tools such as Gradle or Maven are installed.

The structure of an Elasticsearch plugin follows a well-defined format. A plugin is generally composed of:

- **Plugin Class**: The entry point of the plugin, which extends the abstract class org.elasticsearch.plugins.Plugin.
- **Plugin Descriptor**: A file named plugin-descriptor.properties, which provides metadata about the plugin.
- **Java Classes and Resources**: The actual implementation code and any additional resources.

A typical directory structure for an Elasticsearch plugin might look like:

```
my-plugin/
|-- src/
|   |-- main/
|       |-- java/
|           |-- org/
|               |-- example/
|                   |-- MyPlugin.java
|       |-- resources/
|           |-- plugin-descriptor.properties
|-- build.gradle
```

Within the plugin-descriptor.properties file, the following properties must be specified:

```
# Plugin descriptor properties
name=example-plugin
description=An example Elasticsearch plugin
version=1.0.0
elasticsearch.version=7.10.0
java.version=1.8
classname=org.example.MyPlugin
```

The above properties define the plugin's name, description, version, compatible Elasticsearch version, required Java version, and the fully qualified class name of the plugin's entry point.

Next, we define the plugin entry point class. This class must extend org.elasticsearch.plugins.Plugin. Depending on the plugin's purpose (e.g., a custom analysis plugin, a custom search component), it might also need to extend other classes or implement specific interfaces. The following example demonstrates a simple plugin that logs a message during initialization:

```
package org.example;

import org.apache.logging.log4j.LogManager;
import org.apache.logging.log4j.Logger;
import org.elasticsearch.plugins.Plugin;

public class MyPlugin extends Plugin {

    private static final Logger logger = LogManager.getLogger(MyPlugin.class);

    public MyPlugin() {
        logger.info("MyPlugin has been initialized.");
    }

    // Additional plugin functionality goes here
}
```

Depending on the functionality, you may need to override specific methods or provide implementations of various classes to extend Elasticsearch's core capabilities. For instance, if developing a custom analysis plugin, one might need to implement a custom TokenizerFactory:

```
package org.example.analysis;

import org.apache.lucene.analysis.TokenStream;
import org.elasticsearch.index.analysis.AbstractTokenizerFactory;
import org.elasticsearch.index.analysis.TokenizerFactory;

public class CustomTokenizerFactory extends AbstractTokenizerFactory {

    protected CustomTokenizerFactory(IndexSettings indexSettings, Environment env,
            String name, Settings settings) {
        super(indexSettings, name);
    }

    @Override
```

```
    public TokenStream create() {
        // Implement custom tokenizer logic here
        return new CustomTokenizer();
    }
}
```

Finally, you will need to configure your build tool to package the plugin correctly. With Gradle, this involves setting up the build.gradle file to include dependencies and define the packaging task:

```
plugins {
    id 'java'
}

group 'org.example'
version '1.0.0'

repositories {
    mavenCentral()
}

dependencies {
    compile "org.elasticsearch:elasticsearch:${elasticsearchVersion}"
}

jar {
    manifest {
        attributes(
            'Plugin-Class': 'org.example.MyPlugin'
        )
    }
    from {
        configurations.compile.collect { it.isDirectory() ? it : zipTree(it) }
    }
}
```

Once the plugin code is written and configured, build the plugin using the Gradle command:

```
./gradlew clean build
```

This command generates a JAR file in the build/libs directory, which can then be installed in the Elasticsearch plugins directory. After placing the plugin JAR file in the plugins directory, restart the Elasticsearch node to load the new plugin.

Monitoring the logs during startup can provide useful insights into whether the plugin loaded successfully or if any errors occurred. It's important to integrate comprehensive logging and error handling within the plugin to ensure observability and ease of debugging during the development phase.

Developing custom plugins for Elasticsearch involves a thorough understanding of the core functionalities of Elasticsearch and the specific extension points provided by its plugin APIs. It allows users to tailor the search and analysis engine to precise application needs, augmenting the native capabilities with bespoke features that can significantly enhance the overall utility and performance of the Elasticsearch deployment.

10.6 Extending Ingest Pipelines with Plugins

Ingest pipelines in Elasticsearch provide a mechanism to transform and enrich documents before they are indexed. This pre-processing step is essential for tasks such as data normalization, enrichment, and extraction of structured fields from unstructured data. The fundamental building blocks of ingest pipelines are processors, which perform specific transformations on your data. While Elasticsearch offers a broad range of built-in processors, there are occasions when custom transformations are necessary to meet unique business requirements. This is where ingest pipeline plugins come into play.

Plugins extend the functionality of Elasticsearch by adding custom processors to ingest pipelines. These plugins are Java-based extensions that are registered with Elasticsearch during runtime, allowing you to define custom logic for data transformation.

To create a custom ingest pipeline plugin, follow these steps:

1. Set Up Your Development Environment: Ensure you have the necessary tools and libraries to develop and build Elasticsearch plugins, including the Java Development Kit (JDK) and Gradle build system.

```
# Clone the Elasticsearch repository
git clone https://github.com/elastic/elasticsearch.git
cd elasticsearch

# Check out the branch that corresponds to your Elasticsearch version
git checkout <version-branch>
```

2. Define the Plugin Class: Create a new Java class that extends the Plugin class provided by Elasticsearch. This class serves as the entry point for your plugin and includes metadata such as the plugin name and version.

```
public class MyCustomProcessorPlugin extends Plugin implements
    IngestPlugin {

  @Override
  public Map<String, Processor.Factory> getProcessors(Processor.
      Parameters parameters) {
    Map<String, Processor.Factory> processors = new HashMap<>();
    processors.put("my_custom_processor", new MyCustomProcessor.
        Factory());
    return processors;
  }
}
```

3. Implement the Processor: Define the custom processor by implementing the Processor interface. This involves handling the specific transformation logic that your processor will apply to the documents.

```
public class MyCustomProcessor implements Processor {

  private final String field;
  private final String value;

  public MyCustomProcessor(String tag, String description, String field,
      String value) {
    super(tag, description);
    this.field = field;
    this.value = value;
  }

  @Override
  public IngestDocument execute(IngestDocument document) {
    document.setFieldValue(field, value);
    return document;
  }

  @Override
  public String getType() {
    return "my_custom_processor";
  }

  public static final class Factory implements Processor.Factory {

    @Override
    public MyCustomProcessor create(Map<String, Object> config,
        Processor.Parameters parameters) throws Exception {
      String field = (String) config.get("field");
      String value = (String) config.get("value");
      return new MyCustomProcessor(null, null, field, value);
    }
  }
}
```

4. Register the Processor: Register your custom processor in the Plugin class through the getProcessors method. This step makes your custom processor available to ingest pipelines.

5. Build and Deploy the Plugin: Use Gradle to build the plugin JAR

file. Once built, place the JAR file in the plugins directory of your Elasticsearch installation and restart the Elasticsearch node to load the new plugin.

```
# Build the plugin
./gradlew assemble

# Copy the plugin to the Elasticsearch plugins directory
cp build/distributions/my-custom-processor-plugin-1.0.0.zip $ES_HOME/
    plugins/

# Restart Elasticsearch to load the plugin
cd $ES_HOME
./bin/elasticsearch restart
```

6. Configure the Pipeline: Define an ingest pipeline in Elasticsearch that uses your custom processor. This is done by sending a PUT request to the endpoint _ingest/pipeline with the pipeline definition.

```
PUT _ingest/pipeline/my_custom_pipeline
{
  "description": "A pipeline to use my custom processor",
  "processors": [
    {
      "my_custom_processor": {
        "field": "foo",
        "value": "bar"
      }
    }
  ]
}
```

7. Test the Pipeline: Send documents to the ingest pipeline endpoint to ensure that your custom processor is executing as expected.

```
POST my_index/_doc?pipeline=my_custom_pipeline
{
  "foo": "initial value"
}

# Verify that the document has been processed
GET my_index/_doc/<doc_id>
```

In this manner, custom processors enhance the ingest pipelines, enabling complex and specialized data transformations directly within Elasticsearch. This flexibility is pivotal for scenarios where out-of-the-box processors do not suffice, offering a pathway to tailor the ingestion process to specific business logic and workflow requirements.

10.7 Enhancing Search and Query Capabilities

Elasticsearch is renowned for its robust search and query capabilities, and plugins offer a powerful means to extend these functionalities even further. In this section, we will delve into several plugins that enhance search and query capabilities, providing detailed insights on how they work and how to integrate them into your Elasticsearch environment.

Phrase Suggestion Plugin

The phrase suggestion plugin enhances the query completion process by suggesting phrase completions based on indexed text. This is particularly useful for applications where accurate and quick suggestions are critical, such as search engines or predictive text systems.

```
POST /_search
{
  "suggest": {
    "text": "quick brown foks",
    "phrase-suggestion": {
      "phrase": {
        "field": "content",
        "direct_generator": [{
          "field": "content",
          "suggest_mode": "always"
        }]
      }
    }
  }
}
```

In this query, the text "quick brown foks" is corrected to "quick brown fox" based on the content of the indexed documents. The plugin uses a phrase suggester with a direct_generator to produce accurate corrections.

Regex Query Plugin

The regex query plugin allows users to perform searches using regular expressions. Regular expressions offer a powerful method to define search patterns, enabling more flexible and complex search criteria.

```
POST /_search
{
  "query": {
    "regexp": {
      "name": "Jo.* Doe"
    }
  }
}
```

In this example, the regex query searches for documents where the name field matches the pattern "Jo.* Doe", thus capturing variations like "John Doe", "Johnny Doe", etc.

Custom Scoring Plugin

The custom scoring plugin enhances search capabilities by allowing the implementation of custom scoring algorithms. This can be useful for tailoring search results to specific application needs.

Below is an example of how to use a custom script to influence the scoring of search results:

```
POST /_search
{
  "query": {
    "function_score": {
      "query": {
        "match": {
          "content": "elasticsearch"
        }
      },
      "script_score": {
        "script": {
          "source": "doc['popularity'].value * _score"
        }
      }
    }
  }
}
```

In this example, the score is influenced by a custom script where the document's popularity field dynamically adjusts the score during the search.

Percolator Plugin

The percolator plugin, which is integral to the Elasticsearch core, allows for the registration of queries and the subsequent matching of new documents to these queries. This is highly useful in scenarios where analysis or alerts need to be triggered based on the insertion of new documents.

To use the percolator, first register a query:

```
PUT /my-index/_doc/1?refresh
{
  "query": {
    "match": {
      "message": "Elasticsearch"
    }
  }
}
```

Next, to percolate a new document against the registered queries:

```
POST /my-index/_percolate
{
  "doc": {
    "message": "Using Elasticsearch for search and analytics"
  }
}
```

The result indicates which registered queries match the new document, enabling advanced alerting and notification systems.

Query Rewrite Plugin

The query rewrite plugin allows for the rewriting of queries before execution, enhancing the flexibility and precision of search functionality. This can be advantageous for optimizing queries or modifying them based on specific criteria.

```
// Java code for a custom query rewriter:
public class CustomQueryRewriter extends RewriteScript {
    @Override
    public XContentBuilder rewriter(QueryBuilder originalQuery) {
        // Custom logic to rewrite the original query
        QueryBuilder rewrittenQuery = QueryBuilders.matchAllQuery();
        return rewrittenQuery.toXContent(jsonBuilder(), ToXContent.
              EMPTY_PARAMS);
    }
}
```

While adding such a plugin involves additional steps in the development and deployment process, the ability to programmatically control query modification can lead to substantial improvements in search precision and performance.

Phrase Matching with Span Queries

Span queries allow for precise matching of sequences of terms in a flexible manner. The span_near query, for example, can be used to find documents where terms appear in close proximity to each other.

```
POST /_search
{
  "query": {
    "span_near": {
      "clauses": [
        { "span_term": { "content": "quick" } },
        { "span_term": { "content": "brown" } },
        { "span_term": { "content": "fox" } }
      ],
      "slop": 1,
      "in_order": true
    }
  }
}
```

Here, the span_near query looks for documents where "quick", "brown", and "fox" appear in sequence with no more than one intervening term.

Enhanced search and query capabilities in Elasticsearch through the use of these plugins provide users with the tools necessary for precise, efficient, and powerful search solutions suitable for a wide range of applications.

10.8 Monitoring and Performance Plugins

Elasticsearch clusters, while robust and highly scalable, often require monitoring and optimization to maintain optimal performance, especially in production environments. Monitoring and performance plugins offer advanced tools and metrics to ensure clusters operate efficiently. These plugins provide insights into various aspects of Elasticsearch, including resource usage, query performance, indexing rates, and potential bottlenecks.

Monitoring plugins like Elastic's Monitoring, Prometheus Exporter, and Eland help track cluster health and performance metrics. They typically integrate with dashboards such as Kibana and Grafana for visualization. Performance optimization plugins like Search Guard or ReadOnlyREST enhance the efficiency and security of Elasticsearch operations.

When deploying monitoring plugins, it is crucial to understand their data collection processes, integration points, and possible impacts on performance. Here, we delve into several prominent monitoring and performance plugins.

- **Elastic's Monitoring Plugin**

  Elastic's Monitoring plugin, part of the Elastic Stack, provides comprehensive monitoring capabilities. It collects data about cluster health, performance, nodes, indices, and shards, storing this data within Elasticsearch itself for analysis and visualization through Kibana.

  ```
  bin/elasticsearch-plugin install x-pack-monitoring
  ```

  Once installed, the plugin provides metrics such as CPU usage, memory consumption, disk I/O, and network traffic. It also alerts administrators to potential issues like slow queries or node failure.

- **Prometheus Exporter**

  Prometheus Exporter is another popular plugin for monitoring Elasticsearch. It exposes Elasticsearch metrics in a format compatible with Prometheus, which can then scrape these metrics for analysis and visualization in Grafana.

```
bin/elasticsearch-plugin install https://github.com/vvanholl/elasticsearch-
    prometheus-exporter/releases/download/7.10.0.0/prometheus-exporter
    -7.10.0.0.zip
```

  Prometheus Exporter provides a wide range of metrics covering nodes, indices, and cluster-wide statistics. This integration is particularly valuable in environments already utilizing Prometheus for monitoring other services.

- **Eland**

  Eland is a plugin for Elasticsearch focused on simplifying the interaction with Elasticsearch data using Python. While not strictly a monitoring tool, it can be used to track and analyze performance metrics by leveraging Python's data science libraries.

```
pip install eland
```

  With Eland, you can convert Elasticsearch queries into Pandas DataFrames for in-depth analysis. It facilitates efficient data processing and visualization, making it a valuable tool for performance monitoring and troubleshooting.

- **Search Guard**

  For performance optimization, Search Guard offers extensive security features, enhancing authentication, authorization, and encryption within Elasticsearch clusters. Improved security measures can lead to better performance by preventing unauthorized access and reducing the attack surface.

```
bin/elasticsearch-plugin install com.floragunn:search-guard-7:7.x-49.0.0
```

  Search Guard also provides tools for compliance auditing and monitoring, further ensuring the integrity and efficient operation of Elasticsearch environments.

- **ReadOnlyREST**

  ReadOnlyREST is another security-focused plugin that enhances Elasticsearch performance by enforcing strict access controls. It applies filters based on user roles, IP addresses, and other criteria, preventing unauthorized operations that could degrade cluster performance.

  ```
  bin/elasticsearch-plugin install readonlyrest-1.31.0_es7.10.0.zip
  ```

  By managing privileges effectively, ReadOnlyREST minimizes the risk of resource-intensive queries run by unauthorized users, ensuring consistent and reliable cluster performance.

Analyzing data collected by these plugins helps administrators identify and rectify performance issues before they escalate. Effective use of monitoring and performance plugins leads to a proactive approach in maintaining Elasticsearch clusters, ensuring they remain performant and resilient under varying loads.

We can visualize the monitoring data using tools like Kibana, which displays metrics in a user-friendly interface. Below is an example illustrating how to configure monitoring settings in the kibana.yml file:

```
# Monitoring Settings
monitoring.ui.enabled: true
monitoring.kibana.collection.enabled: true
monitoring.elasticsearch.collection.enabled: true
```

Using Kibana, administrators can create dashboards that aggregate various metrics, providing a holistic view of the cluster's performance. Tools like Grafana offer similar functionalities when paired with Prometheus, enabling complex visualizations and alert configurations.

Incorporating these plugins into your Elasticsearch deployment not only aids in identifying performance bottlenecks but also fortifies security and access control, leading to a robust and smoothly functioning search infrastructure.

10.9 Security and Access Control Plugins

When deploying Elasticsearch in a production environment, securing the cluster and controlling access is crucial. Security and access control plugins provide the necessary tools to enforce strong authentication, authorization, audit logging, and data encryption. This section delves into the various plugins available for enhancing the security and access management of your Elasticsearch deployment.

At the core, Elasticsearch offers basic security features in its X-Pack extension, which includes a range of functionalities such as TLS encryption, user authentication, role-based access control (RBAC), IP filtering, and auditing. However, third-party plugins also exist that provide additional capabilities or alternative approaches to security and access control.

Elastic Security (formerly X-Pack Security)

Elastic Security, integrated into the X-Pack extension, is a comprehensive suite that includes several security features essential for protecting your Elasticsearch cluster:

1. **Transport Layer Security (TLS)**: Encrypts communications within the Elasticsearch cluster and between clients to prevent eavesdropping and tampering. TLS ensures data integrity and confidentiality.

```
bin/elasticsearch-certutil ca --out config/certs/ca.zip
bin/elasticsearch-certutil cert --ca config/certs/ca.zip --out config/certs/certs.zip
unzip config/certs/certs.zip -d config/certs
```

2. **User Authentication**: Allows for multiple realms (e.g., native, LDAP, Active Directory) to authenticate users. It supports pluggable authentication mechanisms.

```
# config/elasticsearch.yml
xpack.security.enabled: true

# config/users
# Native user definition
useradd -c "John Doe" -u johndoe -p passwd1234 -r superuser
```

3. **Role-Based Access Control (RBAC)**: Assigns roles to users, defining privileges at a granular level, such as document-level security and field-level security.

```
# config/roles.yml
power_user:
  cluster: [ "all" ]
  indices:
    - names: [ "*" ]
      privileges: [ "all" ]

# config/users_roles
power_user: johndoe
```

4. **IP Filtering**: Controls the IP addresses that can access the cluster, adding an extra layer of security by blocking unauthorized IP addresses.

```
# config/elasticsearch.yml
xpack.security.http.filter.allow: "192.168.0.0/16, 10.0.0.0/8"
xpack.security.http.filter.deny: "0.0.0.0/0"
```

5. **Audit Logging**: Keeps track of security-related events such as login attempts, access control changes, and authentication failures, providing comprehensive audit trails.

```
# config/elasticsearch.yml
xpack.security.audit.enabled: true
xpack.security.audit.outputs: [ "index", "logfile" ]
```

Search Guard

Search Guard is a third-party plugin that offers similar features to Elastic Security but includes additional capabilities and customizable authentication and authorization modules. It provides:

- **Multitenancy**: Allows multiple tenants to securely share the same Elasticsearch cluster, isolating their data, visualizations, and dashboards.
- **Advanced Security Modules**: Includes Kerberos integration, JSON web token (JWT) support, and an enhanced audit logging framework.
- **Compliance Features**: Features such as anonymization, pseudonymization, and field-level encryption that help meet regulatory requirements (e.g., GDPR).

```
bin/elasticsearch-plugin install com.floragunn:search-guard-6:${es.version}
```

```
# config/elasticsearch.yml
searchguard.ssl.transport.enabled: true
searchguard.ssl.transport.keystore_filepath: CN=sgadmin-keystore.jks
searchguard.ssl.transport.truststore_filepath: truststore.jks
searchguard.authcz.admin_dn:
  - CN=sgadmin,OU=SSL,O=Test,L=Test,C=DE
```

Open Distro for Elasticsearch Security

Open Distro for Elasticsearch, an open-source project, also offers extensive security measures. The security plugin includes all the essential features such as TLS encryption, RBAC, and audit logging as well as advanced features:

- **Attribute-Based Access Control (ABAC)**: Extends RBAC by considering user attributes during access control decisions.
- **Document- and Field-Level Security**: Ensures sensitive information is only visible to authorized users.
- **Security Dashboards**: Provides real-time visual insights into security configurations and events.

```
bin/elasticsearch-plugin install opendistro_security
```

```
# config/elasticsearch.yml
opendistro_security.ssl.http.enabled: true
opendistro_security.ssl.http.pemcert_filepath: esnode.pem
opendistro_security.ssl.http.pemkey_filepath: esnode-key.pem
opendistro_security.authcz.admin_dn:
  - CN=admin,OU=SSL,O=Test,L=Test,C=DE
```

Robust security setups ensure that your Elasticsearch cluster is protected against threats and unauthorized access, safeguarding sensitive data and maintaining operational integrity. By leveraging these plugins, you can implement comprehensive security and access controls tailored to meet organizational and regulatory requirements.

10.10 Hands-On: Creating Your First Plugin

Creating your first plugin for Elasticsearch may seem daunting, but with a structured approach, it can be an instructive and rewarding process. The custom plugin development involves understanding the framework provided by Elasticsearch, setting up a development environment, implementing the plugin logic, and testing it thoroughly before deployment. This section will guide you through these steps in detail.

First, ensure that your development environment includes the following prerequisites:

- Java Development Kit (JDK) 8 or newer.
- Elasticsearch source code or a clone of the Elasticsearch repository.
- Gradle, a build automation tool.
- An Integrated Development Environment (IDE) such as IntelliJ IDEA or Eclipse.

Begin by setting up your development environment. Clone the Elasticsearch repository from GitHub:

```
git clone https://github.com/elastic/elasticsearch.git
```

Navigate into the cloned directory:

```
cd elasticsearch
```

Create a new directory within the 'plugins' folder for your custom plugin. Assume we are creating a plugin called 'example-plugin':

```
mkdir plugins/example-plugin
```

Inside this directory, the essential files and directory structure for the plugin must be set up. The structure includes:

- 'build.gradle' - Defines build configurations.
- 'src/main/java' - Contains Java source files.
- 'src/test/java' - Contains test files.
- 'plugin-descriptor.properties' - Plugin descriptor file defining metadata about the plugin.

First, create the 'build.gradle' file with the following content:

```
plugins {
    id 'elasticsearch.esplugin'
    id 'java'
}

description = 'This is an example plugin for Elasticsearch'

dependencies {
    compileOnly 'org.elasticsearch:elasticsearch'
}
```

Next, create the 'plugin-descriptor.properties' file with the following content:

```
plugin.name=example-plugin
plugin.description=A simple example plugin for Elasticsearch
plugin.version=7.10.0
plugin.elastic.api.version=7.10.0
```

The most critical part of the plugin development is the main class that extends 'Plugin' from the Elasticsearch framework. Create a Java class called 'ExamplePlugin.java' within 'src/main/java':

```
package org.elasticsearch.plugin.example;

import org.elasticsearch.plugins.Plugin;

public class ExamplePlugin extends Plugin {

    @Override
    public String name() {
        return "example-plugin";
    }

    @Override
    public String description() {
        return "An example plugin to extend Elasticsearch functionalities";
    }

    // Additional functionality will be implemented here
}
```

At this stage, you can implement the specific logic your plugin aims to extend or modify in Elasticsearch. For instructional purposes, suppose we want to implement a simple custom REST action. Start by creating a new class 'ExampleRestAction.java':

```
package org.elasticsearch.plugin.example;

import org.elasticsearch.client.node.NodeClient;
import org.elasticsearch.rest.BaseRestHandler;
import org.elasticsearch.rest.RestRequest;
import org.elasticsearch.rest.RestController;
import org.elasticsearch.rest.RestStatus;
import org.elasticsearch.rest.RestChannel;

import java.io.IOException;
import java.util.List;
import static java.util.Collections.singletonList;
import static org.elasticsearch.rest.RestRequest.Method.GET;

public class ExampleRestAction extends BaseRestHandler {

    @Override
    public String getName() {
        return "example_rest_action";
    }

    @Override
    public List<Route> routes() {
        return singletonList(new Route(GET, "/_example"));
    }

    @Override
    protected RestChannelConsumer prepareRequest(RestRequest request, NodeClient
            client) throws IOException {
        return channel -> channel.sendResponse(new BytesRestResponse(RestStatus.
                OK, "Example response"));
    }
}
```

Register the custom REST action in the ‘ExamplePlugin.java‘:

```
@Override
public List<CustomRestHandler> getRestHandlers() {
    return singletonList(
        new Supplier<CustomRestHandler>() {
            @Override
            public CustomRestHandler get() {
                return new ExampleRestAction();
            }
        }
    );
}
```

Now, to build and test the plugin, navigate back to the root of the Elasticsearch directory and run the following Gradle command:

```
./gradlew :plugins:example-plugin:assemble
```

This command generates a zip file for the plugin in the ‘build/distributions‘ directory. To install the plugin in your Elasticsearch instance, use the following command:

```
elasticsearch-plugin install file:///path/to/elasticsearch/plugins/example-plugin/build/
    distributions/example-plugin-7.10.0.zip
```

After successful installation, start your Elasticsearch node. You can test the custom REST action by making an HTTP GET request:

```
curl -X GET "localhost:9200/_example"
```

The response should be:

```
{
    "message": "Example response"
}
```

This section delineates the foundational steps in creating and deploying a basic Elasticsearch plugin, laying the groundwork for more complex extensions.

Made in the USA
Monee, IL
05 November 2026

67911518R00174